KANT'S PHILOSOPHY OF
RELIGION RECONSIDERED

THE INDIANA SERIES IN THE PHILOSOPHY OF RELIGION
Merold Westphal, *general editor*

KANT'S PHILOSOPHY OF RELIGION RECONSIDERED

Edited by
Philip J. Rossi and Michael Wreen

INDIANA UNIVERSITY PRESS
Bloomington and Indianapolis

The paper used in this publication meets the minimum requirements of
American National Standard for Information Sciences—Permanence of
Paper for Printed Library Materials, ANSI Z39.48-1984

∞™

Manufactured in the United States of America

Library of Congress Cataloging-in-Publication Data
Kant's philosophy of religion reconsidered / edited by Philip J. Rossi
  and Michael Wreen.
      p. cm. — (Indiana series in the philosophy of religion)
  Includes index.
  ISBN 0-253-35027-1 (alk. paper)
    1. Kant, Immanuel, 1724–1804—Religion. I. Rossi, Philip J.
  II. Wreen, Michael J. III. Series.
  B2799.R4K37 1991
  200'.1—dc20   90-27310

1 2 3 4 5   95 94 93 92 91

In Memory of
Edward D. Simmons

Contents

Editors' Introduction

After decades of neglect, Kant's account of religion and its relationship to morality, culture, and history has once again become a topic of interest to philosophers, historians of philosophy, and theologians. During the past twenty-five years, a number of published works—most notably those by James Collins, Michel Despland, Ronald Green, Gordon Michalson, Philip Quinn, Allen Wood, and Yirmiahu Yovel—suggested the need both for a renewed investigation of the arguments that Kant deploys in his account of religion and for a reassessment of the systematic role that this account plays within his critical philosophy. Their work has raised a number of questions about quite commonly held views that see Kant's treatment of religion as standing at the periphery of his critical project. These views have also usually interpreted his major treatise on religion, *Religion within the Limits of Reason Alone,* as a work that adds little of substance to the account of human moral life and agency developed in the *Grundlegung* and in the *Critique of Practical Reason.* These views, moreover, have generally held that this peripheral status and lack of originality issued from the relentlessly reductionistic character of Kant's account, which sought to make religion—or at least those elements of religion which can be critically justified—wholly identical with or reducible to morality.

This collection of essays continues and enlarges the renewed debate about the shape and significance of Kant's philosophy of religion. To bring the major issues of the debate into focus, it is organized around three questions to which the individual essays set forth and defend a variety of answers. The first question—What is the scope and status of Kant's claims about "rational religion," especially as these claims bear upon notions such as grace, providence, and revelation?—concerns the extent to which Kant's account of religion can be most appropriately construed in reductionistic terms. For this examination, the notions of grace, providence, and revelation provide the most significant test case for the kind of limits Kant sets to "rational religion."

The second question—What impact does Kant's account of "radical evil" have upon his understanding of human agency and subjectivity?—probes the evidence that, within his account of religion, Kant significantly develops or even recasts some of the concepts that are central to his moral philosophy. In the discussion of this question, the interpretation of the way Kant construes human moral agents and moral actions in their relationships to time, history, and culture emerges as particularly crucial.

The third question—What is the systematic significance of the place that Kant gives to religion within the workings of human culture and history?—regards the possibility of situating Kant's account of religion as an integral element of the extended argument that constitutes the critical project. This possibility needs to be considered if, as a number of the essays contend, the nature and the shape of the destiny of the human species emerges as a focal concern for Kant in the latter stages of his critical project.

The first three essays, by Allen Wood, Joseph Runzo, and Nicholas Wolterstorff, focus on the scope and status of Kant's claims about "rational religion." Allen Wood's essay, "Kant's Deism," provides an appropriate introduction to discussion of this issue by clearly setting forth the case for excluding revelation from the purview of Kant's account of religion standing within the boundaries of human reason. To make this case, Wood first argues that Kant is a deist, i.e., a monotheist whose belief in the goodness and the providence of God excludes revealed biblical faith; he then examines some of the arguments Kant offers in favor of deism. Wood takes Kant's rejection of revealed faith to rest on both a theoretical premise—we have no cognition of the supersensible—and a practical one—we have a vocation as rational beings to think for ourselves. Since the exclusion of revelation, however, is not "immediately evident" from these premises, Wood considers dubious the way that Kant, at least in *Religion within the Limits of Reason Alone*, states his argument from these premises. As a result, Wood offers a reconstruction of Kant's argument that rests on the requirement that we are not morally required to believe that for which no one could ever provide adequate grounds; this requirement excludes revelation from the ambit of rational religion inasmuch as no claim for supernatural revelation can pass the test of universality it sets up as a condition for the rationality of a belief.

Wood's account of Kant's deism makes two further points to

which other essays in this collection will devote more detailed discussion. First, he sees the moral thrust in Kant's exclusion of revelation to be a particular application of Kantian autonomy to human intellectual conduct. Denis Savage's essay elaborates this point in terms of Kant's view of the laws that appropriately govern human conduct and volition, and he suggests some of the implications that such moral exclusion of revelation has for interpreting Kant's notion of "radical evil." Second, Wood takes note of the fact that Kant, even while placing revelation outside the limits of "rational religion," acknowledges its function in the empirical—i.e., the social and historical—development of rational religion. Such a function, however, although necessary because of "a special weakness in human nature" (R 103/94), still leaves revelation outside the ambit of rational religion. In the concluding essays in this collection, Sharon Anderson-Gold, Philip Rossi, and Burkhard Tuschling argue that Kant, particularly in his later critical writings, began to show some hesitation in taking the historical and social development of human culture, including religion, to be solely an empirical phenomenon. As a result, such a function may yet place revelation within the limits of Kantian rational religion.

Joseph Runzo, in "Kant on Reason and Justified Belief in God," conducts his examination of the scope and status of "rational religion" within the framework of Wood's reconstruction of Kant's argument. Although Runzo sees a number of "clear advantages" for both the religious believer and for genuine religion in the Kantian appeal to reason and defense of rational religion, he also considers mistaken a crucial premise in the reconstructed argument, viz., "It is *impossible* for revealed religion to provide sufficient epistemic justification for theistic truth claims" (Runzo 25). In Runzo's view, Kant bases his defense of the premises in the reconstructed argument on an evidentialist understanding of epistemic justification. Runzo claims that Kant fails to see another possibility for the epistemic justification of theistic beliefs, i.e., that they can be what some contemporary philosophers, such as William Alston and Alvin Plantinga, have called "basic beliefs." Runzo would thus modify the reconstructed Kantian position to allow for properly "basic beliefs" grounded in the human experience of divine revelation, while also maintaining that rational theology, in Kant's sense, still must be the judge of the truth of any alleged revelation. Runzo notes, moreover, that even with this modification, the status of revelation remains problematic, particularly in view of the relativity of human thought, unless we can provide an account of revelation whose significance does not rest upon its accurately delivering facts about the divine. Runzo suggests that such an account could be developed out of the neo-Reformed view of faith as human confrontation with the divine.

Runzo's proposal that revelation be understood in terms of human confrontation with the divine opens possibilities for enlarging discussion of the scope and status of "rational religion" beyond the epistemic considerations to which both he and Wood principally direct their attention. Nicholas Wolterstorff's essay, "Conundrums in Kant's Rational Religion," explores one of these possibilities. Like Runzo, Wolterstorff sees Kant continuing the evidentialist tradition about religious belief which Locke started, and he notes Kant's conviction that the only hope for finding adequate evidence for religious beliefs rests upon morality. In consequence of this moral focus, Kant concentrates his analysis of Christian religion upon the moral dimensions of its faith in salvation. Wolterstorff singles out one element of this faith— viz., the forgiveness that wipes out the evil we have done—as particularly problematic for Kant. Such undoing of guilt, which is necessary to ground faith in salvation, is beyond human power, so God must be the agent of such undoing; yet this stands in tension with Kant's affirmation of the Stoic maxim that makes the determination of a person's moral worth entirely the responsibility of that individual alone. Despite Kant's use of the language of grace to designate such an act of divine forgiveness, his insistence on the Stoic maxim of individual responsibility makes it something quite different: an act of justice whereby forgiveness is due by right to the person of good moral character. In this Kantian scheme, grace has to be eliminated and God is under a requirement to forgive. Wolterstorff's exploration of this tension indicates that the epistemic issue of the admissibility of revelation within the limits of rational religion cannot be separated from the moral issue of the admissibility of grace within those same limits.

Wolterstorff notes that this tension between what is bestowed by grace and what is due by right is most evident in Kant's exposition of "radical evil" and the conversion from radical evil that reason requires of every human moral agent. Both Denis

Savage and Leslie Mulholland make the moral agent's turn from evil central to their treatment of Kant. Their analyses, moreover, move discussion toward the second focal question of the debate: What impact does Kant's account of "radical evil" have upon his understanding of human agency and subjectivity? Denis Savage, in his essay "Kant's Rejection of Divine Revelation and His Theory of Radical Evil," argues that Kant's precise reason for rejecting revelation can be illuminated by reference to a four-fold classification of law which had been typically made in the Western philosophical tradition that Kant inherited. Kant accepts three of these four types of law as valid for the governance of human volition and conduct—the moral law of our rational human nature, the divine law, i.e., this same moral law understood as having its origin in God, and human, positive laws enacted by the state. He rejects, however, the fourth type: the laws of the special divine providence of the Old and New Testaments which pertain to all persons insofar as they are supernaturally called to a special relationship with God. Savage agrees with Wood's contention that Kant rejects the putative revelation of such laws because they do not have the necessity that is required for them to be, in Kant's sense, universal. Savage supplements Wood's contention on this point by arguing that, according to Kant's account of judgment, propositions claiming revelation as their warrant could only be mere opinion, that is, synthetic judgments lacking justification. This Kantian rejection of revelation, Savage then maintains, provides the context for Kant's account of "radical evil" in *Religion within the Limits of Reason Alone:* Kant takes the biblical story of Adam and Eve and seeks to demythologize this religious myth of the origin of evil to make it accord with the principles of rational ethics. Savage sees this demythologization as adding nothing new to the theory of moral good and evil presented in Kant's ethical works—a point that will be contested by Anderson-Gold, Mulholland, and Rossi.

Mulholland's essay, "Freedom and Providence in Kant's Account of Religion: The Problem of Expiation," provides an explicit link between the question of the scope and status of Kantian "rational religion" and the question of the impact that Kant's account of "radical evil" has upon his understanding of human agency and subjectivity. In making this link, he transposes the locus of discussion of the scope of rational religion from that initially proposed by Wood. For Mulholland, the adequacy of Kant's account of providence, rather than of revelation, will provide the crucial test of the limits placed on rational religion. In Mulholland's view, even though Kant denies that providence is necessary for expiation—i.e., the overcoming of radical evil in human nature—his account is mistaken on this point. Kant places providence outside the limits of rational religion because he sees it as an external force that would compromise the fundamental ground of morality, human freedom, if it were to operate in the turn from evil to good which accomplishes expiation. Mulholland first argues that there is an original account of the human self and of the human condition implicitly contained within the treatment Kant gives to the problem of moral improvement and its relationship to freedom and then that this account provides a basis on which providence can be shown to function in expiation without thereby compromising human freedom. In contrast to Savage, Mulholland sees Kant's treatment of radical evil and its expiation as a significant development in Kant's moral theory, particularly for his concept of the good will.

Like Wolterstorff and Mulholland, Walter Sparn, in his brief essay "Kant's Doctrine of Atonement as a Theory of Subjectivity," also recognizes both the importance and the shortcomings of Kant's effort to encompass the Christian doctrine of the atonement within the limits of rational religion. Sparn provides a useful historical context for assessment of Kant's account by locating it in relation to the discussions of atonement and Christology that engaged the "Neologians," the theologians of "enlightened Protestantism" in eighteenth-century Germany. Sparn notes Kant's fundamental agreement with the Neological view that forbids the transfer of guilt or merit from one agent to another, since this eliminates the agent's subjectivity as well as her responsibility. In keeping with this principle, Kant reconstructs the Christian doctrine of the atonement into a requirement of subjectivity to itself and in itself. In Sparn's analysis, however, the abstractness of Kant's account entails a view of history that makes it insignificant for the moral betterment that atonement requires. In consequence, the continuance of the "Neological" approach to Christology, found both in Hegel and in Schleiermacher, does more justice than Kant's to the theoretical substance of the traditional doctrine of the atonement.

The essays by Sharon Anderson-Gold and Philip Rossi continue discussion of the impact that Kant's treatment of "radical evil" has upon his understanding of human moral agency. Anderson-Gold, in "God and Community: An Inquiry into the Religious Implications of the Highest Good," argues for a religious setting to Kant's ethics. She bases this claim on an analysis of two elements in Kant's account, in *Religion within the Limits of Reason Alone*, of the conflict between good and evil; these two elements are the notions of the highest good and of the disposition, understood as the intelligible act determining both the significance and the order of incentives. For Anderson-Gold, Kant's treatment of these notions in *Religion* marks a significant development in his ethics inasmuch as they enable him to deal with a problem prefigured but not adequately treated in the *Grundlegung:* the meaning and possibility of moral evil. Since a full account of this problem cannot be rendered by an analysis of the particular actions of individuals, the notion of an intelligible disposition enables Kant to shift the focus of moral analysis from individual actions taken at their face value to the principle that brings them into connection with each other. Yet even this focus on an agent's moral life as a whole is not sufficient to provide a full account of evil; for Kant, the question of evil concerns human beings not just as individuals but also as a species. Anderson-Gold argues that Kant develops the notion of the highest good in *Religion* in a way that allows him to address the propensity to evil in terms of its social significance. The moral meaning of the postulate of God's existence is clarified, moreover, by making the social destiny of the human species the focus of the highest good: God is now understood as the common ground for the moral relationships among persons which make possible what Kant terms an "ethical commonwealth." Anderson-Gold concludes that this conception of God's moral function, which bears similarities to the sanctifying activity that Christian theology attributes to the Holy Spirit, provides the religious setting for Kant's ethics.

Philip Rossi's essay, "The Final End of All Things: The Highest Good as the Unity of Nature and Freedom," turns discussion toward the third focal question for debate—What is the systematic significance of Kant's placement of religion within the workings of human culture and history? Rossi locates Kant's elaboration of the "highest good" in *Religion* within the context

of the overall concern of Kant's critical project for delimiting
the mutual relation between the activity of human (moral) freedom and the network of causality constitutive of nature. Rossi
agrees with Mulholland and Anderson-Gold that Kant's efforts
to delineate and address the problem of evil in *Religion* mark
out an important development in his moral philosophy. Rossi
argues that this also has important consequences—which Kant
himself did not always work out—for a number of the concepts
which are basic to the whole Kantian critical project. As Kant
shifts the focus of his analysis of freedom from "spontaneity"
to "autonomy" in the course of the critical project, he modifies
his interpretation of the relationship between the sensible and
the intelligible "worlds" that nature and freedom, respectively,
constitute. Correlative to this shift, moreover, is Kant's tracking
of the implications of the social character of autonomy as it
has concrete impact upon the institutions of human culture.
Attention to the social character of autonomy leads Kant to
characterize the attainment of the highest good not just in "next
worldly" terms of personal immortality, but also in "this
worldly" terms as the historical achievement of human destiny
in and through the institutions of human culture. Rossi sees
these developments leading to a major ambiguity in Kant's
understanding of history which indicates that he had not yet
fully come to grips with the temporality that essentially marks
out the finitude of human reason.

Anthony Perovich's essay, "'For reason . . . also has its mysteries': Immortality, *Religion*, and 'The End of All Things',"
offers an analysis of one pole of the tension between Kant's
characterizations of human destiny in "other worldly" and "this
worldly" terms. In contrast to Rossi, who sees Kant's concept
of human destiny developing in social and "this worldly" directions that highlight its temporality, Perovich maintains that Kant
developed an atemporal conception of our future state based
on the practical (i.e., moral) preferability of viewing our future
existence as eternal rather than temporal. Perovich notes that
the distinction Kant draws in his critical writings between a
discursive and an intuitive intellect allows him to consider both
temporal and atemporal conceptions of the future life. In
Perovich's view, Kant's 1794 essay "The End of All Things,"
which seems initially to leave unresolved the question of which
conception is more critically adequate, does, indeed, indicate

Kant's endorsement of the atemporal one. Kant makes this endorsement on practical grounds even though he maintains that an atemporal concept of immortality is theoretically incomprehensible. Perovich observes that there is something "perplexing" about Kant's view here because it involves accepting an admittedly self-contradictory belief about the supersensible without provoking an effort to explain away its contradictory character. To resolve this perplexity, Perovich appeals to the notion of "mystery" that Kant elaborates in *Religion:* "an article of faith which is hidden from our theoretical yet revealed to our practical reason" (Perovich 171). Kant's endorsement of the atemporal view of immortality, however, calls into question the argument for immortality that he earlier advanced in the *Critique of Practical Reason*, which views it as a life of infinite progress and, thus, of continuous temporal development. Perovich contends that the introduction of the concept of a "disposition"—whose importance in another context was noted by Anderson-Gold—makes it unnecessary to look for a new proof of immortality since it provides us with a fundamentally atemporal conception of ourselves.

The final essay, Burkhard Tuschling's *"Rationis societas:* Remarks on Kant and Hegel," places Kant's account of rational religion within a larger philosophical and historical horizon. Tuschling is concerned to spell out the implications of Kant's basically social conception of the human being, particularly as this involves membership in a totality of free, rational agents. Tuschling first points out the elements in Kant's work that show that the social dimension is not merely an appendage to his practical philosophy but is fully intrinsic to it; he then notes that this also holds true of Kant's philosophy of religion. This "interior systematic" of Kant's practical philosophy, which orders morality and religion toward a destiny of enlightenment and freedom for humankind, is one that Hegel takes over and transforms. Tuschling notes some of the key respects in which Hegel's concept of *Sittlichkeit* diverges from Kant's account of practical reason. Of particular importance is Hegel's contention that Kant's account does not overcome the separation of the moral and the legal order: the formalization of maxims to accord with the idea of a general law of reason is not sufficient to bring about that realization of reason by which the individual makes self-conscious identification with the life of the social whole.

While admitting the cogency of Hegel's criticisms of Kant, Tuschling contends that neither of them solved the problem of freedom and the state. Their rationalistic optimism that reason "manifests itself in absolute individual freedom and private property, in the *Not- und Verstandesstaat* of bourgeois society— or in any other actual society whatever its social constitution may be," cannot be sustained (Tuschling 198–99). Tuschling concludes that their failure, nonetheless, should not prevent us from learning a lesson from "this story of a commonwealth of reason: . . . there is just as much reason, freedom, and humanism in human relations, institutions, actions, and productions as we give to them" (Tuschling 199). The authors and editors of this volume hope that their work will help foster the constant efforts we all must make to keep learning that lesson.

Acknowledgments

A work of this kind requires the commitment of many minds, hearts, and hands for its successful completion. We are particularly grateful for the assistance that the editor of this series, Merold Westphal, has given us in the selection and organization of essays for this volume. Katherine Thome, a theology doctoral student at Marquette University, deserves a special mention in our thanks: she labored many hours in the editorial and technical preparation of the manuscript and we are deeply indebted to the care, precision, and good humor she displayed throughout the demanding process. Richard Edwards, Andrew Tallon, Oliver Olson, and Joseph O'Malley, our colleagues at Marquette, provided essential technical or scholarly advice at crucial stages of this project, and we extend to them our thanks.

The plan for this volume originated at a conference held in November 1987 under the sponsorship of the philosophy and the theology departments of Marquette University. Very special words of thanks are due to Joseph O'Malley, of Marquette's philosophy department, who proposed the idea for the conference, to Jane Linahan, a theology doctoral student at Marquette University, who both cheerfully and effectively administered many of the details of the conference, and to Audrey Martini, administrative assistant in the theology department, who provided indispensable help in many matters great and small in the preparation both of the conference and of this volume. We also thank all the participants in the conference, particularly Alexander von Schoenborn of the University of Missouri, for the advice, interest, and encouragement they offered in pursuing the major questions raised by Kant's philosophy of religion. Other publications have issued from the work of the conference and we consider it appropriate to provide here the bibliographical information about them: Diana Axelsen, "Kant's Metaphors for Person and Community," *Philosophy/Theology* 3 (1989): 301–21; Ronald Green, "The Leap of Faith: Kierkegaard's Debt to Kant," *Philosophy/Theology* 3 (1989): 385–411; John Treloar, S. J., "The Crooked Wood of Humanity: Kant's Struggle with Radical Evil," *Philosophy/Theology* 3 (1989): 335–53; and Wilhelm Vossenkuhl, "The Paradox of Rational Religion," *Pro-

ceedings of the Aristotelian Society, New Series 88 (1987–88): 179–92.

Our final word of thanks, to the late Edward Simmons, is one that is personally most important because it must be offered with sadness. Support from Marquette University and its fund for special programs reflecting Marquette's religious commitment made it possible to hold the conference "Kant's Philosophy of Religion Reconsidered." Dr. Simmons, Marquette's vice president for academic affairs and principal architect of this special fund, died the week after the conference. One of Ed's last official acts before his untimely death was a gracious speech of welcome to the conference participants. We hope the essays in this volume meet the standard of excellence that Ed expected of all activities sponsored by Marquette; it is with gratitude and respect for a life committed to those standards that we dedicate this volume to his memory.

A Note on Citations

The essays and notes in this volume refer to Kant's writings according to the abbreviations listed below. Unless otherwise noted, citations to the German titles provide pagination in the appropriate volume of Kant's *Gesammelte Schriften;* when these citations are followed by a slash (/), the number following is a reference to the pagination of the corresponding English translation. When citations to English translations are followed by a slash (/), the number following is a reference to the pagination in the corresponding volume in the *Gesammelte Schriften*. In the following list, German/English cross-referencing is provided in parentheses at the end of each entry.

A   "Beantwortung der Frage: Was ist Aufklärung?" GS 8 (E).

A/B   *Kritik der reinen Vernunft*, GS 3–4. Unless otherwise noted, trans. Norman Kemp Smith (New York: St. Martin's Press, 1965).

AP   *Anthropology from a Pragmatic Point of View*, trans. Mary J. Gregor (The Hague: Martinus Nijhoff, 1974) GS 7.

CB   "Conjectural Beginning of Human History," in *On History*, trans. Emil Fackenheim (New York: Bobbs-Merrill, 1963) GS 8 (MMG).

CF   *The Conflict of the Faculties*, trans. Mary J. Gregor (New York: Abaris Books, 1979) GS 7 (SF).

CJ-B   *Critique of Judgment*, trans. J. H. Bernard (New York: Hafner, 1951) GS 5 (KU).

CJ-P   *Critique of Judgment*, trans. Werner Pluhar (Indianapolis: Hackett, 1987) GS 5 (KU).

E   "What is Enlightenment?" in *On History*, trans. Lewis White Beck (New York: Bobbs-Merrill, 1963) GS 8 (A).

ED   *Education*, trans. Annette Churton (Ann Arbor: University of Michigan Press, 1960) GS 9.

EF   *Zum ewigen Frieden*, GS 8 (PP).

ET   "The End of All Things," in *On History*, trans. Robert E. Anchor (New York: Bobbs-Merrill, 1963) GS 8.

F   *Foundations of the Metaphysics of Morals*, trans. Lewis White Beck (New York: Bobbs-Merrill, 1959) GS 4 (Gr).

FP   *The Fundamental Principles of the Metaphysics of Ethics*, trans. Otto Manthey-Zorn (New York: Appleton-Century-Croft, 1938) GS 4 (Gr).

Gr   *Grundlegung zur Metaphysik der Sitten*, GS 4 (F, FP).

GS   *Gesammelte Schriften*, Ausgabe der Königlichen Preußischen Akademie der Wissenschaften (Berlin, 1902).

I   "Idee zu einer allgemeinen Geschichte in weltbürgerlicher Absicht," GS 8 (IH).

IH   "Idea for a Universal History from a Cosmopolitan Point of View," in *On History*, trans. Lewis White Beck (New York: Bobbs-Merrill, 1963) GS 8 (I).

KpV   *Kritik der praktischen Vernunft*, GS 5 (PrR).

KU   *Kritik der Urteilskraft*, GS 5 (CJ–B, CJ–P).

L   *Lectures on Philosophical Theology*, trans. Allen Wood and Gertrude M. Clark (Ithaca, N.Y.: Cornell University Press, 1978) (VpR).

MdSR   *Die Metaphysik der Sitten: Rechtslehre*, GS 6 (MMJ).

MdST   *Die Metaphysik der Sitten: Tugendlehre*, GS 6 (MMV, MPV).

MMG   "Mutmaßlicher Anfang der Menschen Geschichte," GS 8 (CB).

MMJ   *The Metaphysical Elements of Justice: Part I of The Metaphysics of Morals*, trans. John Ladd (New York: Bobbs-Merrill, 1965) GS 6 (MdSR).

MMV   *The Doctrine of Virtue: Part II of The Metaphysics of Morals*, trans. Mary J. Gregor (New York: Harper and Row, 1964) GS 6 (MdST).

MPV   *The Metaphysical Principles of Virtue: Part II of The Metaphysics of Morals*, trans. James Ellington (New York: Bobbs-Merrill, 1964) GS 6 (MdST).

O   "Was heißt: Sich im Denken orientieren?" GS 8 (OT).

OT   "What is Orientation in Thinking?" in *The Critique of Practical Reason and Other Writings in Moral Philosophy*, trans. Lewis White Beck (New York: Garland, 1976) GS 8 (O).

PM   *Prolegomena to Any Future Metaphysics*, ed. Lewis White Beck (New York: Bobbs-Merrill, 1950) GS 4.

PP   "Perpetual Peace," in *On History,* trans. John Ladd (New York: Bobbs-Merrill, 1963) GS 8 (EF).

PrR   *Critique of Practical Reason,* trans. Lewis White Beck (New York: Bobbs-Merrill, 1965) GS 5 (KpV).

R   *Religion within the Limits of Reason Alone,* trans. Theodore M. Greene and Hoyt H. Hudson, with a new essay by John Silber (New York: Harper and Row, 1960) GS 6 (RGV).

RGV   *Religion innerhalb der Grenzen der bloßen Vernunft,* GS 6 (R).

SF   *Streit der Facultäten,* GS 7 (CF).

TP   "Über den Gemeinspruch: Das mag in der Theorie richtig sein, taugt aber nicht für die Praxis," GS 8.

VpR   *Vorlesungen über die philosophische Religionslehre* (hrsg. Pölitz) 2. Ausgabe (Leipzig: Taubert, 1830) (L).

VpS   "Von der philosophischen Schwarmerey," GS 18.

KANT'S PHILOSOPHY OF
RELIGION RECONSIDERED

Kant's Deism

Allen W. Wood

1. What Is Deism?

Kant defines a "deist" as someone who admits only a "transcendental theology," that is, who ascribes to God only properties which can be derived from a priori concepts; by contrast, a "theist" is someone who also admits a "natural theology," applying to God, by analogy, the properties of creatures known to us through experience (VpR 15–16/29–30, 53/54).[1] In his concept of God, says Kant, the deist "understands merely a blindly working eternal nature as the root of all things, an original being or supreme cause of the world" (VpR 96/81). A deist, therefore, will say that God is supremely perfect, necessarily existent, a single extramundane substance, immutable, impassible, all-sufficient, omnipresent, omnipotent, timelessly eternal, and a cause of the world (VpR 67–95/62–79). But only a theist predicates of God the qualities drawn from the human mind; only the theist can say that God lives, knows, and wills (VpR 96–122/81–99).

In this sense, of course, Kant is a theist and not a deist. He thinks that we are justified in ascribing to the *ens realissimum* the predicates of finite things, especially of the human intellect and will, so long as we do so by analogy (VpR 97–98/90–91) and are careful not to ascribe human imperfections to God; and Kant insists that only the idea of God as a living, knowing, and willing being is adequate for the purposes of our moral faith in providence (VpR 16/30). Kant's definition of "deism," however, is idiosyncratic, less a reflection of common seventeenth- and eighteenth-century usage than a device to deflect reproach from Kant's own heterodox religious views.

The first known use of the term in a sense opposed to "theism" is found in the Calvinist theologian Pierre Viret's *Instruction chrestienne* (1563). Viret characterized deists as "those who profess belief in God as creator of heaven and earth, but reject Jesus Christ and his doctrines."[2] Edward Stillingfleet, Bishop of Worcester, probably best known for his exchanges with John Locke, described the addressee of his polemical "Letter to a Deist" (1677) as "a particular person who owned the Being and Providence of God, but expressed mean esteem of the Scriptures and the Christian religion."[3] The poet John Dryden, in the preface to his poem "Religio Laici" (1682), defined "deism" as "the opinion of those that acknowledge one God, without the reception of any revealed religion."[4] In his *Dictionary* of 1775, Samuel Johnson defined deism as "Belief in a God, but rejection of all other articles of religious faith."[5]

All these characterizations are given by people who are trying to display deism in an unattractive light. Nevertheless, the main significance of the term is clear enough from them, and Dryden's definition, at least, is both clear enough and fair enough to be quite usable. A deist is a monotheist who believes in the goodness and providence of God but refuses to embrace a revealed faith based on the biblical traditions of Christianity. In other words, a deist is a believer in a natural religion, a religion founded on unaided reason, but not in a revealed religion, a religion founded on a supernatural revelation through scripture.

My purpose here is to consider how far Kant is a deist in this sense and to examine some of Kant's arguments in favor of deism. The very title of Kant's principal work on religion, *Religion innerhalb der Grenzen der bloßen Vernunft*, clearly raises the issue. In that title, the word *"bloß"* means "unassisted" or "unaided," that is, without the aid or assistance of supernatural revelation. The reference of the title, therefore, is precisely to the deist's natural or rational religion: a religion within the boundaries of unassisted natural reason, religion without the supernatural aid of miracles, signs or other divine revelations through mystical experience, ecclesiastical tradition, or holy scripture. But the title by itself does not necessarily imply that Kant embraces the deistic position that religion can get along without revelation. Some of Kant's own formulations are meant to appease those who think it cannot. In the Preface to the Second Edition of 1794, Kant has this comment on the book's title:

> Since *revelation* can at least comprehend pure *rational religion* within itself, but, conversely, the latter cannot include what is

> historical in the former, I will be able to consider the former as
> the *wider* sphere of faith, which includes within itself the latter
> as a *narrower* one (not unlike two circles placed outside of one
> another, but like concentric circles). (R 12/11)

Moreover, at crucial junctures Kant indicates that the religion
of reason has need of revealed traditions: owing to "a special
weakness in human nature," he says, a church cannot be
grounded solely on the religion of unassisted reason but requires
an "ecclesiastical faith" based on an empirical revelation (R
103/94). The preservation of pure religious faith unchanged
over long periods of time, he says, has been best facilitated not
by tradition alone but only with the help of revered scriptures
or holy books which, he wryly adds, are treated with the greatest
reverence by those who do not read them (R 107/98).

2. Ecclesiastical Faith and Human History

As these remarks indicate, Kant thinks of the necessary function
of revealed religion as social or historical, and so his conception
of the relation of revealed or ecclesiastical faith to the religion
of pure reason must be understood in the context of his philosophy of history. Kant does not think that experience enables
us to resolve the question whether in its history the human race
is improving, getting worse, or remaining about the same; but
he does hold that we can look at the evidence in light of our
practical vocation to improve ourselves and try in this way to
form conjectures about the way nature or providence might
contrive the progress of our species (SF 81–84, I 29–31/23–26).
According to the *Idea for a Universal History from a Cosmopolitan Standpoint* (1784), the chief goal nature has set for the
human race is the fashioning of a "universal civil society" which
is able to protect the freedom to which rational beings have a
fundamental right and thereby enable them fully to develop and
perfect their manifold capacities (I 22/16). The means nature
has used in working toward this end is the human trait of
"unsociable sociability," the human passion to "achieve a rank
among one's fellows, whom he cannot *suffer* but also cannot
leave alone" (I 21/15). People are thus driven together into
societies, all seeking dominion over the others, abusing such
freedom as they have and struggling to violate the freedom of

others. This struggle leads to the founding of states, in which a supreme authority achieves mastery over the lawless wills of its subjects, forcing them to obey a law that is universally valid and confining each within its rightful sphere (I 23/17). The remaining task of the human race in the political realm is to establish a constitution in which the powers of the state are administered with complete justice; Kant is convinced that this task cannot be fulfilled completely until states establish a lawful order regulating their external relations with each other—and this is something which Kant thinks there are definite historical tendencies for states to do (I 24–26/18–21).

Nearly a decade later, in *Religion*, Kant attempts an analogous historical conjecture as regards a purely ethical society founded not on public laws of external right but on moral laws which ought to govern people's inner dispositions. "The species of rational beings is determined objectively, in the idea of reason, to a common end, namely the furthering of the highest good as the good of a community" (R 97/89). Kant claims that the highest moral good cannot be brought about only through individuals striving after their own moral perfection; rather, the highest moral good requires them to unite into a whole for the promotion of the moral improvement of each and all, a "universal republic according to laws of virtue" (R 98/89). Because the laws of this community have to do with morality rather than strict right, membership in it must be optional (R 96/87), and the scope of this community should be in principle universal, extended to the whole of humanity rather than limited to any one people (R 97/88).

Just as Kant finds in the political state the empirical ectype of a realm of external justice, so he finds the empirical ectype for the universal ethical republic in the churches of various empirical religious faiths (R 100/91). And as empirical states have been highly imperfect, often straying far from their rational end of establishing external justice, so churches and ecclesiastical faiths have regularly fallen short of their task. Their chief failing has been to encourage not morally good conduct of life, which is their proper office, but rather the performance of statutory observances, in themselves morally indifferent. Instead of cultivating a disposition to moral freedom, they have typically promoted cult and prayer, often combining such activities with superstitious belief in miracles, enthusiastic pretensions to supersensible experience, and fetishistic attempts to produce super-natural occurrences through ritual acts (R 53/48, 86/81, 106/97, 174/162, 177-78/165-66). Worst of all, they have subjected the consciences of individuals to a hierarchy of priests, under-mining the individual freedom of conscience which is the very essence of rational religion and enslaving the very soul itself, where the proper function of true religion is precisely to liberate it (R 134n/124n, 175-80/163-68, 185-90/173-78).

The historical function of ecclesiastical faith is to serve as the *vehicle* for pure rational religion (R 106/97). But it is also the *shell* in which rational religion is encased and from which it is humanity's historical task to free the religion of reason (R 121/112, 135n/126n). It is not Kant's view that this must involve the actual abolition of ecclesiastical faiths: "Not that [the shell] should cease (for perhaps it will always be useful and necessary as a vehicle) but that it will be able to cease" (R 135n/126n). Kant does, however, look forward to the time when "the form of a church itself is dissolved, the viceroy on earth steps into the same class as the human being raised to a citizen of heaven, and so God will be all in all" (R 135/126).

The plain intent here is eventually to abolish the church's hierarchical constitution and, with it, the tutelage of humanity to a class of priests who (in Kant's view) usurp the authority of individuals over their own beliefs and consciences. To think for oneself, Kant says, is the vocation of each and every human being (A 36/4). When someone's thinking is subject to the guidance or direction from others, as the thought and conduct of children is to the direction of their parents, then that person is in the condition of "tutelage" or "minority" *(Unmündigkeit)* (A 35/3). The greatest human indignity occurs when free adult human beings are also in a state of tutelage. There is nothing offensive, of course, about acquiring information and advice from others, or in listening to and being persuaded by their arguments, or treating the informed opinion and wisdom of others with the deference and respect it deserves. What disturbs Kant is the way that people tend simply to let others do their thinking for them, the way they substitute deference to the authority of others for the critical use of their own reason in matters of central importance to the conduct of their lives. To do that is not to show due respect for the wisdom and expertise of others but utter disrespect for oneself as a rational being.

Religious faith is not the only form taken by such degrading tutelage; people put themselves in tutelage not only to priests but also to teachers, lawyers, physicians, and the printed page (A 35/3). (This last, of course, was virtually the sole medium of mass communication available in Kant's day. The list of media threatening critical thought would have to be greatly expanded to apply to the late twentieth century.) But Kant lays stress on religious tutelage because, of all the forms of tutelage, he regards it as "the most harmful and degrading" (A 41/9). Hence the most fundamental change which Kant demands in ecclesiastical faith is what he calls "enlightenment." Kant defines "enlightenment" as "release from self-incurred tutelage." Tutelage is "self-incurred" when it is due not to the immaturity or incapacity of one's faculties but to the lack of courage and resolve to think for oneself (A 35/3). This does not mean, however, that Kant lays the blame for tutelage entirely on the individuals subject to it. He recognizes that ecclesiastical faiths have devised highly effective means of inculcating "pious terror" into people and powerful means of playing on the human propensity to a "servile faith in divine worship" (gottesdienstlich Frohnglauben). Such methods regularly destroy people's confidence in their own capacities, frightening them away from honest doubt and thus preventing them from ever acquiring a faith free of servile hypocrisy (R 133n/124n, 188–90/176–78). Kant is confident that in the long run, the powers of "inner compulsion" must inevitably yield to the progressive forces of moral insight; but he urges the secular authority not to hinder this progress by "supporting the ecclesiastical despotism of some tyrants in his state over his other subjects" (A 40/8).

Perhaps there was a time when most human beings benefited by the paternal guidance of priests and could do no better than to follow the revealed statutes of the church, handed down by tradition and recommended on the supernatural authority of divine revelation. But to be in such a condition is to be treated both by oneself and by the authorities as less than a human adult, less than a fully rational being. Kant sees the highest vocation of his age as that of putting an end to this condition, which still harms and degrades the vast majority of people. That is why Kant describes his own time (soberly) not as an enlightened age but (optimistically) as an age of enlightenment (A 40/8).

The leading string of holy tradition, with its appendages of statutes and observances, which did good service in its time, gradually becomes dispensable, and finally becomes a shackle when humanity reaches its adolescence. "When he [the human species] was a child, he understood as a child" (1 Cor. 15:28). "But when he becomes a man, he puts away childish things" (1 Cor. 13:11). The demeaning distinction between *laity* and *clergy* ceases, and equality arises from true freedom; but there is no anarchy, because each obeys the (non-statutory) law which he prescribes to himself, and which he at the same time must regard as the will of the world-ruler, revealed through reason, combining all invisibly under a common government in one state, already prepared for and inadequately represented by the visible church. (R 121–22/ 112)

3. Rational Religion

Essential to any deism is the view that there is such a thing as rational or natural religion, religion based on natural reason and not on supernatural revelation. Kant clearly holds that there is rational religion in this sense. Kant defines "religion" as "the cognition of all duties as divine commands" (R 153/142). But this definition is in need of commentary on several counts. Kant understands religion not as a matter of theoretical knowledge but as a matter of subjective practial disposition (KpV 129/134, KU 481/376, SF 36, VpR 10/27; cf. A 818/B 846). Thus the definition must be understood in the sense that religion is "the moral disposition to observe all duties as [God's] commands" (R 105/96). Kant is emphatic that there need not be any special duties to God in order for there to be religion; he also denies that theoretical cognition of God's existence is required for religion—naturally enough, since he thinks that no such cognition is available to us (R 153–54n/142n). What does seem requisite to religion is that (1) we have duties, (2) we have a concept of God, and (3) we are capable of regarding our duties as something God wills us to do.

Now Kant holds that these three requirements for religion can all be met solely through reason. That we have duties is presumably proven in rational moral philosophy. That we have a concept of God as a supremely perfect being is argued in detail and with sophistication by Kant in the unjustly neglected second section of "The Ideal of Pure Reason."[6] That God wills the fulfillment of our duties follows from his supreme perfection as the ideal of pure reason and the fact that duties are imperatives of reason. A purely rational or natural religion, therefore, is possible.

Of course, Kant plainly associates religion in this sense with rational or moral faith in God's existence, in the immortality of the soul, and in God's forgiving grace, which makes it possible for us to satisfy the demands of the moral law despite the propensity to radical evil in our nature. He holds that while we cannot have theoretical cognition or knowledge of any of these matters, we can attain to practical cognition, rational conviction, or faith in them through the famous (or infamous) moral proofs with which Kant's name is associated.[7] But although Kant himself credits these proofs and sees them as harmonizing with rational religion (R 3–7/3–7), it is far from clear that he regards the acceptance of his proofs—or any other rational arguments, theoretical or practical, for their conclusions—as necessary for a rational "religion" in the strict sense. Kant is emphatic in *Religion* that for religion "no assertoric knowledge (even of God's existence) is required; . . . but only a *problematic* assumption (hypothesis) as regards speculation about the supreme cause of things." Though Kant refers to this requisite as a "free *assertoric* faith," he explains that "this faith needs merely *the idea of God* . . . only the *minimum* cognition (it is possible that there is a God) has to be subjectively sufficient" (R 153–54/142; cf. VpR 10/27). Apparently I can be a religious person in Kant's sense even if I am an agnostic, so long as my awareness of moral duty is enlivened with the thought that if there is a God, the fulfillment of my duties is commanded by him. Kant wants to broaden rational religion in this way because he thinks that a religion of reason must be open to all rational beings who use their reason honestly. To demand an "assertoric knowledge," even of God's existence, as a prerequisite for rational religion would be to demand for religion more in the way of theoretical faith than that "to which all morally serious (and therefore faithful) striving for the good must inevitably lead." It would be to demand "a confession which might be hypocritical" due to "our lack of insight into supersensible objects" (R 153–54n/142n).

It is worth emphasizing the extreme modesty of the theoretical demands for Kantian rational religion, because the usual strategy of deism's most formidable religious opponents, from the acute Bishop Butler in the eighteenth century down to the present day, has been to charge that if revealed religion stands on shaky epistemic foundations, so equally does the deist's natural religion.[8] It has always seemed to me that this line of argument would better suit the aims of those who want to reject all religion than those who want to affirm revealed religion rather than natural religion. As a way of shoring up conspicuously shaky claims to knowledge, this strategy of indiscriminate skepticism— which has been aptly called the strategy of "poisoning the wells"[9]—is surely bound to fail, since it does not alter the relative strength of the evidence for different views but only raises dust in the faces of us who are examining the evidence.

But however all this may be, Kant seems to be very much aware of the skeptical strategy and intends to counter it by emphasizing how modest the claims of rational religion are and how little they need to strain the intellect of an honest person. Of course, the standard anti-deist response at this point is to ridicule natural religion for its aridity and emptiness as compared with the fulsome heart-swelling fantasies of revealed faith. But such reproaches miss the mark at least partly, since the point for Kant is to guarantee the flexibility, not the poverty, of rational faith. Kant regards the content of rational religion for any given individual as including whatever that individual may believe through reason about the God whom we regard as commanding the fulfillment of moral duties. Some may be led by rational reflection only to the "minimum of theology" necessary for rational religion, while others may be able to convince themselves of considerably more than this: Kant himself, for instance, is convinced of immortality, divine providence, and even of God's forgiving grace. Kant's *Religion* itself exhibits a concerted effort to provide a rationalist interpretation of Christian doctrine and imagery so as to include as much as possible of it within the religion of pure reason.

The only unequivocal concession which Kant must make at this point concerns the *uniformity* of belief in rational religion. But as Kant sees it, genuine religious solidarity does not rest on the confession of a uniform symbol or creed anyway; Kant suspects such credal formulas of contributing more to a spirit of hypocrisy within people and between them than to anything else. What unites believers in rational religion is not the content of their beliefs but the morality of their dispositions and their propensity to associate their moral vocation with the thought of God. On what they believe, rational believers may differ, each being led by reason to a wholly personal creed. But as Kant sees it, this is quite as it should be in a religion which encourages us to regard ourselves as free adult rational beings whose basic convictions should always be the results of our own thinking.

4. Rationalism and Deism

A deist is someone who believes in a natural or rational religion rather than a religion based on supernatural revelation. We have seen that Kant does believe in a natural or rational religion. What we have now to examine is his attitude toward the claims of revealed religion.

The authority of ecclesiastical faith rests on its claims to empirical or historical revelation as preserved in scriptural documents and ecclesiastical tradition. Hence Kant's views about the claims of revelation, and consequently his position as regards deism, are intimately bound up with his view of the function and the shortcomings of ecclesiastical faith. Kant provides us with what is probably the most explicit account of his position on revelation at the opening of Book IV, Part I of *Religion* (R 153–55/142–43). But the account is a bit confusing, and Kant is a trifle coy about exactly where he stands.

Kant begins with a flurry of definitions. Religion in general is the recognition of one's duties as commands of God. A religion in which my knowledge of something as a duty depends on my knowledge of it as a divine command is a *revealed* religion, whereas a religion in which my knowledge of something as a divine command depends on my knowledge of it as a duty is a *natural* religion. Kant calls a "rationalist" anyone who holds that natural religion alone is morally necessary. A rationalist may either believe or deny that there is revealed religion. A rationalist who denies the reality of all supernatural revelation is a *naturalist*, whereas one who accepts the reality of such revelation (while of course regarding it as morally unnecessary) is a *pure rationalist.* Someone who not only believes in revealed religion but also holds it to be morally necessary is a *pure supernaturalist.*

Though he does not avow it in so many words, it seems clear that Kant's position is a rationalist one. From this it follows that he is committed to denying pure supernaturalism, since pure supernaturalism affirms, while rationalism denies, that a revealed religion is morally necessary. But it is equally clear that Kant is not a naturalist: he insists that it would transcend the limits of human insight to claim that supernatural revelation has not occurred (R 155/143). What may be less clear is Kant's attitude toward pure rationalism, the view that recognizes the reality of supernatural revelation but nevertheless denies that belief in it is morally necessary. But "pure rationalism" seems scarcely deserving of its name, and it is hard to imagine anyone who would hold it. For it apparently takes the position that God has given us certain commands supernaturally while denying that we are morally bound to carry them out. This surely cannot be a position Kant intends to embrace. Kant's only purpose in mentioning pure rationalism at all seems to be the rhetorical one of cushioning his evident denial of pure supernaturalism.

Kant is plainly a rationalist because he is simply an agnostic about supernatural revelation. Kant's disavowal of all claims to transcendent knowledge justifies his refusal to assert that there is no such thing as supernatural revelation. On the other hand, it justifies equally his refusal to admit the possibility that anyone might have adequate grounds for claiming the authenticity of any particular putative revelation. This is stated most clearly in *The Conflict of the Faculties:* "If God actually spoke to a human being, the latter could never *know* that it was God who spoke to him. It is absolutely impossible for a human being to grasp the infinite through the senses, so as to distinguish him from sensible beings and be *acquainted* with him" (SF 63). Kant's position, then, is that there may be such a thing as supernatural revelation but, if there is, no human being can ever know that there is and no particular claim to supernatural revelation can ever be deserving of our rational assent. For that very reason, belief in supernatural revelation cannot be required of us as a duty: for it would be a duty which one could fulfill only by holding a belief which no human being could ever be theoretically justified in holding.

In his own terms, then, Kant's position is simple rationalism: natural religion alone is morally necessary. He rejects not only pure supernaturalism, which holds that belief in supernatural revelation is morally necessary, but also naturalism, which denies that there is such revelation; and he eschews pure rationalism, which affirms that there is such revelation while denying that it is morally necessary to accept it. Of these four positions, naturalism most clearly deserves to be called a "deist" view, since it alone positively rejects the existence of supernatural revelation. But Kant's rationalism also fits Dryden's definition of deism as "the opinion of those that acknowledge one God, without the reception of any revealed religion"; for although Kant does not deny the possibility of a supernaturally revealed religion, he seems plainly not to accept such a religion himself, and he denies that it can be morally necessary to accept it. In that sense, it seems accurate to say that Kant acknowledges one God, but his position involves no "reception" of revealed religion; and so I think we ought to conclude that Kant is accurately described as a deist.

5. Reason and Revelation

We have already become acquainted with two of the main premises on which Kant's deism rests: the theoretical premise that our faculties afford us no cogntion of the supersensible and the practical premise that the vocation of every rational being is thinking for oneself. But it is now time to look at Kant's arguments for deism in a bit more detail. For it is not immediately evident that the two premises just mentioned preclude the possibility of a revealed religion or even the possibility that such a religion might belong to what God might morally require of us. Kant himself acknowledges that rational thinking, in the form of the moral arguments for faith in God, justifies a religious faith which goes beyond what our powers of theoretical cognition can afford us. Why might not such thinking also justify us in embracing a faith in supernatural biblical revelation as a consequence of our predicament as moral beings? Such a direction was actually given to Kant's doctrine of rational religious faith by Hegel's sometime teacher, the Tübingen biblical theologian Gottlob Christian Storr (See R 13/14).[10] Does Kant have good grounds for rejecting Storr's alternative?

The main lines of *Religion*'s argument on this point are clear and are repeated a number of times in the book: only that can be morally required which is universal and common equally to all human beings. The commands of rational morality and the modest requirements of rational religion can meet this universality test, but the claims of an empirical revelation cannot.

> *Pure* [*rational* religious faith] alone can found a universal church, because it is a faith of unassisted reason, which may be communicated with conviction to everyone; but a historical faith, insofar as it is grounded merely on facts, can extend its influence no further than the news of it, in respect of time and circumstances, can acquire the capacity to make themselves worthy of belief. (R 102-03/94)

Kant's claim is apparently that rational morality, and the religion founded on it, is equally credible to all people, irrespective of time and circumstance, but any faith based on empirical (historical) facts about a putative divine revelation is necessarily more credible to those more closely acquainted with the facts and the tradition which preserves the record of them than to those who have the misfortune to be less well acquainted with these matters. From this Kant concludes that if we regard belief in a revealed faith as morally necessary, we are committed to giving the historically learned an inherent moral advantage over the unlearned, a consequence Kant regards as morally unacceptable (R 164/152; VpR 9–10/26–27).

This line of argument seems to me rather dubious. First, it seems empirically false that any kind of knowledge or human capacity is distributed to people with perfect equality, so that if the only moral demands on people were those resting on completely equal capacities, then the conclusion would have to be that nothing whatever could be morally demanded of people. But even worse, it also seems untrue that rational religion holds any advantage over revealed religion as regards the empirical extent of its accessibility. If there is a determinate history to the dissemination of the Christian message, and determinate temporal and geographical limits to the credibility of this tradition, a morality founded on reason seems equally to belong to a determinate culture and its dissemination has a determinate tradition, much more limited in spatial and temporal extent than that of Christian revelation.

Part of the trouble with Kant's argument is the tempting and characteristically Kantian but sadly unrealistic idea that before the cosmic bar of moral judgment, all must somehow ultimately stand as perfect equals, to be judged solely on their intrinsic merits. But its even more obvious and flagrant defect is the way in which it seems to insist on taking the spatiotemporal extent of a faith's dissemination as the sole measure of its credibility. This seems neither plausible in itself nor likely to bring out the advantages which rational religion might reasonably claim over revealed religion. For if the contest turns solely on historical pedigree and control over the cultural engines of dissemination, the victory will of course go not to the religion of reason but to revealed faith, and even within revealed faith the rankest and most pernicious popular superstitions are likely to score higher than the traditions representing wisdom and goodness. (We need only to consider the forms of revealed faith which have greatest access to the media of mass communication today.) Moreover, despite being deprived of the opportunity to watch the "700 Club" on television, Kant seems acutely aware of these regrettable facts (VpR 221/161); and this should make us wonder whether we have misunderstood his argument or whether perhaps he has misstated it.

Of course the basic issue raised by the argument is not how widely religious doctrines are disseminated but rather how rationally credible they are. Kant's statement of his argument seems encumbered with a certain tact, or even fear, which makes him reluctant to express with perfect candor what he really thinks about this issue. Kant's real view is expressed clearly enough on occasion, when he asserts that a revealed faith "can never be universally communicated so as to produce conviction," so that when a church founds itself on claims to supernatural revelation, it "renounces the most important mark of truth, namely a rightful claim to universality" (R 109/100). But for the sake of tact, Kant tries to pretend that this defect of revealed teachings is due only to the indisputable fact that their dissemination is spatially, temporally, and culturally limited. But as we have seen above, this is not what Kant really thinks. He thinks that even for those who are most intimately acquainted with a putative revelation, and even supposing the revelation to be wholly genuine, there could never be sufficient grounds for a human being to attain a justified conviction of its authenticity.

This defect of claims to supernatural revelation has nothing to do with the fact that they are based on historical reports or with the fact that not everyone has access to these reports. Historical evidence, if it is strong enough, is surely capable of convincing any rational being who is in possession of it, and it has this virtue even if many people do not have access to it (O 141/300). The problem with supernatural revelation is rather that because the idea of a God or supremely perfect being is an idea of reason, to which no experience can ever correspond, it follows that no empirical evidence that a finite being may possess is capable of licensing the conclusion that some empirical event is the special revelation of a supremely perfect being (O 142/301).

Kant's real argument, then, depends on neither of the two dubious premises we looked at earlier. Instead, the argument is that belief in supernatural revelation cannot be morally required. In Kant's view, the morally required cannot extend beyond what a rational being might justifiably be convinced of, and no rational being could ever be justifiably convinced of any claim to supernatural revelation. The argument does not require that people cannot be morally judged on matters where one person may possess more morally relevant information than another; it requires only that people should not be morally required to hold a belief for which no person could ever, under any circumstances, have adequate grounds. And the argument does not depend on the claim that rational religion is more widely available to people than revealed religion; it depends instead on the claim that it is possible in principle for any rational being to be justified in holding the extremely modest and highly flexible tenets of rational religion but impossible in principle for any human being to authenticate any alleged case of supernatural revelation. It is this line of argument, I suggest, which is really intended in *Religion*. But it is expressed much more clearly several years later in *The Conflict of the Faculties*:

> It is a contradiction to demand *universality* for an ecclesiastical faith (*catholicismus hierarchicus*) because unconditioned universality presupposes necessity, which occurs only where reason itself sufficiently grounds the propositions of faith, and so these are not mere statutes. On the other hand, pure [rational] religious faith has a rightful claim to universality (*catholicismus rationalis*). Sectarianism in matters of faith will therefore never occur with the latter, and where it is met with it always arises from an error

of ecclesiastical faith: that of holding one's statute (even a statute of divine revelation) for an essential piece of religion . . . and so passing off something contingent for what is necessary in itself. (SF 49-50)

In the passage just quoted, however, Kant's explicit reason for denying the universality of revealed faith is the equivalence of universality with necessity, and the claim, familiar from the first critique, that only reason and not experience is capable of supplying either one (A 1-2/B 3-6). "Universality" here refers to the fact that rational grounds for belief apply universally to all rational beings, that when I am convinced of something by rational grounds, I am convinced by grounds which would be valid for any rational being who happened to be in possession of them. It is apparently Kant's view that the claims of rational religion are universal in this sense, but claims to supernatural revelation cannot be. Those who are convinced by such a claim may hold it sincerely and fervently, but they do not hold their conviction on grounds which would be valid for any rational being who had them.

In Kant's view there is a close connection between the universality of reason in this sense and Kant's fundamental principle of the ethics of belief, the principle of enlightenment or of thinking for oneself. This connection is made explicit in Kant's 1786 essay, "What is Orientation in Thinking?":

> *Thinking for oneself* means seeking the supreme touchstone of truth in one's self, i.e., in one's own reason; and the maxim of always thinking for one's self is *enlightenment* . . . To make use of one's own reason means nothing more than to ask oneself with regard to everything that is to be assumed whether he finds it practicable to make the ground of the assumption or the rule which follows from the assumption a universal principle for the use of one's reason. (O 145-46n/305n)

The principle of thinking for oneself is nothing but a special case of the Kantian principle of autonomy applied to our intellectual conduct. The moral test is to ask oneself whether the grounds on which one holds one's belief could serve as a universally valid principle of reason. Thinking for myself no more licenses me in believing whatever I please than the principle of autonomy licenses me in doing whatever I please. Kant apparently thinks that it is consistent with the principle of thinking for oneself to hold certain beliefs in the absence of sufficient theoretical evidence for them if there exist practical or moral considerations, valid universally for all rational beings, that are capable of sufficiently grounding one's belief. But it would be a violation of the principle of thinking for oneself to permit oneself to believe something in the absence of any grounds, or from grounds which do not proceed according to a rule which might be a universally valid principle of reason.

Beyond this, however, I confess it is obscure to me what consequences Kant intended this to have. We might give it a lenient intepretation analogous to the universal law formula of the categorical imperative, which says that one is permitted to follow any rule which would not involve any impossibility or any contradictory volitions if it became a universal law of nature. On this reading, the principle might license beliefs which are not grounded on reasons universally valid for all rational beings, so long as no contradiction results from supposing that all rational beings might hold the same belief on the same grounds. It is not clear to me what would have to be true about the grounds of a belief for it to violate the principle on this interpretation, but it seems likely that at least some beliefs based on empirical revelation might turn out to be morally permissible. But presumably the denial of any such belief would be equally permissible, and this would yield Kant's rationalist conclusion that no belief based on empirical revelation can be morally required.

Alternatively, however, we might interpret the principle of thinking for oneself more strictly as saying that a belief is not permissible unless it is held on grounds which actually are universally valid for any rational being who possesses them. In other words, it would be immoral to hold a belief unless one held it on rationally adequate grounds, grounds which would be sufficient to convince any rational being who had them. Kantian rational religious faith would still be permitted by the principle in this interpretation, because Kant's moral arguments, though practical rather than theoretical in character, are supposed to be universally valid for all rational moral agents. In effect, Kant's principle of thinking for oneself would entail a variant of W. K. Clifford's renowned principle that it is wrong for anyone ever to believe anything on insufficient evidence.

The only variation would be that for Kant a belief could be grounded, and thus rendered morally permissible, by practical grounds as well as by theoretical evidence. But in this interpretation the consequences of the principle for ecclesiastical faith based on empirical revelation would be dire. For Kant holds, as we have seen, that no universally valid grounds can be given for beliefs based on empirical revelation. In this more stringent interpretation of the principle, then, any religion which goes beyond the boundaries of unassisted reason is not merely gratuitous; it is also necessarily immoral.

6. Revelation through Reason

Kant does provide one way of rescuing revealed religion, however, or at least certain parts of it. For he holds that supernatural, empirical, or external revelation, revelation through scriptures or extraordinary experiences, is not the only kind or even the most important kind.

> Revelation is either *external* or *inward.* An external revelation can be of two kinds: either (1) through works, or (2) through words. Inward divine revelation is God's revelation to us through our own reason. It must precede all other revelation and serve as a judge of external revelation. It has to be the touchstone by which I know whether an external revelation is really from *God;* and it must give me proper concepts of him. (VpR 220/160)

It may seem a wretched subterfuge for a shameless rationalist such as Kant to lay claim to divine revelation simply by identifying revelation with the deliverances of human reason. But this reaction is too hasty. For in the first place, Kant does not describe just any result obtained by human reason as a case of divine revelation. Principally, he identifies inward revelation with our pure rational concept of God as a most real being; but he also identifies inward revelation with our knowledge of our moral duties, since these can be represented as divine commands and thus go to make up our concept of God (R 87/81–82). And in the second place, we are justified in regarding all rational knowledge of God as an instance of revelation because it hardly makes sense to suppose that we might acquire any knowledge of God whatever except through revelation. No doubt we are capable of finding out many things about the natural world solely through our own initiative; and through similar ingenuity we are often able to discover the truth about other people against their will, by spying on them or by interpreting the hints they give us unintentionally through slips of the tongue or other such behavior. But in the case of an omnipotent and omniscient being, no such ingenious prying could possibly avail us. Any knowledge of any kind which we might acquire of such a being would have to depend on the decision of such a being to reveal itself to us.

Kant also regards our rational concept of God as a case of divine revelation because he is convinced that there is no other source from which we can derive a suitable concept of Deity: "The *concept* of God and the conviction of his *existence* can be met with only in reason; they can come from reason alone, and not from inspiration or from any tidings, however great their authority" (O 142/301). Of course Kant is aware that the concept of God possessed by many people, perhaps by most, derives from some other source: from the contemplation of the works of nature, for instance, or from some religious tradition claiming supernatural authority. But these are precisely the concepts of God against which we should be especially careful to guard ourselves: "Of what use is the natural concept of God as a whole? Certainly none other than the use actually made of it by most peoples: as a terrifying picture of fantasy, and a superstitious object of ceremonial adoration and hypocritical high praise" (VpR 221/161; cf. R 168–69/156–57).

Just as the principle of thinking for oneself is the touchstone of morally permissible belief generally, so inward revelation is the touchstone of permissible belief about God. As such, it can also serve in a certain sense to authenticate claims of revelation based on nonrational illumination and the external revelation claimed on the authority of scripture by ecclesiastical faiths. We cannot prove whether such experiences and records are in fact the result of special divine deeds, but we can judge whether, as regards the content communicated, they could have been. "If I encounter an immediate intuition of a sort that nature, so far as I know, cannot afford, a concept of God must still serve as a criterion for deciding whether this appearance agrees with the characteristics of the divine" (O 142/301; cf. R 169n/157n).

The inward revelation of reason is also our only criterion for the possible authenticity of external revelation. And in this connection Kant views it as the sole legitimate interpreter of any scripture or ecclesiastical tradition which claims divine authority (R 109–10/100; SF 46–48). Kant is very blunt about what this entails: "If [a scripture] flatly contradicts morality, then it cannot be from God (for example, if a father were ordered to kill his son who is, as far as he knows, perfectly innocent)" (R 87/82). "Frequently in reference to the text (the revelation) this interpretation [given by reason] may appear to us forced, it may often really be so; and yet it must be preferred to the literal interpretation if the text can possibly support it" (R 110/100–101).

But by now Kant's God may seem to some very far from omnipotent. For it now appears that God is incapable of revealing himself to human beings except through the operations of their reason. Kant appears not to admit the possibility that God might take it upon himself to make his presence known or to reveal his saving truth to us, simply by causing us to believe in that presence, irrespective of our rational scruples, to believe by faith through a grace which transcends and humbles the feeble powers of human reason. For were God to do this, as orthodox Christianity insists that he has and does, Kant would deny us the capacity to receive such a gift. Worse yet, he would blasphemously forbid us to accept it.

It is quite true, I think, that Kant would be reluctant to admit that God ever provides us with revelation in any such way. But it would be an error to think that Kant denies to God the *power* to provide it. Instead, Kant would have us reflect on what sort of being it is that would create free, rational creatures, with the vocation to self-legislation and to thinking for themselves, and then exhibit contempt for this vocation in his own conduct toward them. An omnipotent being surely has the power to take such a degrading course with its rational creatures, but the real blasphemy would consist in asserting that a good God actually chooses that course.

NOTES

1. All translations from Kant's writings are my own, but standard English translations are cited along with the German for the reader's

convenience, with the German pagination preceding the English, separated by a slash (/).

2. Pierre Viret, *Instruction chrestienne* (Geneva, 1563), vol. 2, Epistle dedicatory.

3. Edward Stillingfleet, Bishop of Worcester, *A Letter to a Deist* (London: Moses Pitt, 1682).

4. John Dryden, *Religio Laici; Or, a Layman's Faith* (London: J. Tonson, 1682), Preface.

5. Samuel Johnson, *A Dictionary of the English Language* (London: W. Strahan for J. and P. Knapton, 1775). See also my article "Deism," in Mircea Eliade, et al., eds., *The Encyclopedia of Religion* (New York: Macmillan, 1987), vol. 4, 262–64.

6. See my book *Kant's Rational Theology* (Ithaca, N. Y.: Cornell University Press, 1978), 25–94.

7. These moral arguments are expounded sympathetically in my book *Kant's Moral Religion* (Ithaca, N. Y.: Cornell University Press, 1970).

8. Joseph Butler, Bishop of Durham, *The Analogy of Religion to the Constitution of the Course of Nature* (New York: Frederick Ungar, 1961).

9. Bernard Williams, *Descartes: The Project of Pure Inquiry* (Harmondsworth, U. K.: Penguin, 1978), 26n.

10. Gottlob Christian Storr (1746–1805), *Annotationes quaedam theologicae ad philosophicam Kantii de religione doctrinam* (Tübingen: Typus Fuestianus, 1793).

Kant on Reason and Justified Belief in God

Joseph Runzo

At the beginning of the *Dialogues Concerning Natural Religion*, David Hume addresses the relation between reason and justified belief in God. In the voice of Philo, he proposes as a central epistemic thesis that

> If we distrust human reason we have now no other principle to lead us into religion. [For, Hume warns] . . . sceptics in one age, dogmatists in another—whichever system best suits the purpose of these reverend gentlemen in giving them an ascendant over mankind—they are sure to make it their favorite principle and established tenet.[1]

Kant "openly confesses" that in metaphysics, it was the works of Hume which "first interrupted my dogmatic slumber and gave my investigations in the field of speculative philosophy a quite new direction" (PM 8). Kant might have as appropriately acknowledged Hume's precedence in articulating the thesis that "apart from human reason we have no principle to lead us into religion," a thesis which lies at the heart of Kant's own philosophy of religion. As we analyze this foundational thesis of Kant's we should be forewarned, though, by its presence in Hume's work. For we should approach Kant's proposed reliance on reason to justify belief in God with some of the same suspended credulity with which we read Hume's only half-jesting suggestion, under the guise of a reference to Lord Bacon, that "a little philosophy . . . makes a man an atheist; a great deal converts him to religion."[2]

In "Kant's Deism,"[3] Allen Wood addresses this key idea in Kant's philosophy of religion, that reason alone justifies theistic belief. Wood does so by offering a lucid account of the sense in which Kant is a *deist*—though Kant regards himself as a *theist*—and an insightful explication of the reasons why Kant held this deist view. I will first explain the issues that Kant is centrally addressing and set out what I take to be the fundamental argument which Wood identifies for Kant's deist solution to those issues. After noting advantages of Kant's defense of deism, I will also argue that there are several trenchant problems with Kant's position. Finally, extending Wood's analysis, I will suggest how Kant's deist position might be amended to take account of these difficulties and so offer a stronger basis for the epistemic justification of belief in God.

1.

Kant regards himself as a *theist* because he defines a "theist" as one who allows for natural theology as a means for divine predication (L 29–30). Kant thinks this is essential for comprehending God because to limit oneself to "transcendental theology"—i.e., to concepts derivable purely a priori—results in a "wholly idle and useless" concept of God, one which is insufficient for understanding God and hence insufficient for rational, including moral, action (L 30).[4] Transcendental theology does have negative utility since in providing the means for predicating pure concepts of God, untainted by experience, it offers a sure means of avoiding anthropomorphism. However, to advance beyond this, we need to derive positive content for divine predications by means of a three-stage process (L 52–54). We must initially employ negative predication (follow the *via negationis*) to identify the divine attributes. This separates out the sensible and imperfect. Second, we must then proceed *via eminentiae* in order to know the "quantity of reality *in God.*" For God possesses, for instance, not just power and knowledge but *infinite* power and knowledge. Third, we must fill out the concepts of the infinite attributes which we have thus arrived at by using *analogical* predication, by regarding "the whole world as a consequence of its ground *in God*" (L 54). Thus, underlying Kant's appeal to transcendental and natural theology are two important theoretical concerns: the desire to avoid anthropomorphism, on the one side, and yet to give substantive content to the idea of God, on the other. But as Wood points out, Kant's emphasis on reason forces him into holding a deist position, in the seventeenth- and eighteenth-century sense of this term. As he succinctly states in the very title of *Religion within the Limits of Reason Alone*, Kant essentially rejects *revealed theology* in his defense of transcendental and natural theology.

Now, Kant's appeal to transcendental and natural theology is also based on *practical* concerns which are related to the two theoretical concerns we have just noted. He is deeply disturbed by the means and the manner in which the common religious person approaches the divine. The religious institutions of humankind function as the primary means by which the vast majority of believers comprehend and experience the divine and, what is worse in Kant's view, the ordinary believer consequently regards ecclesiastical directive and declamation as authoritative in matters of faith. It may be socially and historically necessary, because of our human weaknesses, to have institutional religion convey rational religion, but it is imperative ultimately to break out of the debilitating restraints which those very institutions impose on the human will and understanding.

This is reminiscent of Karl Barth's acknowledgment that "the catastrophe of the Church [is] inevitable."[5] But Barth concludes that for all the inherent faults of the church, "there is no friendly lifeboat into which [the believer] can clamber and row clear of the imminent disaster,"

> for the Church, situated on this side of the abyss which separates men from God, *is the place* where the eternity of *revelation* is transformed into a temporal, concrete, directly visible thing in the world.[6]

This is precisely what Kant denies. For in Kant's view, God comes to us through reason, not revelation—at least not revelation in Barth's sense—and the church, rather than being the instrumental cause of our receptivity to God, is instrumental in inhibiting our potential receptivity. Hence, the most important change for which we must strive is "enlightenment": breaking the bondage of the intellectual "tutelage" to ecclesiastical authority, a tutelage which denies our fundamental and divinely created nature as free, rational beings. (See Kant's essay, "What Is Enlightenment?")

2.

This brings us to the central lines of Kant's argument against revealed theology and for rational religion and the concomitant transcendental and natural theology, which, he feels, we can only fully develop as free beings outside the confines of a church wedded to the notion of a revealed truth that is putatively bolstered by the *magisterium* and its Protestant counterparts. At the beginning of Book IV of *Religion within the Limits of Reason Alone*, Kant defines genuine religion as "the recognition of all duties as divine commands." Genuine religion further divides into "revealed" and "rational" religion. In "revealed religion," after first coming to know (by revelation) that something is a divine command, one then recognizes it as a duty. In "rational religion" the reverse is the case: one must first know (by reason) what one's obligations are, and then one can infer that those duties are divine commands (R 142–43). Kant argues that only rational religion is warranted, alone enabling us to recognize our duties as divine commands.

In his interesting analysis in "Kant's Deism," Wood argues that Kant's own argument that revealed religion is deficient because it depends on historical knowledge is not, in fact, his central argument. Rather, the central argument for this conclusion involves a negative thesis and a positive thesis: on the negative side, Kant argues that it is *impossible* in principle to have sufficient epistemic warrant to support any claim of supernatural revelation; on the positive side, it *is possible*, in principle, for every rational being to be epistemically justified in the truth-claims of rational religion.

In general Kant argues for the principle of "thinking for oneself"—i.e., that one is only epistemically justified in a belief if one arrives at that belief on the basis of one's own uncoerced reasoning (OT 305n). Using this epistemic principle, I think that Kant's argument in defense of deism, which Wood identifies as central, can be formulated as follows:

(1) There are only two types of religion: revealed religion and rational religion.

(2) It is *impossible* for revealed religion to provide sufficient epistemic justification for theistic truth-claims.

(3) It is *possible* for rational religion to provide sufficient epistemic justification for theistic truth-claims.

(4) Therefore only rational religion can provide sufficient epistemic justification for theistic truth-claims.

(5) It is the practical vocation of every rational person to think for oneself.

(6) Rational religion encourages thinking for oneself.[7]

(7) Therefore rational religion is the only epistemically justifiable form of religion, and it promotes the proper vocation of any rational person.

Before assessing the strengths and deficiencies of this line of reasoning, let us consider one obvious objection which the defender of revealed theology will immediately mount against this argument. For Kant appears to have totally discounted the tradition of revelation and offered in its place the thin solace of depending on the finite, fickle, and corrupt human mind to apprehend the divine.

Kant holds that even *if* people were the recipients of external divine revelation—i.e., if they experienced external acts, including speech-acts, of the divine—and even *if* they were in the best possible position to comprehend those divine acts—e.g., if they were able to consider the evidence thoughtfully, and were not distracted by emotionalism or misled by dogmatic ideology accepted solely upon authority—they still *could not know* that their experiences were genuinely revelatory. Later we will analyze Kant's grounds for this claim. But it is important to note that it does not follow from this claim that there is no place for revelation in humanity's relationship to God. And in fact Kant responds to this problem by distinguishing *external* from *internal* revelation, where *internal* revelation is "God's revelation to us through our own reason" (L 160). Internal revelation provides our concept of God as most perfect being. As such, it takes precedence over and is properly used to judge external revelation. Yet, although it is epistemically dependent and secondary, *external* revelation has a certain value, for

> an external divine revelation can be an occasion for man to come for the first time to pure concepts of God which are pure concepts of the understanding; and it can also give him the opportunity to search for these concepts. (L 161)

3.

There are a number of clear advantages of Kant's appeal to reason and his defense of rational religion. I will focus on four. The first advantage, which lends support to premise (3) of the argument above, is Kant's general conception of the sort of potential access which *all* humans have to God. Kant thinks it is pernicious to suppose that genuine religion is restricted to the cultured or specially educated. He is not endorsing, of course, the extreme Tolstoyan view that educated religiosity inhibits one's faith and that only simple, trusting faith is genuine.[8] But Kant *is* opposed to the sort of division, which we find, for example, in Maimonides, between the common religious person, incapable of truly knowing God, and the person of superior intellectual and hence superior spiritual development. For in Maimonides's view,

> the true perfection of man [is] the possession of the highest intellectual faculties; the possession of such notions which lead to true metaphysical opinions as regards God. With this perfection man has obtained his final object; it gives him true human perfection; it remains to him alone; it gives him immortality; and on its account he is called man.[9]

Kant points out that the claims of revealed religion are limited either to the direct recipients of revelation or to those who possess the requisite critical understanding of the historical record of reputed revelatory events. In contrast, he feels that the claims of rational religion are universally valid, that any rational being who possesses the appropriate conceptual resources will arrive at the same, fully epistemically justified conclusions. Hence, one requirement of the true church (which exhibits the moral kingdom of God on earth) is universality:

> although divided and at variance in unessential opinions, [the church] is none the less, with respect to its fundamental intention, founded upon such basic principles as must necessarily lead to a general unification in a single church (thus, no sectarian divisions). (R 93)

In this manner Kant is attempting to support a view which it seems to me is clearly theologically sound—viz., that genuine religion is not the privilege of the few but the right of all.

The second and third advantages of Kant's appeal to reason are related to this first advantage, but more directly support premise (2), by denying the sufficiency of revealed theology. In the view Kant presents, true piety does not require a detailed knowledge of God. Otherwise,

> the small body of textual scholars (the clerics) . . . would drag

along behind itself the long train of the unlearned (the laity) who, of themselves, are ignorant of the Scripture . . . But if this, in turn, is to be prevented from happening, recognition and respect must be accorded, in Christian dogmatic, to universal human reason as the supremely commanding principle in a natural religion, and the revealed doctrine, . . . must be cherished and cultivated as merely a means, but a most precious means, of making this doctrine comprehensible, even to the ignorant. . . . (R 152–53)

Surely Kant is right that genuine religion does not require a thorough knowledge of God, which would after all be impossible. He concludes that

faith needs merely the idea of God, to which all morally earnest (and therefore confident) endeavor for the good must inevitably lead; it need not presume that it can certify the objective reality of this idea through theoretical apprehension. Indeed, the minimum of knowledge (it is possible that there may be a God) must suffice, subjectively, for whatever can be made the duty of every man. (R 142n)

Yet while faith does not require—and certainly is not reducible to—a thorough knowledge of God, knowledge of God is still possible. Using natural theology, we can properly ascribe attributes to God by analogy, and, importantly, we are able to ascribe those attributes which derive from the notion of personhood—e.g., that God wills and knows.

Directly related to this second strength of Kant's view is a third advantage: the specific claim that we do not need the *historically* grounded truths of revealed theology. There are two reasons why it is essential that theistic truth-claims need not be historically grounded. In the first place, in Kant's general epistemology the mind is not a tabula rasa; rather, all experience is structured by the mind of the perceiver. Thus Kant points out vis-à-vis religious experience that "even if God were to make an immediate appearance, I would still need rational theology as a presupposition. For how am I to be certain that it is God himself who has appeared to me, or only another powerful being?" (L 161). Since all our experiences are conceptualized, we could never know directly from our experiences that what appears to us to be the case, vis-à-vis God, is the case. Hence, neither direct external experience (which later becomes a historical event) nor historical inquiry regarding already past religious experiences could ever be sufficient for knowing that a putative act of God is an act of God. In the second place, historical inquiry is itself delimited both by the sociohistorical context of the inquirer and by the historical context of the original record. Consequently, no historically based truth-claim could itself provide sure knowledge of the most perfect being, God.

Both of these reasons for trying to separate theistic belief from any reliance on historical inquiry are central to the genesis of the influential "neo-Reformed" movement in theology in this century. Thus we find Barth, the progenitor of this movement, asking in his seminal *Epistle to the Romans* whether we cannot escape "from the accursed relativity of every merely human possibility . . . [for] even our thinking is conducted within the sphere of relativity."[10] And following out this theme, Tillich explicitly declares that

> it is a disastrous distortion of the meaning of faith to identify it with the belief in the historical validity of the biblical stories. . . . Faith does not include historical knowledge about the way in which [significant religious events] took place.[11]

Tillich himself bases this view on two points. First, he thinks that every cultural activity of humans, such as historical inquiry, involves an inherently finite perspective and so cannot tell us about matters of ultimate concern.[12] And second, he thinks that the historian always starts from certain philosophical (and therefore relative) presuppositions in order to discover the "historical facts."[13] Therefore, Tillich is able to draw the conclusion, propitious in the face of modern historical-critical biblical analysis, that "faith cannot be shaken by historical research even if its results are critical of the traditions in which the event is recorded."[14]

4.

The fourth strength of Kant's position is the central emphasis which he places on the role of reason in the religious life. If God has fully revealed Godself in scripture and / or personal religious experience, then, so it would seem, there is no need to attempt to reason about God. But reasoning about God will make sense on certain assumptions: (a) it will make sense if one assumes, as Kant does, that God's revelation is not directly accessible to the human mind and that we can never know, even when God does reveal Godself, that God has done so; (b) the attempt to reason about God will also make sense if one assumes that the person of faith needs to reason about God in order to address newly arising issues which were not or could not have been addressed in past tradition or within the historical context of revelatory events; and (c) most importantly, reasoning about God will make sense if one assumes that all revelation and experiential contact with God is necessarily mediated by the world-view, and shaped by the needs and desires, of the human percipient.

We have already noted Kant's reasoning for (a) in holding that rational theology (transcendental and natural) must serve as the judge of revealed theology; (b) and (c) explain why we must engage in rational theology. For it is unlikely that God's past revelation can be applied directly, without reasoning, to uniquely modern ethical issues arising from medical technology, for example, or the threat of nuclear holocaust, ecological disaster, and so on. And, even if one believed that God's revelation is complete and final in scripture, or that the experience of God is ever present, what is revealed and what is experienced about God will be unavoidably structured by the world-view[15] of the human recipient. Consequently, reasoning about God is necessary not only for achieving an initial, pure concept of God and as a check on the validity of the content of putative revelation; human reasoning about God is an inseparable element of the very content itself of the revelation and experience of God.

Without the conceptual resources to understand and experience God, and without the unifying conception which our schemas bring to our beliefs and experiences, it is not possible to engage in an explicitly theistic life. In other words, having a theology is a necessary condition for the life of faith in God. Hence, reason does not serve as just one among many elements in the religious life. Reason is foundational to any genuinely religious life. Since this essential reasoning about God must be autonomous, the centrality of theology also shows the importance of Kant's defense of the principle of "thinking for oneself" in matters of genuine religion.

In general, humans cannot have purposes and cannot live autonomous lives successfully unless they have a basic unifying conception of the world in which they live. Otherwise, sustained action would be literally aimless and understanding chaotic. The total system of ideas and beliefs—the world-view—of a monotheist provides precisely such a unifying schema for purposive activity. Although the common religious person does not think of it this way, the implicit claim of the person of faith is that theology provides the best unifying cognitive structure for an ultimately purposive life—i.e., a life oriented wholly toward God.

5.

However, this very strength of Kant's emphasis on the role of reason in the religious life is also a major weakness. For Kant overemphasizes the importance of reason, to the detriment of significant elements of genuine religion. In Kant's view, one can be religious as long as one is aware of one's moral duties, and that awareness includes the idea that if God exists, he commands those moral duties. One does not need knowledge of God or even of God's existence. One only needs to be committed to the assumption that it is possible that God exists. Thus in the *Prolegomena* Kant says that

> we are compelled to consider the world as if it were the work of a Supreme Understanding and Will. . . . [But] by means of this analogy, however, there remains a concept of the Supreme Being sufficiently determined for us, though we have left out everything that could determine it absolutely or in itself; for we determine it as regards the world and hence as regards ourselves, and more do we not require. (PM 106)

Substantive theological content is thus incidental and not essential to genuine religion. And reason, particularly reason regarding the moral point of view, is preeminent over theological belief.

This conception of monotheism runs the risk of reducing theology to ethics and the religious life to the moral life. Yet there is an even more fundamental danger here. True, Kant is recognizing that if there is a God, it would be unreasonable as well as irreligious to think that God gave us reason and then does not expect us both to employ and abide by this faculty. This is reminiscent of Descartes's notions that God would be a deceiver if we could not utterly rely on "the light of nature" and that the light of nature dictates that "the understanding should always know before the will makes a decision."[16] But Kant's complete reliance on reason to justify belief in God falls prey to the problems of evidentialism.

I think Kant is mistaken to suggest that "it is *possible* for rational religion to provide *sufficient* epistemic justification for theistic truth-claims" (premise [3]), and I think he misleadingly overstates the negative assertion that "it is *impossible* for *revealed religion* to provide sufficient epistemic justification for theistic truth-claims" (premise [2]). For Kant's defense of these premises is based on an understanding of epistemic justification which is—even though in a weak sense—evidentialist.[17]

An evidentialist holds that in order for a belief to be epistemically justified, it must be rational, and to be rational, it must be supported by evidence.[18] Typically, evidentialists are also foundationalists. Putting these two epistemic principles together in terms of theistic belief, evidentialism can be variously characterized as the view that it is either irrational or unreasonable or intellectually dishonest to believe in God unless either (a) one has *sufficient* evidence or (b) the belief is a foundational, or "properly basic," belief—i.e., a belief which is epistemically justified even though it is not based on other beliefs as reasons. And for the *classical* foundationalist, a belief is only properly basic if it is self-evident, evident to the senses, or incorrigible.

Kant does not hold this strong evidentialist thesis, since he holds that we could never have *sufficient* evidence or proof for theism (nor is theistic belief self-evident, evident to the senses, or incorrigible). But since he endorses natural theology, he allows for either pure reason or a posteriori considerations, adjudicated by pure reason, to provide reasons or evidence for theistic belief. In either case, he insists that theistic belief must be based on some (in fact moral) reasons, reasons which would be universally valid for any rational being who is able to possess them. Although this is not as unremittingly strong as the evidentialist's demand for sufficient evidence, what Kant fails to see is the possibility that theistic beliefs could be properly basic beliefs,

beliefs that are epistemically justified without evidence, or other beliefs as reasons. More precisely, theistic beliefs could be properly basic beliefs even though, contrary to the classical foundationalist's view, they are neither self-evident, nor evident to the senses, nor incorrigible.

Now, again, a basic belief is a belief which is held immediately and is not based on other beliefs as reasons, and a properly basic belief is a belief which one can hold as basic without violating any fundamental epistemic principles. Yet, to say that one does not need reasons for theistic beliefs, that they could be basic beliefs, is not to say that these beliefs are *groundless.* The sorts of beliefs typically appealed to as paradigmatic basic beliefs are ordinary perceptual beliefs, memory beliefs, and beliefs ascribing mental states to other persons. So, for instance, immediately coming to believe that a rugby player is in pain as one watches him writhing on the ground after running headlong into another player, or groggily recalling last night and immediately forming the belief that one suffered a bout of insomnia, is to form a properly basic belief. For being justified in believing that someone is in pain, or that one could not sleep last night, does not depend on having other beliefs as reasons, such as believing that rugby players are often in pain or that the sheets lying rumpled on the floor indicate a sleepless night. Rather, these beliefs are justified because they are formed under, and therefore grounded in, the proper circumstances.

In the same manner, a theist can properly believe, without inferring this from other beliefs as reasons, that "God created nature" or "God should be thanked." For a theist often comes to hold these beliefs not on the basis of evidence or inference but immediately—e.g., while observing the works of nature, or while hearing sacred music, or while in quiet prayer. And in such instances, being awed by the Alps, or by the wondrous complexity of an Alpine meadow, or by Bach's *B Minor Mass,* or feeling the (putative) presence of God during prayer, could serve as *grounds* for belief about God and God's relation to the world.[19]

If I am right about this, then Kant's observation that no experience can ever correspond to, and no empirical evidence could ever be sufficient to justify, belief in God as the supremely perfect being turns out to be beside the point. Evidence, whether theoretical or empirical, is not needed to justify basic beliefs. If theistic beliefs can be basic beliefs, then they can be properly basic beliefs *grounded* in the human experience of the revelation of the divine. (So this is not to endorse *groundless* beliefs, to which Kant would rightly object.) And revealed theology, then, has a place in genuine religion, even if, as I would agree with Kant, rational theology must serve as the arbiter of the truth of purported revelation.

6.

This brings us to a second major difficulty with Kant's position. We have already noted that Kant shows an awareness of the problem of historicity, particularly as it concerns, in Kant's mind, the deficiencies of revealed theology. But Kant's reliance on reason will not help him evade the problem of historicity. Kant assumes that there is a universally valid basic conception of God which is trans-historically and cross-culturally comprehensible by anyone who honestly pursues rational thought. This seems highly doubtful, especially for us in the twentieth century with our pluralist understanding of the great world religions as well as the recognition of the enormous variety of world-views in general, nonreligious as well as religious. If anything, we have better grounds for supposing that not all rational people *will* come to hold the same pure concept of the divine. However, at the least it is safe to say that while it might be true that all rational beings would come to the same concept of the divine, we cannot *know* this to be true.[20]

Kant argues that within his epistemology of religion one "will no longer be in danger of forming an incomplete concept of God from mere nature." For, he says, "I have already received from my reason a thoroughly determinate concept; and by means of this concept I can judge all God's works in this world insofar as He has revealed Himself in them" (L 161). But the relativity of human understanding to one's own historical place and cultural context affects both the concepts which one will form *via rational theology* and the sorts of judgments which one will make as to what those conceptual-schema-relative concepts tell one about revealed theology. For as in every human inquiry, what will count as facts and what will be accounted significant events—in this case, facts about God and revelatory events—depends on such factors as what questions one is trying to answer, what issues are taken to override all others, and

what is regarded as a sufficiently comprehensive system of explanation. And these factors are relative to one's particular world-
view: how they are assessed will vary from person to person.
Hence, we have good reason neither to suppose that there is a
universally valid pure concept of God nor for supposing that,
even if there were such a concept, all rational people would
apply it to the natural order in the same way to determine, by
analogical predication, the nature of God and the relation of
Godself to humanity.

This is a point which Friedrich Schleiermacher, following much
of Kant's epistemology in his own work, was perhaps the first
to make explicit when he observed that, "regarded from the
outside, according to the definite attitude and form it assumes
in particular cases, [religion] is a product of time and history."[21]
Put in other words, all religions are inherently subject to the
historicity of human perspective. And as Barth suggests and
Kant would agree, "religion compels us to the perception that
God is not to be found in [institutional] religion." But the very
problem of the relativity of human thought, which undermines
the possibility that institutional religion can bring one to God,
likewise undermines the notion that where religion fails, human
reason succeeds. For as Barth notes,

> We dispose ourselves upon our appropriate shelf in the emporium
> of religion and ethics, ticketed and labeled with this or that
> philosophy of life. . . . From time to time we change our position;
> but this only suggests to those gifted with acute powers of obser-
> vation the triviality of any particular position.[22]

While which world-view we hold is not a trivial matter, the fact
that we change our views, and the fact that there are alternative
views, indicates the conceptual-schema-relativity of the notion
of what is reasonable and what should be considered epistemically warranted.

7.

How might we amend Kant's position to preserve the strengths
of his appeal to reason and yet meet the problems raised by
his reliance on reason? The direction we must take here is
precisely one which, as Wood notes at the end of "Kant's Deism,"

Kant himself leaves no room for: the divine grace of God's self-revelation beyond the operations of human reason alone. As we have seen, we need to allow for revelation, particularly insofar as it could ground theistic beliefs as basic beliefs, and therefore we need to allow for revealed theology. And we cannot depend on rational religion *alone*, because that both incurs the problems of evidentialism and ignores the relativity of human thought and perception. Regarding the problems of evidentialism, we have seen that Kant's argument (1)—(7) fails, because premise (2) is false and premise (3) is overstated and hence misleading. Regarding the relativity of human thought and perception, if revealed theology is to have a place, revelation cannot be a matter of the mere conveyance of propositions about the divine. For *anything* which we can comprehend as humans, including any revealed truths, we must necessarily comprehend in terms of our own world-view. So if revelation is thought of as essentially involving the delivery of correct facts about God, we will be driven back into the problem of relativism.[23]

What we need, then, is an account of revelation where its significance does not depend on the accurate delivery of facts about the divine. And indeed this sort of view is offered in the neo-Reformed tradition which I have been contrasting with Kant's own position. Thus, Karl Barth suggests that "Religion brings us to the place where we must wait, in order that God may *confront* us . . . "[24] and Tillich defines revelation as "the experience in which an ultimate concern grasps the human mind. . . . "[25] In the same vein, Rudolf Bultmann talks about God "confronting us" in a "demand for decision." In this view, revelation is the *self*-manifestation of God. This supports an alternative to the evidentialist emphasis in Kant's appeal to reason. Instead of one foundation, justified belief in God has two essential epistemic foundations: reason and *faith*—where faith is the (uncoerced) human response to God's self-manifestation.

True, Kant holds that he "found it necessary to deny *knowledge* [of God, freedom, and immortality], in order to make room for faith." But he does so because he feels that the alternative, "dogmatism of metaphysics, . . . wars against morality." Thus it is in the interests of morality—it is rationally required by morality—that belief in God is faith rather than theoretical knowledge. Because Kant places an evidentialist emphasis on reason, he arrives at a highly restricted notion of faith: theistic faith is moral faith. And at the same time, that restrictive, evidentialist emphasis precludes precisely the means for a richer notion of theistic faith: an autonomous response to God's self-revelation through God's grace. Where Kant moves from reason to faith, I am suggesting a move from reason to faith and revelation. This offers broader grounds for, and a stronger view of, faith. For Kant, faith is epistemically justified on practical, rational, moral grounds. Against this, I am suggesting that reason is insufficient to ground theistic faith. For if it is justified, faith will be epistemically justified on the grounds of God's self-revelation, grounds which will include but are not reducible to moral grounds. Faith becomes, then, the ultimate commitment that one has indeed confronted God. And this in turn makes it rational to suppose that religious experience can provide grounds for theistic beliefs as properly basic beliefs.

The church constitutes a human attempt to deal systematically and authoritatively with the human confrontation with the divine—in ritual and liturgy, creed and theology. As a human endeavor, it of course fails to achieve its goal. But we should not aim, as Kant would have it, to phase out the authoritative character of institutional religion because of that failure. For institutional religion is by nature authoritative. Rather, its very failure can help us realize the ultimacy of God over and against our own finitude and relativity. For even pure reason, let alone the empirical facts of the natural order, cannot bring one to God. Yet, in keeping with Kant's own concerns, *through faith* and God's grace, God's self-revelation will be available to *all* rationally honest people who possess the appropriate conceptual resources.

This is not to suggest that the sort of radical appeal to faith which much of the neo-Reformed movement proposed should be accepted in place of Kant's appeal to reason. On the spectrum of views which appeal to either revelation or reason as the epistemic justification for theistic belief, the Barthian neo-Reformed view is just as extreme on its side as Kant's is on the other. Rather, I am suggesting a middle course in which the neo-Reformed identification of the inextirpable place of faith *and* God's self-revelation counterbalances Kant's recognition of the centrality of reason, and vice versa. Kant is right, that without reason there can be no faith. Apart from a monotheistic world-view, the experience of God would be incoherent and faith contentless. Yet it is faith that must bring one to God, because it is faith in God's grace that God has indeed *revealed* Godself in our conceptual-schema-relative conceptions and experiences, which can take us beyond the limits of reason alone.[26]

NOTES

1. David Hume, *Dialogues Concerning Natural Religion*, Nelson Pike, ed. (New York: Bobbs-Merrill, 1970), 17-18.

2. Ibid., 16-17.

3. Printed in this volume, 1-21.

4. This, in Kant's terms, is a "deist."

5. Karl Barth, *The Epistle to the Romans*, trans. Edwyn C. Hoskyns (Oxford: Oxford University Press, 1972), 336.

6. Ibid., 336 and 332 (italics mine).

7. Note that rational religion—recognizing, *apart* from revelation, all duties as divine commands—does not *per se* require thinking for oneself.

8. See, e.g., Leo Tolstoy, "My Confession," in E. D. Klemke, ed., *The Meaning of Life* (Oxford: Oxford University Press, 1981), 9-19; for a clear example of this view in Tolstoy's literary works, see "Master and Man."

9. Moses Maimonides, *The Guide for the Perplexed*, trans. M. Friedlander (New York: Dover Publications, 1956), 395.

10. Barth, 255, 436.

11. Paul Tillich, *Dynamics of Faith* (New York: Harper and Row, 1958), 87, 89.

12. Ibid., 76.

13. Ibid., 93.

14. Ibid., 89.

15. As I am using this term, a world-view consists in the total web of concepts and beliefs, interconnected by past reasoning and the present structure of our process of reasoning, which the mind brings to experience.

16. René Descartes, *Meditations on First Philosophy*, trans. Laurence J. LaFleur (New York: Bobbs-Merrill, 1960), Meditation IV, 57.

17. In saying this, I am taking Kant's notion of "thinking for oneself" in the stricter sense which Wood identifies in "Kant's Deism."

18. For an excellent analysis of evidentialism and its historical background, see Nicholas Wolterstorff's Introduction to *Faith and Rationality: Reason and Belief in God*, Alvin Plantinga and Nicholas Wolterstorff, eds. (Notre Dame, Ind.: University of Notre Dame Press, 1983), 5-7, and his article "Can Belief in God Be Rational If It Has No Foundations?" in the same volume, 136-40.

19. Two philosophers who have recently developed strong arguments

against an evidentialist account of religious belief are Alvin Plantinga and William Alston. See Plantinga, "Is Belief in God Rational?" in *Rationality and Religious Belief*, ed. C. F. Delaney (Notre Dame, Ind.: University of Notre Dame Press, 1979), 7–27; "Is Belief in God Properly Basic?" *Nous* 15 (1981): 41–51; "Reason and Belief in God," in Plantinga and Wolterstorff, eds., 16–93; and "On Taking Belief in God as Basic," in *Religious Experience and Religious Belief: Essays in the Epistemology of Religion*, Joseph Runzo and Craig K. Ihara, eds. (Lanham, Md.: University Press of America, 1986), 1–17; see also Alston, "Religious Experience and Religious Belief," *Nous* 16 (1982): 3–12; "Christian Experience and Christian Belief," in Plantinga and Wolterstorff, eds., 103–34; and "Religious Experience as a Ground of Religious Belief," in Runzo and Ihara, eds., 31–51. While I agree with Alston and Plantinga that theistic beliefs can be basic beliefs, I think they do not take full account of the relativizing effect of our world-views on our beliefs, basic or otherwise. On this point, see my "World-Views and the Epistemic Foundations of Theism," *Religious Studies* 25 (March 1989): 31–51.

20. For an explanation of the problem of relativism for theology, and an analysis of the relativity of truth-claims to world-views, see my *Reason, Relativism and God* (London: Macmillan, 1986; New York: St. Martin's Press, 1986), chapters 1 and 2, respectively.

21. Friedrich Schleiermacher, *On Religion: Speeches to Its Cultured Despisers*, trans. John Oman (New York: Harper and Row, 1958), 13.

22. Barth, 230.

23. For an analysis of this issue vis-à-vis the neo-Reformed appeal to the *kerygma* to avoid the problem of relativism, see my "Relativism and Absolutism in Bultmann's Demythologizing Hermeneutic," *The Scottish Journal of Theology* 32 (1979): 401–19.

24. Barth, 242 (italics mine).

25. Tillich, 78 (italics mine).

26. I am indebted to Allen Wood and Nick Wolterstorff for their helpful comments on the original version of this paper, and I am grateful to the National Endowment for the Humanities for support for this paper through a Summer Stipend Fellowship.

Conundrums in Kant's Rational Religion

Nicholas P. Wolterstorff

In his *Critique of Practical Reason*, Kant argued that the *Summum Bonum* is a necessary ideal of practical reason. Acknowledging morality as real requires that we also think of such a state as real. One aspect of the *Summum Bonum* is that in it, each person's happiness is directly proportioned to that person's moral worth. Obviously this present life does not qualify as such a state, nor are we as human beings capable of bringing about such a state. Accordingly, Kant drew the conclusion that, for there to be such a state, there must be a God who proportions happiness to virtue, and we ourselves must enjoy some sort of "immortal" existence transcending this present physical/historical existence of ours. Another aspect of the *Summum Bonum* is that, in it, each person can endlessly progress in the direction of ideal moral worth—hence also in the direction of complete happiness.[1] Or to put the same point differently, the *Summum Bonum* is that state in which it is possible for us, whatever we may have done in the past, to advance toward becoming persons entirely well-pleasing to God. God will express pleasure over our advance in moral worth by granting to us ever greater happiness.

In *Religion within the Limits of Reason Alone*, Kant speaks again of the *Summum Bonum*, only now from the side of religion rather than from the side of morality. He assumes that religious belief, if it is to be justifiably held, must be based on adequate evidence. Religious belief is not self-justifying. It must receive its justification from elsewhere. Thus Kant continues the tradition of evidentialism concerning religious belief which was initiated by John Locke.[2] Furthermore, Kant was convinced that *morality* is the only area of human existence in which there is any hope of finding the adequate evidence. Adequate reasons for religious beliefs will always prove to be moral principles. It would be a serious mistake to say of Kant that he tried to *reduce* religion to morality. What he tried to do, rather, was show that morality provides us with *reasons* for holding certain central religious beliefs, thus making us *justified* in holding them. Kant regarded the moral principles in question as *necessary* truths—albeit *synthetic*, not analytic, necessary truths. Thus Kant was not only an evidentialist concerning religious belief; his particular way of trying to carry out the evidentialist requirement satisfies the demands of classical foundationalism.

In discussing the justification of religious belief, Kant had his eye especially on Christianity. He did not think that everything in the Christianity of the churches could be rationally grounded. But he did think that the core, the kernel, of Christianity could be justified and, conversely, that Christianity was, above all religions, a religion of morality. The ritualistic side of Christianity should be seen, he thought, as having merely historical worth: rituals are necessary, for a time, if humanity is to progress to the point where it can discard a faith of divine worship and make do with a purely rational religion. Furthermore, some passages in the Bible may have to be interpreted in a somewhat forced manner. Yet Kant thought that, overall, no serious violence would be done to the New Testament, at least, if we interpret it as proclaiming a religion which can, in fact, be grounded on moral foundations—if we interpret it, "as regards its essential content, in line with the universal moral dogmas" (R 101).[3]

The main element of Christianity on which Kant had his eye in *Religion* was faith in salvation. Are we warranted, he asked, in holding out salvation—endless increase in happiness—as a genuine possibility for ourselves? If faith in the possibility of salvation is to be justified, we must be entitled, Kant said, to believe two specific things about our moral status and moral progress: we must be justified in believing "that we can become well-pleasing to God through a good course of life in the future" and we must be justified in believing that our guilt for our past wrongdoing will somehow be undone—in other words, that there will be atonement for us, reparation for guilt, redemption, and thus reconciliation with God (R 106).

As to the first of these, Kant saw no problem. Even the

person characterized by radical evil is capable of a change of heart; for "a change of heart such as this must be possible, because duty requires it" (R 60). And though having a good moral character does not yet guarantee that each of one's individual actions will be good, that too must be seen as a theoretical, if not a practical, possibility—again, on the *ought implies can* principle. But the very concept of God implies that insofar as a person's character and actions are good, that person will be well-pleasing to God.

It is that other conviction, that other component of faith in salvation, which Kant found deeply problematic and which, as I read *Religion*, haunted him throughout. How can our evil past be made well-pleasing to God? How can guilt for our *prior* wrongdoing be "undone" (R 106), "wiped out" (R 172)? And if somehow it can be undone, what reason is there for thinking it *will* be undone? Yet unless it can be undone, and unless we have reason for thinking it will be undone, faith in salvation is groundless. For none of us is without wrongdoing. So if our guilt is not wiped out, the proportioning of felicity to moral worth will result in our happiness being limited rather than endlessly expansible.

Clearly, says Kant, the wiping out is beyond human capabilities. Suppose that a person, having had a character of radical evil, undergoes a conversion, conversion being, for each of us, as we have seen, always a real possibility.

> Whatever a man may have done in the way of adopting a good disposition, and indeed, however steadfastly he may have persevered in conduct comformable to such a disposition, he nevertheless started from evil, and this debt [*Verschuldung*, guilt] he can by no possibility wipe out. For he cannot regard the fact that he incurs no new debts subsequent to his change of heart as equivalent to having discharged his old ones. Neither can he, through future good conduct, produce a surplus over and above what he is under obligation to perform at every instant, for it is always his duty to do all the good that lies in his power. (R 66)

So too,

> this debt which is original, or prior to all the good a man may do—this, and no more, is what we referred to in Book One as

the *radical* evil in man—this debt can never be discharged by another person, so far as we can judge according to the justice of our human reason. For this is no *transmissible* liability which can be made over to another like a financial indebtedness . . . ; rather is it *the most personal of all debts*, namely a debt of sins, which only the culprit can bear and which no innocent person can assume even though he be magnanimous enough to wish to take it upon himself for the sake of another. (R 66)

Are we then each forever laden with the guilt we have acquired by the radical evil of our character? Is there no way in which we, past as well as future, can become well-pleasing to God? Is hope for salvation mere illusion? Must all mankind "look forward to *endless punishment* and exclusion from the kingdom of God" (R 66)?

No, says Kant. Though "satisfaction must be rendered to Supreme Justice, in whose sight no one who is blameworthy can ever be guiltless" (R 67), right there *in* the act of conversion we can spy the satisfaction rendered to divine justice (R 67).

The good principle is present quite as much in the desertion of the evil as in the adoption of the good disposition, and the pain, which by rights accompanies the former disposition, ensues wholly from the latter. The coming forth from the corrupted into the good disposition is, in itself (as "the death of the old man," "the crucifying of the flesh"), a sacrifice and an entrance upon a long train of life's ills. These the new man undertakes in the disposition of the Son of God, that is, merely for the sake of the good, though really they are due as *punishments* to another, namely to the old man (for the old man is indeed morally another). (R 68)

In short, the moral life here in this present existence of ours requires that we repeatedly reject what promises to give happiness, in favor of the call of duty. It requires that we choose sorrow and suffering. It is this giving up of happiness, this painful embrace of sorrow, that constitutes punishment for the guilt of our former adoption of an evil character.

But the person who, by strength of will, has undergone conversion and thereby painfully entered a life of suffering—this pain making satisfaction for the guilt of the radical evil which characterized him or her before conversion—is not yet in the clear, not typically so, anyway. For though one's heart may now be pure, it does not follow that all one's actions will be pure. On the contrary, she is called to moral *progress*. Good characters come in varying degrees of strength (R 42, 43, 69n). So what is to be done about the guilt of the person of good character who performs incidental acts of wrongdoing? Though the guilt of evil character may not haunt us throughout eternity, provided we change our heart, will the guilt for evil actions do so, in particular, the guilt for evil actions done *subsequent* to our conversion?

No, says Kant. Divine forgiveness will undo such guilt. In the first place, "although the man (regarded from the point of view of his empirical nature as a sentient being) is *physically* the self-same guilty person as before and must be judged as such before a moral tribunal and hence by himself; yet, because of his new disposition, he is (regarded as an intelligible being) *morally* another in the eyes of a divine judge for whom this disposition takes the place of action" (R 68). And secondly, "what in our earthly life (and possibly at all future times and in all worlds) is ever only a *becoming* (namely, becoming a man well-pleasing to God) is credited to us exactly as if we were already in full possession of it . . . " (R 70).[4] Just as the punishment consisting in the pain of choosing a good character wipes out the guilt one has acquired because of one's evil character and the deeds which flowed from it, so divine forgiveness wipes out, for those who have a good but weak character, the guilt they acquire as the consequence of episodically falling into evil actions.

This divine forgiveness of the evil deeds done by persons of good but weak character, granted on the ground of their goodness of character—or as Kant puts it, this making good by God "in consideration of an upright disposition, the deficiency of the deed" (R 110)—is called by Kant an act of *grace*. Obviously in calling it this he is suggesting that his account has captured an important dimension of Christianity. It is problematic, however, whether there is anything at all "gracious" in God's act, as Kant conceives it. What Kant is doing, in his entire argument, is probing the implications of our human rights and obligations. But something is an act of grace on someone's part only if the rest of us have no *right* to his or her performance of that act. If we have a moral claim on someone's doing something, then for that person to do that is not for the person to act graciously but for the person to grant what is due us. It is to act *justly*, not to act *graciously.*[5] We may of course be *distressed* over a person's failure to act graciously; perhaps the source of our distress is that we do not like what that failure reveals about the person's character. But what it reveals is not a deficiency in the acknowledgment of legitimate claims on him. Thus Kant cannot have it both ways: he cannot hold that we can expect God's forgiveness, since God's failure to forgive would violate the moral order of rights and obligations, and also hold that God's granting of forgiveness is an act of grace on God's part. But since Kant's project is to ground religion rationally in the deliverances of morality, that is, in the structure of rights and obligations, it is grace that will have to go. God must be understood in the Kantian scheme as *required* to forgive. Of course this means that a gap begins to open between Christianity, on the one hand, and Kant's rational religion, on the other.

There is one passage which appears to say something quite different from what I have just interpreted Kant as holding. It appears to say that even those of good character *do not* have a moral claim on God's forgiveness of the guilt of their incidental wrongdoings. That passage reads:

> That what in our earthly life (and possibly at all future times and in all worlds) is ever only a *becoming* . . . should be credited to us exactly as if we were already in full possession of it—to this we really have no legal claim, that is, so far as we know ourselves . . . and so the accuser within us would be more likely to propose a judgment of condemnation. Thus the decree is always one of grace alone, although fully in accord with the divine justice, when we come to be cleared of all liability by dint of our faith in such goodness; for the decree is based upon a giving of satisfaction (a satisfaction which consists for us only in the idea of an improved disposition, known only to God). (R 70)

The language of this passage is scarcely lucid. But if we interpret Kant as really holding that those of good character have no claim on God's forgiveness for their acts of incidental wrongdoing, then we would have to conclude already that Kant has failed in his own project of grounding faith in salvation in the domain of morality. Accordingly, I propose that we take as the crucial clue for interpreting this passage the qualification "so far as we know ourselves," which follows the words "to this we really have no legal claim," along with the words at the end, "known only to God." It was one of Kant's doctrines that one can never know with surety whether one has a good character (cf. R 56–57; 71). If one does have a good character, one does have a claim on divine forgiveness; the moral order would be violated if such forgiveness were not forthcoming. In fact, though, no one knows whether he or she has a claim on divine forgiveness, for no one knows whether he or she has such a character. Only God knows.

A more serious question to raise about Kant's appeal to divine forgiveness is why, in Kant's scheme, God would ever do such a thing as forgive. In the Christian vision, divine forgiveness, though indeed an act of grace, is not unmotivated. It is grounded in God's love. God, out of love for God's human creatures, transcends the entitlements of justice and forgives. Kant does, on occasion, speak of "the love . . . of God toward men" (R 110). That seems entirely gratuitous, though. In the Kantian scheme, all we know of God is that God honors and ensures the requirements of morality—i.e., of rights and obligations. Kant himself emphasizes, indeed, that "we must place God's beneficence not in an unconditioned *goodwill* toward His creatures but in this, that He first looks upon their moral character, through which they can be *well-pleasing* to Him, and only then makes good their inability to fulfill this requirement of themselves" (R 132). Here is Kant's thought: to have rejected one's evil character and chosen a good character is to be committed to an endless progress in goodness. Though for us it is impossible to know with surety whether we have indeed adopted a good character, God's sight penetrates to the heart. If God sees there a good disposition, then God "judges" the sequence of individual actions, ordered overall in the direction of moral progress, "as a completed whole" (R 60-61); and God does this on account of the good disposition "from which this progress itself is derived" (R 61). What is in fact "ever only a becoming" is by God "credited to us exactly as if we were already in full possession of it" (R 70)—on the ground that "because of his new disposition, man is . . . morally another in the eyes of God for whom this disposition takes the place of action" (R 68).

Kant distinguishes here betweeen, on the one hand, the person's underlying character or disposition and, on the other, the person's sequence of actions which, in the case of the person of good character, exhibits moral progress. And he then says that God judges *the moral ideal as attained*, on the ground that the underlying disposition is pure. There are two ways of interpreting "judges" here. In one interpretation, God affirms that the person has reached perfection of action, and this because that person's character is good. But this would be to attribute the assertion of falsehood to God. I think, accordingly, that we should be extremely reluctant to conclude that this is what Kant had in mind. The other interpretation is that God, because of the person's purity of heart, *treats* the person as if the person's actions had reached perfection.

This latter, more plausible interpretation raises the question: Why would God do a thing like that? Ultimately Kant's answer has to be: the person of pure heart has a claim on God to such treatment. If—per impossible—God did not treat the person thus, the moral order would be violated, subverted.

But, to understate the point, it is far from evident that this is so. Would *we* be obligated, if we believed someone to be of good character, to treat the person as if she had attained moral perfection in her actions—thus to practice Kantian forgiveness? It hardly seems so. But in the Kantian universe, God and humanity live under the same moral order.

Further, imagine two persons who have undergone conversion, one of whom now lives in total consistency with her new maxim of character and the other of whom repeatedly falls into wrong-doing; the person's character, though good, is weak. Surely the former is more virtuous. Can it really be the case, in the Kantian scheme, that God is obligated to treat these two alike? Would *we* be obligated to treat them alike?

But let us press on. Thus far I have spoken of divine forgiveness, in the Kantian scheme, as consisting of God's treating persons of good but weak character as if they were of good and morally omnipotent character and God's doing so simply on the ground of their goodness of character. But I do not think that this is in fact how Kant thinks of forgiveness; nor would it be sufficient for his project to think of it thus. Kant describes forgiveness as the *undoing* of guilt, as the *wiping out* of guilt. It is necessary that he think of it thus. For he holds that in the *Summum Bonum*, happiness is proportioned to worth; and he holds further that in the *Summum Bonum* there is no limitation in principle on our attainment of moral perfection, and hence of unadulterated happiness, in spite of the fact that we are all wrongdoers. Indeed, Kant thinks of punishment the same way; it too wipes out guilt.

Two things must be said about this. In the first place, the claim seems necessarily false. How can guilt possibly be removed, undone, wiped out? If at some time one violates the moral law and becomes guilty for so doing, then forever after it is the case that at that time one violated the moral law and was guilty for so doing; one remains guilty for having done so. And secondly, if in fact God wipes out the guilt for the evil actions of the person of good character, on the ground of the person's goodness of character, *then in fact* that person has attained the moral ideal in his actions; and all of Kant's insistences that the actions of the person of good character are at best a matter of moral *progress* are just mistaken. Since persons of good character have the guilt for their evil actions wiped out, presumably as soon as they perform the evil actions, every such person satisfies the moral ideal: there is no tinge of guilt about them.

Christianity also, of course, speaks much about forgiveness. But its conception of forgiveness is different. To forgive a person is to declare that the person's prior wrongdoing will not be held against her. It is to declare that one's moral interactions with the person will be what they would be if she had never done the ill deed. To forgive a guilty person is not to declare that she is not guilty but to declare that the person will be treated as not guilty. So too, punishment does not *remove* guilt. Rather, when punishment is completed the punished person is received back into the community and treated as one not guilty. What Christianity claims is that God, by an act of grace, forgives us, with the consequence that our fitness for membership in God's kingdom is not judged by our moral status. Kant, by contrast, insists that our fitness for God's kingdom is always judged by our moral status; accordingly he attributes to God the power of making the person who is guilty not guilty.[6]

We have in effect been noticing that Kant's religion, so far from being entirely rational, is riddled with irrationalities. That is true in yet one more way. Kant repeatedly affirms the Stoic maxim that a person's moral worth is determined entirely by that person himself. "Man *himself*," he says, "must make or have made himself into whatever, in a moral sense, whether good or evil, he is or is to become" (R 40). Yet it is essential to Kant's particular project of a rational religion that *God* be able to alter our moral status for the better. Here then we have not just implausibility or tension, but internal contradiction.

Kant himself was aware of the difficulty. He says:

> The concept of supernatural accession to our moral, though deficient, capacity and even to our not wholly purified and certainly weak disposition to perform our entire duty, is a transcendent concept, and is a bare idea, of whose reality no experience can assure us. Even when accepted as an idea in nothing but a practical context it is very hazardous, and hard to reconcile with reason, since that which is to be accredited to us as morally good conduct must take place not through foreign influence but solely through the best possible use of our own powers. (R 179)

What then was Kant's resolution, or attempted resolution, of the difficulty? What he goes on to say is this:

> the impossibility thereof (i.e., of both these things occurring side by side) cannot really be proved, because freedom itself, though containing nothing supernatural in its conception, remains, as regards its possibility, just as incomprehensible to us as is the supernatural factor which we would like to regard as a supplement to the spontaneous but deficient determination of freedom. (R 179)

In effect, what Kant does here is appeal to what, in other passages, he calls the "mystery of atonement." We do not understand how God could forgive guilt. Reason tells us that God will, but "without presuming to determine the manner in which this aid will be given or to know wherein it will consist: it may be so mysterious that God can reveal it to us at best in a symbolic representation in which only what is practical is comprehensible to us..." (R 159). It seems clear, however, that such an appeal is illegitimate here. To affirm the Stoic principle is to affirm something which *contradicts* the claim that God wipes out guilt.[7] Our situation is not that we do not know *how* God wipes out guilt. Our situation, given the Stoic principle, is that we know God does not.

Reason, says Kant, may conclude that "in the inscrutable realm of the supernatural there is something more than she can explain to herself, which may yet be necessary as a complement to her moral insufficiency," and may further conclude that this is "available to her good will" (R 48). Therein, Kant adds, we find consolation.

> Reason does not leave us wholly without consolation with respect to our lack of righteousness valid before God. It says that whoever, with a disposition genuinely devoted to duty, does as much as lies in his power to satisfy his obligation (at least in a continual approximation to complete harmony with the law), may hope that what is not in his power will be supplied by the supreme Wisdom *in some way or other* (which can make permanent the disposition to this unceasing approximation). (R 159)

But surely this is an entirely hypothetical consolation: we can be assured that *if* someone has a good will, that person's deficiency in action will be made good by God. Given that no one can be certain whether she has a good will, the Kantian system gives no actual consolation to any actual human being. Quite to the contrary. As Kant himself remarks, "If this question as to the verdict to be pronounced upon a person is addressed to the judge *within* a man he will pronounce a severe verdict upon himself . . . " (R 72). "The accuser within us would be more likely to propose a judgment of condemnation" (R 70). In the Kantian scheme, this much is clear: for the unconverted there is no mercy.

It may be said that the tenability of the interpretation I have offered of Kant, and of the criticisms I have lodged, requires ignoring the antinomy to which Kant calls attention in Book III of *Religion.* So let us, in conclusion, look briefly at that. Either we must assume, says Kant, "that the faith in the absolution from the debt resting upon us will bring forth good life-conduct, or else that the genuine and active disposition ever to pursue a good course of life will engender the faith in such absolution according to the law of morally operating causes" (R 106–07). This, he says, is "a remarkable antinomy of human reason with itself." He adds that its solution or adjustment "can alone determine whether an historical (ecclesiastical) faith must always be present as an essential element of saving faith, over and above pure religious faith, or whether it is only a vehicle which finally . . . can pass over into pure religious faith" (R 107).

It seems clear, however, that in Kant's view this is not a true antinomy. Indeed, he himself calls it "only apparent" (R 110). For though he lays out both lines of thought—for the view that atonement must precede good life-conduct and for the view that good life-conduct must precede atonement—he makes it emphatically clear, as he has already in Book II, that in his judgment only the latter is correct. It is quite impossible, he says,

> to see how a reasonable man, who knows himself to merit punishment, can in all seriousness believe that he needs only to credit the news of an atonement rendered for him, and to accept this atonement *utiliter* (as the lawyers say), in order to to regard his guilt as annihilated,—indeed, so completely annihilated (to the very root) that good life-conduct, for which he has hitherto not taken the least pains, will in the future be the inevitable consequence of this faith and this acceptance of the proffered favor. No thoughtful person can bring himself to believe this. . . . (R 107)

It is true, indeed, that the issue cannot be settled "through insight into the causal determination of the freedom of a human being, i.e., into the causes which bring it about that a man becomes good or bad; hence it cannot be resolved theoretically . . ." (R 108). But as a matter of fact, says Kant, a reflective person cannot bring himself to believe that atonement would be extended to the unconverted; that would be a violation of our moral intuitions. "Where shall we start, i.e., with a faith in what God has done on our behalf, or with what we are to do to become worthy of God's assistance (whatever this may be)? In answering this question we cannot hesitate in deciding for the second alternative" (R 108).

In short, when Kant's discussion of the "antinomy" is scrutinized, it proves not to upset our interpretation but to confirm it. God, in the Kantian system, wipes out the guilt of our wrongdoing if we present God with a good character; God is, in fact, morally required to do so. We have seen that such wiping out, if it were possible, would, in its indiscriminateness, raise a serious issue of justice. Further, we have seen that the claim that God can alter our moral status conflicts with Kant's repeated insistence that only we ourselves can do so. But in fact such wiping out is not possible. Forgiveness is not the declaration that the guilty are no longer guilty but the declaration that the guilty will no longer be treated as guilty. Forgiveness, in that sense, is eminently possible. Often, when it occurs, morality is transcended. The forgiven have no moral claim on forgiveness; it comes to them as grace.

What Kant affirms is that only the worthy are saved—and that God, so as to bring it about that some are saved in spite of the wrongdoing of all, makes those of worthy character worthy in action as well. Kant affirms this without ever surrendering the affirmation that each can make only himself or herself worthy. What Christianity affirms is that the unworthy are saved—saved by the grace of divine forgiveness.

NOTES

1. Though without ever reaching it: "if after this life another life awaits [the man of good disposition], he may hope to continue to follow [the course of moral improvement] . . . and to approach ever nearer to, though he can never reach, the goal of perfection" (R 62; cf. 60).

2. See my "The Migration of the Theistic Arguments: From Natural Theology to Evidentialist Apologetics," in *Rationality, Religious Belief, and Moral Commitment*, R. Audi and W. J. Wainwright, eds. (Ithaca, N.Y.: Cornell University Press, 1986), 38–81.

3. An essential part of Kant's overall interpretative strategy was to treat biblical narrative as a "vivid mode of representation" (R 78) of moral truths: "since the sacred narrative, which is employed solely on behalf of ecclesiastical faith, can have and, taken by itself, ought to have absolutely no influence upon the adoption of moral maxims, and since it is given to ecclesiastical faith only for the vivid presentation of its true object (virtue striving toward holiness), it follows that this narrative must at all times be taught and expounded in the interest of morality . . ." (R 123).

4. Cf. R 71: "We learn from this deduction that only the supposition of a complete change of heart allows us to think of the absolution, at the bar of heavenly justice, of the man burdened with guilt." (See also R 60–61 and 61n.)

5. This appears to be also how Kant understands grace. In one passage he says that "a superior's decrees conferring a good for which the subordinate possesses no legal claim but only the (moral) receptivity is called *grace*" (R 70n). And in another he says that "it is customary (at least in the church) to give the name of *nature* to that which men can do by dint of the principle of virtue, and the name of *grace* to that which alone serves to supplement the deficiency of all our moral powers and yet, because sufficiency of these powers is also our duty, can only be wished for, or hoped for, and solicited . . ." (R 161–62). Kant does not indicate disagreement with this customary practice.

6. Further reflections on these matters would do well to take account of this passage from Hannah Arendt's *The Human Condition* (Chicago: University of Chicago Press, 1958), 241: "The alternative to forgiveness, but by no means its opposite, is punishment, and both have in common that they attempt to put an end to something that without interference could go on endlessly. It is therefore quite significant, a structural element in the realm of human affairs, that men are unable to forgive what they cannot punish and that they are unable to punish what has turned out to be unforgivable. This is the true hallmark of those offenses which, since Kant, we call 'radical evil' and about whose natures so little is known, even to us who have been exposed to one of their rare outbursts on the public scene. All we know is that we can neither punish nor forgive such offenses and that they therefore transcend the realm of human affairs and the potentialities of human power, both of which they radically destroy wherever they make their appearance." I think that Arendt quite clearly misunderstands Kant's notion of radical evil. Yet her contention that only what can be punished can be forgiven, and that there are some crimes which human beings cannot punish, is eminently worth considering.

7. Kant himself, in one passage, spoke of these claims as *contradicting* each other: "Man, as we know him, is corrupt and of himself not in the least suited to that holy law. And yet, if the goodness of God has called him, as it were, into being, i.e., to exist in a particular manner (as a member of the kingdom of Heaven), He must also have a means of supplementing, out of the fullness of His own holiness, man's lack of requisite qualifications therefore. But this contradicts man's spontaneity (which is assumed in all the moral good or evil which a man can have within himself), according to which such a good cannot come from another but must arise from man himself, if it is to be imputable to him" (R 134).

Kant's Rejection of Divine Revelation and His Theory of Radical Evil

Denis Savage

In order to understand why Kant rejects divine revelation, it is important to realize that his opposition to it is placed within the context of his affirmation of three other types of rules or laws concerned with human volition and conduct: laws of ethics, laws of the state, and laws of rational religion. In this sense Kant is very much part of the Western philosophical tradition that through the centuries has dealt with these various types of law. This tradition concerning types of law has been clearly and succinctly summed up in the work of Thomas Aquinas. In Part 1 of this paper I propose, therefore, to illuminate Kant's overall position on law by comparing it with that of Aquinas, for this comparison will set the framework for understanding the precise reason why Kant rejects revelation.

1. Four Types of Law

Aquinas holds there are four types of law: the natural law, the eternal law, the human or positive law, and the divine law.[1] Kant holds the first three of these but rejects the fourth.

Take first the natural law, in the sense of the moral laws of our human nature. For Aquinas, this is the set of basic principles that is to govern human beings insofar as they have a formal, rational nature. They are the teleological laws of our freedom, our moral nature qua rational beings. The primary precepts of the natural moral law are enunciated in propositions that are self-evident for anyone who has reached the age of reason; that is to say, they are known by rational insight and are unconditionally necessary, given the fact of our rational nature.[2] Hence, if we disobey them, by giving way to our lower, sensory appetite, we contradict our nature as humans.

Kant entirely agrees with this. The moral laws are the laws of our human nature qua rational beings (*Menschheit*), and if we go against these laws, by freely giving way to our sensory appetite for pleasure, we go against our formal, rational nature. The moral laws are easily discoverable by anyone who reaches the age of moral reasoning, and all who discover them must obey them, regardless of the consequences of pleasure and pain, for they are the universal and unconditionally necessary laws of our nature qua rational persons (*Persönlichkeit*).

It may be objected that to align Kant's ethics with that of Aquinas is a serious error, for Aquinas is one of the main proponents of the theory that moral laws are laws of human nature, whereas Kant insists in all of his works on ethics that the moral laws are not to be sought in "the nature of man" or in a knowledge of "human nature" (F 5,26/389,410; PrR 70–74/67–71; MMJ 16–18/217–18). In reply to this objection it must be understood that when Kant speaks in this manner, he is referring to our lower, sensuous nature, not to our rational, supersensible nature. As he says in the *Metaphysics of Morals*, "the concept of man is not thought of in only one sense" (MPV 79/418). For Kant, as for Aquinas and the natural law tradition of ethics in general, we have unconditionally necessary moral laws precisely because, in addition to our sensuous or animal nature, we have a supersensible, rational nature:

> Nature, in the widest sense of the word, is the existence of things under laws. The sensuous nature of rational beings in general is their existence under empirically conditioned laws, and therefore it is, from the point of view of reason, heteronomy. The super-sensuous nature of the same beings, on the other hand, is their existence according to laws which are independent of all empirical conditions and which therefore belong to the autonomy of pure reason. (PrR 44/43)[3]

Heteronomy occurs when reason takes its rule of action from outside itself, from the sensory appetite for pleasure; autonomy occurs when reason takes its rules from itself, its own formal nature.

In this connection, it should also be pointed out that for Kant the term "natural law" or "law of nature" also has more than one meaning. By this phrase he means, first, the mechanistic laws of physical bodies and, second, the hedonistic law of our sensory appetite; but in a third acceptation he also uses it to designate the a priori moral laws of our higher nature. For example, in distinguishing between the ethical laws of strict duty toward others and the positive, human laws of the state, Kant expressly refers to the basic ethical laws as the "natural law": "Law considered as a system can be divided into natural law, which rests on nothing but a priori principles, and positive (statutory) law, which proceeds from the will of a legislator" (MMJ 43/237; see also 44, 48, 65/238, 242, 256). In this third use of the term, Kant places himself in the great tradition of ethics stemming from Socrates and Plato which holds that moral rules are not simply laws by "contract" or "convention" (*nomoi*), that is, laws made by humans for their mutual advantage and pleasure, but are laws inherent in "nature" (*physis*)—that is, in our higher, supersensible nature.[4]

For Thomas Aquinas, the eternal law is God as author, and therefore eternal exemplar of the laws of our rational nature, as well as of the laws of physical nature. Thus, the moral laws which are our unconditional precepts have their ultimate origin in God; they are commanded to us by God, and if we disobey them we at the same time disobey the eternal law of God, the author of finite nature.

Again Kant agrees: when we consider the laws of our humanity, our personality, as coming from God, the creator both of the noumenal world of things in themselves and of ourselves as persons, we in effect hold the notion of the eternal law. Kant calls this assent on our part pure rational religion: it is the consideration of the laws of our moral nature as laws derivative from and thus commanded by God. The only difference between Kant and Aquinas on this point is that Aquinas thinks we have a valid theoretical proof of God's existence, whereas Kant thinks we have, at best, only a moral, practical proof.

The third type of law is human or positive law, the laws of the state. Here again, Kant is in basic agreement with the position held by Aquinas. For Aquinas, people need to supplement the natural moral laws with statutory laws, which partly duplicate and partly extend the moral laws and which assign physical sanctions to their implementation. Thus the laws of the state are rooted in, and in serious matters should not contravene, the laws of our rational nature. The authority for making these positive laws is vested in the people, with the prince or government officials being simply vice-regents or representatives of the people.[5] The human or positive laws concern only external actions whereby all are to live in society with one another (legal justice); they are not concerned with the fact that such actions should also be done out of the moral motive of doing justice for its own sake (moral justice).[6] Thus, the moral intention of the agent (virtue as an end in itself) is an important consideration in our obeying the moral natural law and the eternal law of God, but it plays no role in our obeying the positive laws of the state. Here we may well act out of fear of punishment or considerations of advantage and pleasure.

Kant agrees: in a state of nature we are bound by the formal, teleological laws of our free rational nature, but in order to provide a proper setting for obeying these laws and thus indirectly to foster the development of our human potentialities or talents, we are morally bound to form a social contract, equipped with powers of coercion, for the common good of all (MMJ 76/312; 70–71/306–307). The sovereign authority of the state resides in the person of the legislator, who is none other than the people united together in the contract (MMJ 78/314). Many of the positive laws of the state reduplicate the ethical laws of our rational nature, but legal justice is distinct from moral justice by the fact that morality requires us to do justice as an end in itself, whereas legality is satisfied if we do justice out of the motive of pleasure/pain.[7]

It is on the fourth type of law, the divine law, that Kant disagrees with the position of Aquinas. By "divine law" Aquinas means two things: the law of the Old Testament and the law of the New Testament. The eternal law is already, of course, a divine law, a general divine providence, but the laws of the Old and New Testaments are laws of special divine providence, first to the Jews and then to all persons insofar as they are called, supernaturally, to a special relationship with God. This is religion in the sense of revelation, religion as historical religion, and here Kant forthrightly disagrees with the position of Aquinas. For Kant, all such supernatural revelation, although logically possible, is ruled out as being objectively, materially impossible. This denial is what makes him a deist and a resolute opponent of historical faiths based on revelation. True religion is not the religion of special divine providence, but is merely rational religion, in which we consider the moral laws inherent in our rational nature as issuing from God as creator of the universe. Kant thinks that any statements purporting to be a divine revelation are, at best, either a repetition or a symbolic expression of the moral laws of our rational nature, laws that we can discover by reason alone. We may, and even should, consider these laws to be God's commands, but all duties alleged to be of special divine revelation are to be rejected if taken for anything more than a restatement or imaginative representation of the ethical duties of reason.

2. Kant's Rejection of Divine Revelation

But why does Kant reject all special divine providence in the sense of supernatural revelation? In his paper entitled "Kant's Deism," in this volume, Allen Wood states that one of the reasons why Kant says he rejects revelation is that it is not universal, that the revelation to the Jews or Christians, or to any individual or people, is not to all of humankind, and therefore no statement or law contained in that revelation is universal, which for Kant is a mark or criterion of any true law. On the other hand, the ethical laws of our rational human nature are, Kant maintains, truly universal and knowable by all humans. Hence, ethical rules qualify as laws but revelation does not; the so-called revealed laws are true laws only insofar as they repeat, often in a symbolic manner, the laws of our rational nature, which is to say, no laws or statements of revelation are to be taken at their face value as revealed truths coming from God.

To this reason that Kant gives for denying revelation, Wood responds (see above, Wood 13–14) that certain concrete instances of revelation are promulgated at least as widely, and perhaps even more widely, than the knowledge of Kant's rational ethics. Hence, if the criterion be that of universality, then at least one particular revelation, the Christian revelation, qualifies as law even more than Kant's ethical laws.

What would Kant reply to this objection? I will sketch out what I think his answer would be. The laws of morality, Kant insists, are laws of our rational, formal nature. These laws are discoverable by anyone who reaches the age of reason in the sense of moral reason. It certainly helps if children in infancy and early childhood are raised in a propitious environment where they find it advantageous and pleasant to do out of subjective motives what they will soon discover by reason that they must do because these are the laws of their rational nature. But in any case, when children start to use reason they will find it fairly easy to discover, by themselves and without instruction, the basic laws of their nature,[8] for these are, indeed, "facts of reason" (PrR 47,55/48,57): for example, that a human being qua living being is to live (and not commit suicide); that a human being, as endowed with potentialities or talents, is to develop those talents; that a human being, as an end in itself among other ends in themselves, is to be social; or that a human being, as endowed with sexual organs whose essential nature is to procreate, may use those organs only in a procreative situation, etc. These laws, Kant maintains, are universal laws for everyone who shares in or has rational human nature (*Menschheit/Persönlichkeit*). It is in this sense that they are universal: they are the laws of everyone, without exception, who has this formal, supersensible nature. The so-called laws of revelation, on the other hand, are quite different. For Kant, even if everyone in the world knew and believed a religious revelation in the sense of a historical revelation ("if the gospel were to be preached to all men"), still this would not qualify those statements to be universal laws. Such statements would be *universal* in the logical sense that they would in fact be held by all the members of the universe of discourse, but they would not be *universal laws* of the formal nature of those members, for the notion of law, as Wood correctly points out, requires not only universality but also necessity.

Thus, Kant's real reason for rejecting a given revelation is not that not everyone believes it but rather that there is no necessity, and therefore no reason, no basis, for anyone to believe it. Now why does Kant think this to be the case?

To see why he thinks this, we must examine the notion of necessity and of necessary judgments. For Kant, as for anyone who follows logic, whatever is said to be necessary is expressible in a judgment in which a predicate is assigned to a subject and cannot not be so assigned without contradiction: S is P and cannot not be P. But there are two types of necessity: absolute or unconditional necessity and hypothetical or conditional necessity. All cases of absolute necessity are expressible in what Kant calls analytic judgments, in which the predicate must unconditionally be affirmed of the subject because it is already contained in the concept of the subject. Among the instances of such absolutely necessary judgments are Kant's moral laws: humans are to do action X, and if they do not do action X they will to that extent contradict their humanity or personality.[9]

All statements that are not analytic judgments are synthetic judgments, in which the predicate is not already contained in the subject but is added over and above to it. Now, there are two and only two types of synthetic judgments: those for which we have a third or mediating factor for joining the predicate to the subject and those for which we do not. Judgments for which we have a mediating factor are hypothetically necessary: given the subject and predicate and the third factor or condition that joins them together, the synthetic judgment is necessary—with conditional necessity: if some necessary condition(s) is (are) granted—e.g., if S is M, and if M is P—then S is and cannot not be P. But we can also make synthetic judgments for which we have no third factor with which to join the predicate to the subject; such judgments are mere opinions, unsubstantiated assertions, for which we have no evidence or proof and which therefore are to be rejected as not having objective validity by any person respectful of logic and reason.

This line of reasoning Kant establishes in the first *Critique*, in the Introduction and in the section dealing with the postulates of empirical reason and the notions of possibility, actuality, and necessity. In these latter texts he shows how certain concepts, such as fate, chance, foreseeing the future, and mental telepathy (and he would include here the notion of miracles and divine revelation), are logically, formally possible, for they involve no contradiction, but they are nevertheless materially, objectively impossible—and therefore must be completely rejected—for they occur in synthetic judgments for which we simply have no third factor, no proof, no evidence, for joining the predicate to the subject. In other words, they are merely surreptitious assertions, opinions, which have for us no necessity and therefore no objectivity, i.e., no objective reference. Such judgments, he says, are indistinguishable from the judgments we make in pure fantasizing, in dreams (A 221–22 / B 268–70; also A 201–202 / B 246–

47). So far as we know, they are on a par with the statements we form about make-believe worlds. Hence, if we assert them as having objective validity, we quickly fall prey to superstition, to charlatanism, to fanaticism—in short, to living in a subjective world of make-believe.

This is the reason why Kant rejects, not the logical possibility of supernatural revelation, but the objective truth-value of such a revelation. For Kant, the statements of revelation, and the rules or commands expressed in those statements, are mere opinions, synthetic judgments for which we have no evidence beyond our mere wish for them to be true. It is in this sense that revelation can never be universal: the so-called divine laws or rules expressed in revelation, even if known and believed by every human being, have no true universality, no force as law or as truth, for they have no necessity, neither the unconditional necessity of analytic, per se known propositions nor the hypothetical, grounded necessity of synthetic propositions for which we have a third or mediating factor (i.e., evidence) for joining the predicate to the subject.

Kant in effect says this: take any judgment alleged to be a judgment of revelation. Is it an analytic judgment? No. Is it therefore a synthetic judgment? Yes. Can you produce any third or mediating factor that will force you, on pain of contradiction, to join the predicate to the subject? No. Well, then, it is but a mere opinion which has, so far as one can know, no objective reference.

In his late work entitled *The Conflict of the Faculties* (1798), in which he discusses the relationship between theology and philosophy, Kant takes as an example of an unfounded opinion the statement that lies at the heart of the Christian revelation, namely that God is incarnate in the human Jesus (CF 67/39). Is this judgment logically possible? Yes, for there is no contradiction between the concept of the subject (God) and the concept of the predicate (the human Jesus); that is to say, there is no contradiction in the notion that God, in addition to his own divine nature, might assume a human nature. Is it a necessary judgment in the sense of being analytic? No, for the concept of God does not already contain the concept of the human Jesus nor of any human. Is it a hypothetically necessary judgment in the sense of being a synthetic judgment for which we have a third or mediating factor that will force us to join the predicate to the subject? Kant's answer is no; for such a judgment we have no evidence whatever beyond the mere assertion of those who choose to affirm it. Kant puts it this way: if the union of God's nature with the nature of a human is possible in one case, then it is possible in all cases, and it thus may be that every human is the God-human. Why not? The one judgment is logically as possible as the other. Both judgments are synthetic, and for neither of them do we have the slightest evidence for joining the predicate to the subject.

Kant pushes the point even further. Suppose a person claims to be the recipient of a divine revelation; does not that individual have good reason to believe in the truth, i.e., the objectivity, of the revelation? Since the judgment that states the revelation is seen to be true neither by being analytic nor by being synthetic but proven by some third factor that would be evidence for it, how is one to distinguish its objective validity from the mere subjective validity of the synthetic judgments we invent in the play of fantasy? There is no possible way to distinguish them, Kant asserts. Even "if God should really speak to man, man could still never know that it is God speaking to him" (CF 115/ 63) and not just his own imagination doing the talking. Hence all revelation, taken in the strict sense as objectively valid judgments which we could not know by reason alone, must be rejected as unfounded opinion.

Kant's position here is, indeed, a harsh indictment of the notion of divine revelation. Interestingly, Thomas Aquinas approaches the question of revelation in exactly the same way as Kant. In *Summa Theologiae*, II-II, Q. 1, Art. 4, and Q. 6, Art. 1, and in his work on truth, *De Veritate*, Q. 14, Art. 1, Aquinas asks whether the strict judgments of revelation are per se known, i.e., analytic, propositions. He answers, No. Are they therefore synthetic? Yes. Can we prove them through some third factor, some demonstration, as hypothetically necessary conclusions of arguments? No. Are they then to be classified as mere opinions? Here Aquinas differs from the position of Kant; he maintains they are not mere opinions but rather fall midway between demonstrated conclusions and opinions. For Aquinas, the third factor that somehow mediates between the subject and the predicate in the judgments of historical revelation is twofold: miracles, which, as Aquinas thinks, do occur but which nevertheless are not sufficient to cause belief, and grace, which is a free gift from God that supernaturally enables the believer to assent to the non–self-evident and non-demonstrated judgments of revelation with complete certitude. In his response to the seventh objection of the *De Veritate* article, Aquinas distinguishes two senses of certitude: "firmness" of assent (on the part of the will) and "evidence" for assent (on the part of the intellect or reason). He admits that we simply have no certitude in the sense of intellectural evidence for assent, but we do have certitude in the sense of firmness on the part of the will in believing. This firmness—in spite of the fact of complete lack of evidence—is produced in us by God's grace.

For Kant, miracles are defined as "events in the world, the *operating laws* of whose causes are, and must remain, absolutely unknown to us" (R 81/86; see also 82–84/87–89). Like the concepts of fate or pure chance, they are logically possible (i.e., not self-contradictory) but are ruled out for the reason given above: we cannot distinguish statements asserting miracles from statements of mere daydreams or wish fulfillments. For us to assert that a miracle has occurred, that is, that an event in the world has been caused by God or an angel and not by some cause in its own order, is the same as to say that an event has occurred by fate (by some unknown cause in another order— the Greek "Moirae," the "fates," "fairies") or by pure chance (by no cause whatever). For Kant, if we indulge in this kind of thinking we cripple reason in its dealing with lawful events in the world and are engaged, so far as we can know, in pure fantasy.

As for grace, in the Thomistic sense of a divine gift that enables one to assent to a proposition for which there is no evidence, Kant does not discuss the problem of religious belief under this rubric but restricts his discussion of the concept of grace to the notion of a divine aid that assists humans to overcome evil and to desire virtue for its own sake.[10] However, since, as we have just seen, he thinks that even if God should really speak to humans, there is no way for them to know that God is speaking to them, it is clear what his response to Aquinas would be: how is one to know that one has the grace to believe? Or, what amounts to the same thing: to which unsubstantiated synthetic judgment is grace to apply? To the fabled accounts of the gods recorded in the literature of the Greeks and Romans? To the visions and revelations granted the Jewish prophets? To the revelations of the New Testament concerning Christ as the son of God? To the revelations given to Muhammad by the archangel Gabriel and faithfully transcribed in the Koran? To the belief of the shaman who, as Kant recounts in *Religion*, begins the day by placing the paw of a bearskin on his head and saying the prayer, "Strike me not dead!" (R 164/176)? These examples, and the great number of other examples that could be taken from the claims to revelation on the part of individuals and religious groups throughout history, differ greatly among themselves, Kant maintains, inasmuch as some of them can be purified, that is, rationalized, demythologized, to square with the precepts of our rational ethics, while others cannot. But in principle, Kant says, they are the same (R 164/176): they are mere opinions, synthetic judgments for which we have no justification. Insofar as they purport to tell us something more than what reason can discover on its own, there is no more reason to affirm them than there is to deny them.

Now, for Kant, since human beings have reason, one of their unconditionally necessary duties is to reason and not to abuse reason. But it would be to contradict reason, Kant thinks, to accept something as certain for which we have no evidence. Hence revelation cannot possibly be accepted as a law of our behavior. One who does so accept it is, Kant asserts, a hypocrite, dishonest (i.e., immoral), and has violated one's own conscience: "*The hypocrite regards as a mere nothing* the danger arising from the dishonesty of his profession, *the violation of conscience*, involved in proclaiming even before God that something is certain, when he is aware that, its nature being what it is, it cannot be asserted with unconditional assurance" (R 177/188–89).

3. Radical Evil, or the Demythologization of Original Sin

For Kant, the most that can be said for divine revelation is that we can accept it only insofar as its statements can be purified and seen to coincide with the moral laws of our rational nature, with our acceptance being based not on the fact that such statements have been revealed but on the fact that we can discover their truth on our own. This is the main thesis of his book *Religion within the Limits of Reason Alone*. In this work he takes as a prominent example of a religious belief the Judaeo-

Christian story of Adam and Eve and their fall from the state of innocence and grace into the state of sin, with the result that all humans are now born in evil. This same myth, Kant believes, has been present in all cultures in the form of a story of a "golden age," that is, the idea that humankind in its origin was morally much better and happier than it is today. Kant's philosophical interpretation of the biblical story of the temptation and fall is an excellent example of how he would deal with any alleged divine revelation.

In what sense, Kant in effect asks, can this religious myth of the origin of evil be desymbolized, demythologized, so as to accord with the principles and concepts of rational ethics? On the one hand, we must purify the story of any feature that contradicts those principles and concepts. In this regard we must reject the idea that we have inherited moral evil, or the guilt of the moral evil, from a set of original parents. If individuals or the entire race are in some sense morally evil, this must be due to the exercise of our freedom and cannot be explained through inheritance from another: "However the origin of moral evil in man is constituted, surely of all the explanations of the spread and propagation of this evil through all members and generations of our race, the most inept is that which describes it as descending to us as an inheritance from our first parents . . ." (R 35/40). For Kant, moral evil, as well as moral worth, is imputable solely to the exercise of each one's personal freedom.

On the other hand, we must ask in what positive sense individuals may be said to be born in evil and at the same time be responsible for being evil. In his explanation, Kant appeals to his theory of our double nature, sensuous and rational, and to the teleological structure of his ethics.

To start with, we are not, properly speaking, born in evil but are rather born with a predisposition to good. This predisposition has three levels, which become manifest in each individual in time and which Kant calls the predisposition to animality, to humanity, and to personality (R 21–23/26–28).[11] Animality refers to the fact that we are born with senses and sensory appetite, by which we receive sensations and desire pleasure and dislike pain. At this level, Kant believes, reason is not yet operative. Humanity refers to the innate capability we have of developing reason and of using it to know objects in the world and to figure out which actions and objects bring pleasure and which bring pain. Here reason is functioning in its theoretical capacity (of knowing objects and of discovering means to ends) but is indirectly practical insofar as it is being put to the service of the sensory appetite whose natural end is pleasure. Personality refers to the innate capability we have of using reason to discover the teleological laws of our rational, moral nature and thus of recognizing that certain actions—those of virtue or duty—are desirable simply because we are the type of being that we are. Here reason is seen to be directly practical, that is, capable not only of knowing but also of desiring virtue or duty as an end in itself.[12] In a fully developed individual, all three levels of our being will be operating simultaneously: our senses and sense appetite in passively receiving sensations and feelings of pleasure and pain; our empirical reason in knowing objects and other people and using them as means to attain our projects and satisfy our inclinations to pleasure; and our moral or practical reason in discovering and acting in accord with the unconditional laws of our rational nature.

Kant himself does not present these three levels as temporal stages in a child's development, for as predispositional capabilities or potencies all are equally present in human nature from the beginning; nevertheless, it seems clear there is a definite temporal sequence in their activation. The activation of the first level begins at birth, with the impingement upon our nervous system of both internal and environmental stimuli. In early infancy we operate purely on the pleasure/pain principle: we sense and desire pleasure and wish to be free of pain, but we have not yet formed concepts of objects in order to know things in the external world. The activation of the second level has its beginning, Kant thinks, sometime around the age of three months.[13] At this time we start to develop some of the basic concepts and principles requisite for knowing our own bodies, other people, and objects in the world,[14] and we use our reason to discover which actions and objects bring pleasure and which bring pain. This is the beginning of the formation of our commonsense view of the world as a world composed of three-dimensional objects with sensory qualities and external relationships. In these early years we come to know and desire real objects, but our choices are all governed by the pleasure principle. In Freud's terminology, the "reality principle" (governing our choice of actions, objects, and other people in the real world) is gradually added to the pleasure principle (the desire for plea- sure sensations in us), but it remains, he insists, subordinate to that earlier principle. In Kant's terminology, the young child in his choice of actions and objects operates exclusively with hypo- thetical imperatives, that is, he uses objects purely as means to the satisfaction of his desire for pleasure/happiness: he learns that if he wants to have pleasure and avoid pain, he must do action X, get the help of person Y, avoid object Z.

With the activation of the third level, starting roughly around the age of three to four years, we begin to make the great discovery of the teleological purposes of things, in the sense that everything, and especially our own body and person, is gradually seen to have a proper function or purpose—eyes are to see, ears are to hear, sex organs are somehow intimately connected with the question of where babies come from, speech is for communicating our thoughts, and so on. At this level and at this time in our lives, we begin to recognize the moral laws of our personality and are thus increasingly faced with the unconditional, categorical imperatives of our beings as moral agents: eyes (now defined as seeing organs) are for seeing; ears (now defined as hearing organs) are for hearing; sex organs (gradually recognized as procreative organs) are for procreation, etc. Such judgments refer to our own persons and are seen to be unconditionally necessary, for the concept of the predicate is seen to be already present in the concept of the subject. Hence they are universal laws and are to be obeyed—on pain of contradicting our very nature—whatever be the consequences of pleasure or pain.

At this point a major decision is imposed upon us. Prior to reaching the third level, our choices were neither morally good nor morally bad. They were, indeed, regulated by the hedonism of the pleasure principle and its subordinate principle, the reality principle, but this was a "time of innocence," a time of amorality, for we were unaware of any further demands, not having dis- covered as yet the moral laws of our higher nature. As Kant says in his treatise on the education of children:

> But is man by nature [i.e., at the first two levels] morally good or bad? He is neither, for he is not by nature a moral being. He only becomes a moral being when his reason has developed ideas of duty and law. (ED 108/492)[15]

But as we discover our formal teleology we are faced with a major decision: Are we going to continue to take as our general maxim of conscious willing the hypothetical imperatives of the pleasure principle, or are we going to follow the newly discovered principle of desiring certain actions, the actions of virtue or duty, purely as ends in themselves? If we choose the second alternative, we set ourselves on the path of unconditional duty and virtue, even though we will continue to be faced with the ever-present allurements of our sensory appetite. If we choose the first alternative, we set ourselves on the path of moral evil, for we in effect declare that we have no respect for our newly discovered formal nature.

This attitude of deliberately choosing to make all our moral decisions purely on the basis of the pleasure/pain principle is what Kant calls the tendency or propensity to radical evil. Insofar as humans in general may be thought to have adopted this tendency, it may be said to be natural or innate to the human species or race. But such a manner of speaking (which is the manner sometimes used by theologians) is not to be taken literally, for properly speaking we are not evil by nature, neither in our sensory appetite nor in our reason and rational appetite, both of which are dispositions to good. The tendency to evil, if present, is something acquired through a deliberate act of free choice (R 26–27, 30/31–32, 34–35).

Kant does not argue from the concept of the species of humankind (*aus seinem Gattungsbegriffe*) that every individual has chosen as supreme maxim the pleasure principle over the moral principle, for this would mean that we are necessarily evil—that is, evil by nature. Instead, he appeals to the disheartening experience of overt human actions in both primitive and civilized societies and in international relations between states to conclude that the human race as a whole may be said to have chosen to follow the hedonistic path (R 27–30/32–34). Hence it may be said that humans are, indeed, born in evil—not in the sense that they are evil by nature or that they have inherited an evil tendency from primal parents but in the sense that they have freely chosen to regulate their choices according to the hedonistic principle of their lower, sensuous nature instead of according to the unconditional teleological laws of their rational nature. Thus there is a truth to the mythical story of Adam and Eve and their fall from a state of innocence into a state of evil.

Their story is the story of each one who, upon reaching the age of moral reason, is called upon to choose between leading a life based on the pursuit of pleasure and a life based on the pursuit of virtue, with pleasure being conditioned by, i.e., subordinated to, virtue.

To understand why Kant thinks this is indeed the fundamental ethical choice that all must make, it is important to know that for Kant, as for all the great ethicians of the natural law tradition (e.g., Socrates, Plato, Aristotle, the Stoics, Cicero, Aquinas), there are two and only two basic ways of doing ethics (F 59–64/440–46; PrR 41–42/39–42) and that this is so because there are two and only two things that are good (i.e., desirable) in and of themselves: virtue/duty (the teleology of our formal nature) and pleasure/happiness (see, for example PrR 59–64/57–62). In addition to these two per se goods, however, there are also relational goods (i.e., things good *per aliud*, through something else), which are desired not for their own sake, as ends, but as means to an end. Anything can be regarded as a relational good—any object, action, other person, or even one's own self. In all, therefore, there are three senses of "good": (1) the virtue good (in the philosophical tradition called the honorable good, or honesty—the *bonum honestum, honestas);* (2) the pleasure good (the *bonum delectabile);* and (3) the useful good (the *bonum utile).* The first two are intrinsic goods, that is, ends in themselves; the third good is an extrinsic or relative good, that is, a means to an end.[16]

Now, it is clear from this division of goods (i.e., desirables) that actions can be desired in two different ways: either as ends in themselves (and these are the virtuous actions, the excellent actions, which are identical with the proper functions, the duties, of our formal, rational nature) or as means to pleasure. Following from these two different ways of desiring actions, there are two basic ethics: either an ethics according to the unconditional imperatives of our rational nature (autonomy) or an ethics according to the conditional imperatives of the pursuit of pleasure/happiness (heteronomy). We have two intrinsic ends, duty and pleasure, and the fundamental question of moral conduct is which of the two is to be subordinated to which. If we subordinate duty/virtue to pleasure/happiness, we are followers of Epicurus and of hedonism, which for Kant, as for all natural law moralists, is the denial of true morality. If we

subordinate pleasure/happiness to duty/virtue, we align ourselves with those who distinguish a higher and a lower human
nature and who regard moral imperatives as unconditional laws
of our being.

Kant thus sees the crucial question of morality for every
individual as being that of freely deciding to follow the dictates
of the unconditional laws of rationality (and to seek pleasure
only as the natural consequence of virtue) or to follow sensuous
inclinations for pleasure (and to define and seek virtue in terms
of actions that produce pleasure). Should one decide to follow
sensory appetite, the fault is not with the sense appetite, which
of itself is a potency for good (in this case, the amoral tendency
to the pleasure good), but with the rational appetite or will,
which by its very nature is called upon to follow the dictates
of teleological reason. When individuals reach the age of moral
reason and become aware that certain actions are per se good,
that is, unconditionally desirable for such beings as they themselves are, they have an insight, Kant thinks, that can never be
lost.[17] If at this time, or at any time in the future course of life,
they decide to seek those actions because they accord with the
essential ends or laws of their nature, they show respect for
their humanity or personality in the sense of their formal,
rational nature. Should they fail to take this moral stance, they
will contradict their formal nature and reduce themselves to the
subhuman level of their animality.

Thus, the biblical notion of radical evil or wickedness as
being inherited by us from the sin of our first parents is seen,
once it is demythologized, to be the tendency, freely chosen by
each individual, to subordinate reason and will to the lower
appetite for pleasure. Even if one chooses actions which happen
to be dutiful, but does so purely as a means to pleasure, one
is radically evil in intention, for one has inverted the true
ordering of one's higher and lower natures. Such individuals,
though they perform an action of duty, have no respect for their
rational, teleological nature; they obey according to the letter
of the law but not according to its spirit. If the actions which
they desire purely as means to pleasure were contrary to their
higher nature, they would choose them anyway, for the sole
maxim or principle of their choosing is the pleasure principle.

For Kant, such an attitude is an inversion, or perversion, of
the true order of our double nature, rational and sensuous. It

is the attitude adopted by the morally indifferent, by the vicious, by the criminals and tyrants of history, an attitude whose basic lines were drawn by Callicles and Thrasymachus in Plato's *Gorgias* and *Republic*. But it is also the attitude adopted by the mechanistic/hedonistic, social contract ethicians of our Western tradition—Epicurus, Hobbes, Rousseau—who deny any moral laws inherent in human nature and who therefore proceed to operate purely according to the hypothetical imperatives of the pleasure principle. For such thinkers, humankind has no teleology laid down in a formal nature but only the teleology of pleasure; so too, human reason is not per se practical but only indirectly practical, insofar as we put reason to work to discover the means of seeking pleasure and avoiding pain. In other words, for social contract ethicians, virtue/duty is reduced to the juridical duties of the contract, whose end is not virtue for its own sake but mutual happiness for all, with virtue being simply the means to that end.

In a text in his treatise *The Metaphysical Principles of Virtue*, Kant briefly entertains the idea of such a reduction when he asks, as a casuistical question, "Would it not be better for the world's welfare [i.e., happiness] if all morality in human beings were restricted exclusively to juridical duties (but done with the greatest conscientiousness) . . . ?" (MPV 122–23/458). But for Kant this would mean the denial of true morality. As he sees it, we must be true to the fact of the teleology of our formal, rational nature; hence we must subordinate pleasure/happiness to virtue/duty. This means, first, that we recognize the moral laws as being the laws of our formal nature and, second, that we strive to follow those laws for their own sake and look to pleasure only as the consequence of (and not as the main incentive for) doing virtue.

If we do this, we will be good not only in the sense of doing the right actions, that is, of being "well behaved" (*bene moratus*), but also in the sense of being "morally good" (*moraliter bonus*) (R 25/30). Moreover, if we do the right actions for the right intention, this does not mean that we have to forget about pleasure or pretend it isn't there. For Kant, as for Plato, Aristotle, and Aquinas, so long as we desire virtue/duty for its own sake, the pleasure which is a natural consequence of acts of virtue is a perfectly natural and morally legitimate end. As Kant says both in the *Critique of Pure Reason* and in the *Critique of Practical Reason,* the ideal is when we get pleasure in exact proportion to virtue (A 806–14/B 834–42; PrR 115/110). The important point for Kant, as for all natural law moralists, is that virtue be seen as the condition for pleasure, and not the other way about. If we invert the two ends, that is, if we subordinate virtue to pleasure, we in effect deny the teleological nature of humanity and reduce ourselves to the level of our animality, albeit an animality that includes reason as theoretical and indirectly practical.

From Kant's description of the tendency to evil, it is clear that it can be acquired only when a person has reached the third level of the predisposition to good, the level where two motives present themselves for doing a virtuous action: the incentive of pleasure as an end in itself and the incentive of virtue as an end in itself. With this distinction in mind, Kant then analyzes the tendency into three degrees or stages: (1) weakness of nature or intention: one wills as one's general principle of action to will virtue for its own sake, but in actual practice the desire for pleasure is often stronger; (2) impurity of intention: one wills as one's general maxim to seek virtue for its own sake, and in actual practice does so, but often, perhaps always, one deliberately mixes in with this pure intention the motive of pleasure; (3) depravity or wickedness of intention: one deliberately chooses hedonism as one's general maxim and wills actions, even virtuous actions, purely as a means to pleasure. It is only when we freely choose to take this third attitude as our supreme principle of action that we become radically evil. Although we continue to recognize the demands of the moral law upon our persons, we nevertheless go against those demands by freely choosing to regulate our concrete acts of choice by the principle of hedonism.

Who are the individuals who have chosen this attitude of radical evil? Kant does not venture to say, for it is impossible perfectly to discern others' intentions or, for that matter, even our own. What Kant clarifies are the abstract possibilities: either a holy will, perfectly desiring virtue for its own sake (which he believes is never fully achievable by humans), a radically evil will, taking pleasure alone as its end and desiring actions merely as means to pleasure, or some combination of the two, where we either through weakness or by deliberation mix the two motives together.

If we have chosen the principle of hedonism as our maxim, and consequently are radically evil, we are nevertheless called upon by our rational nature to undergo a change of heart (intention) by desiring virtue for the sake of virtue. But even if we achieve this conversion of intention and take as our maxim to desire duty as an end in itself, we will never achieve a total purity of intention. The reason for this is that we have, and always will have, two natures. If we had just our higher nature of reason and will, we would be doing virtue purely for its own sake in full act. If we had just our lower nature of senses and sense appetite, we would be acting as an amoral animal, desiring actions and objects purely as means to pleasure and the avoidance of pain. But we are not mere animals, nor are we pure reason subsisting completely apart from animal nature; rather, we have two natures, the higher of which is called upon to dominate the lower. Thus we are called to complete virtue and complete purity of intention, but we can never attain such perfection.

In the Christian religion, Kant believes, we have the symbol of such a calling in the figure of Christ, the Son of God. For Kant, Christ is not really God (though this is logically possible) but is rather the symbol of the demand within each of us to have a holy will—that is, to will duty for its own sake. Just as Adam and Eve are symbols of our choosing to regulate our desires by the principle of pleasure/pain, so too Christ is the symbol, the personification, of the call in each of us to will duty, i.e., our own formal teleology, as an end in itself (R 54–59, 69, 78/60–66, 74, 83). In this sense Christ, like Adam, is each of us. As Kant says, in citing Horace, *mutato nomine de te fabula narratur:* "Change but the name, and of you the tale is told" (R 37/42).

In conclusion, it must be said that Kant's theory of radical evil presented in *Religion* contains nothing basically new as compared with his theory of moral good and evil presented in his ethical works, the *Foundations of the Metaphysics of Morals*, the *Critique of Practical Reason*, and the *Metaphysics of Morals*. And this is as it should be, for the whole idea of the work

Religion within the Limits of Reason Alone is to show that all statements of revealed religion, if they have any objective validity at all, are completely translatable—without remainder—into the concepts and expressions of rational ethics.

NOTES

1. See Thomas Aquinas, *Summa Theologiae,* I–II, Q. 91, Arts. 1–5; see also QQ. 93–100 and 106–12.

2. See especially *S. Th.,* I–II, Q. 94, Art. 2, where Aquinas presents the definition of man according to genus (animal) and specific difference (rational) and shows how the primary precepts of the moral law are per se known propositions implicit in that definition. I take this text to be based on Aristotle, *Nicomachean Ethics,* I, 7, 1097b 23–1098a 25, and on Cicero, *De Officiis (On Duties),* I, 4.

3. Cf. R 50n/57n: "These philosophers [the Stoics] derived their universal ethical principle from the dignity of human nature, that is, from its freedom (regarded as an independence from the power of the inclinations), and they could not have used as their foundation a better or nobler principle."

4. See, for example, Plato, *Gorgias,* 489a–b; see also 482e–483e.

5. *S. Th.,* I–II, Q. 90, Art. 3c and Q. 97, Art. 3 ad 3.

6. *S. Th.,* I–II, Q. 99, Art. 5; Q. 100, Arts. 2 and 9.

7. On this point, both Kant and Aquinas are in agreement with the position of Aristotle in his *Nicomachean Ethics* 2, 4: 1105a 27–b12; 5, 8: 1135b 2–9.

8. See PrR, "Methodology," 156–60/152–56; see also PrR 38/36: "What is required in accordance with the principle of autonomy of choice is easily and without hesitation seen by the commonest intelligence. . . . That is to say, what duty is, is plain of itself to everyone. . . ."

9. This statement seems directly to contradict Kant's express judgment that the moral laws are *synthetic* judgments, but actually it is in full agreement with his overall position. The only judgments that are unconditionally necessary are analytic judgments, and Kant insists that the moral laws are unconditionally necessary. For example, humans, whose speech apparatus has the natural teleology of communicating thoughts, are to use that speech apparatus to communicate thoughts (and not to lie) (MPV 91/429), which is an analytic judgment. On the other hand, it is also true that humans may choose to act in accord or disaccord with the moral laws; in this sense the moral laws are synthetic. The reason for the ambiguity here is that, for Kant, a human being has two natures. Thus, from the point of view of human beings insofar as they have a higher, rational nature, the concept of the predicate of a moral law is already in the concept of the subject: (a human being qua X-doer) is (to do X). But from the point of view

of human beings insofar as they have a lower, sensuous nature, the concept of the predicate is not already in the concept of the subject: (a human being qua pleasure-seeker) is (to do X). For Kant, as for natural law ethicians in general, a human being is a hierarchical unity of two natures, and it is up to the higher nature (reason and will) to make the lower nature (sensuous appetite) obey by actually choosing the action (the X) that is already written in the higher nature. See F 72–73/453–54.

10. The problem with grace in this latter sense is as follows: How can divine grace (e.g., Christ's atonement for our sins) assist us to overcome evil and desire virtue for its own sake when such moral endeavor is purely a matter of each person's own responsibility? Kant's answer is ambiguous. On the one hand, he finds here a contradiction (R 19n, 134, 180/23n, 143, 192), for we thus assert that we both are and are not fully responsible for our moral intentions. On the other hand, he states there is no logical impossibility (and thus no contradiction), for perhaps the two (grace and our own efforts) work side by side (R 179/191). It remains incomprehensible, however, just what divine grace could add to our efforts if it is true that we are solely responsible for our moral intentions.

11. This same distinction of three levels is also presented in MPV 78/418.

12. It should be pointed out that Kant's use of the word "humanity" (*Menschheit*) in the second formulation of the categorical imperative in the *Foundations* ("So act that you treat humanity, whether in your own person or in that of another, always as an end and never as a means only") designates level three of the present text of the *Religion*.

13. See AP 9–10/127–28; see also ED 48/460.

14. These concepts and principles are elaborated by Kant in the first *Critique* as the synthetic a priori principles of the understanding. Like the principles of morality, they are universal and necessary, but there is a major difference between the two. Whereas the principles of morality are unconditionally necessary, the principles of knowing objects are only conditionally, hypothetically necessary (A 228/B 280): *if we are to know objects*, we must assume the principles necessary to know them. For Kant, the laws of morality are not conditional upon some "if."

15. See also 49/465: "We often say to a child [who has not yet reached the age of moral reason]: '*Fie, for shame!* you shouldn't do that,' etc. But such expressions are futile in this early stage of education; for the child has, as yet, no sense of shame or of seemliness. He has [at this early age] nothing to be ashamed of, and ought not to be ashamed."

16. It should be noted that under the virtue good as end in itself there are also included one's own self and other persons as the subjects of virtue. Thus, acts of virtue (duty), one's own person, and other persons are all per se good and therefore worthy of unconditional respect.

17. "Man (even the most wicked) does not, under any maxim what-

ever, repudiate the moral law in the manner of a rebel (renouncing obedience to it). The law, rather, forces itself upon him irresistibly by virtue of his moral predisposition; and were no other incentive working in opposition [i.e., the incentive of pleasure on the part of his sensory appetite], he would adopt the law into his supreme maxim as the sufficient determining ground of his will" (R 31/36).

Freedom and Providence in Kant's Account of Religion: The Problem of Expiation

Leslie A. Mulholland

My aim in this paper is to show that in religion, we need to appeal to providence in order to explain how expiation is possible, although Kant thinks that such an appeal would be incompatible with the ground of morality, freedom. I shall argue that the appeal to providence is not incompatible with Kant's claim that any good or bad deed must be done freely.

In the *Metaphysics of Morals*, Kant states that "there is no room for [religion] in ethics as pure practical philosophy" (MMV 163/488). The reason is that, because religion unavoidably involves some reference to God as given in experience through revelation, it has an empirical content (MMV 163/487) and is not pure. Nevertheless, the discussion of *Religion within the Limits of Reason Alone* suggests that the underlying question is whether pure practical philosophy is enough. The problem is whether human persons can of themselves become good, or whether something given from history and revelation is necessary for them to become good. This is particularly a difficulty because Kant contends that although being bad is a product of free action, it is empirically evident that humanity has chosen, at the earliest possible point of choice, to be bad (R 27–28/32). Indeed, Kant presents us with the possibility that humanity is forever alienated from goodness (R 66/72). I shall refer to the problem of changing from a fundamentally bad character to a fundamentally good character as that of "radical" or "fundamental" moral improvement. It is, as we shall see, to be distinguished from the problem of relative moral improvement. The latter is the kind of improvement required to bring one's dispositions into accord with the principle of goodness.

Kant rejects all claims that a fundamental change of character from bad to good can be a consequence of magic or ritual acts demanded by the rules of a religion. These claims, he finds, are outside the limits of reason alone (R 189/201). Kant argues that the change from a bad to a good character is possible only through a free act whereby a person's cast of mind is transformed and a new supreme maxim is adopted as the basis of all practical behavior. In this position, Kant is claiming that so far as religion is consistent with pure practical reason, a change in the moral state of the individual (from a bad to a good will) cannot be regarded as produced by external divine influence, through grace, or through predestination. I shall consider the question of whether he succeeds in his claim.

Before proceeding, however, it is important to clarify a problem in Kant's treatment of radical moral improvement. Kant's treatment is sometimes seen as containing an unintelligible account of grace. Some of the best commentaries on Kant's *Religion* have misunderstood his treatment of grace.[1] For example, John Silber insists that if radical moral improvement arises from freedom, the individual "does not need grace." On the other hand, if the individual has not done all that is possible to merit grace, "even Kant agrees he should not get it."[2]

However, Kant has a clear answer to the question of the role of grace in religion. To begin with, he defines "grace" as "a superior's decree conferring a good for which the subordinate possesses nothing but the (moral) receptivity" (R 70n/76n). Grace supplies the acknowledgment of moral improvement that is a condition for the attainment of the highest good, i.e., of the possession of "happiness in exact proportion to morality" (PrR 115/110). Kant argues that happiness is not identical with morality and is not caused by virtue (PrR 115/111). Hence, for the highest good to be brought about, a being with the power to produce it (God) must exist (PrR 129/124). But for God to produce the highest good, he must know that a moral improvement has taken place. Since human beings cannot see into noumenal nature and know whether they have actually taken the main moral step to improvement, God's judgment that anyone has done this is an act of grace. Kant's treatment of grace then shows grace to involve the knowledge of moral improvement, which is necessary for the highest good when a person has taken the main moral step to improvement (R 70, 70n/75–76, 75n).

Thus no one needs grace for the act of radical moral improvement. Rather grace is necessary because only God can know the true state of character of the individual. And thus, only God can determine when a person deserves happiness. As Kant remarks, the deduction of "the idea of a justification of an individual who is indeed guilty but who has changed his disposition into one well-pleasing to God" possesses no practical use at all. It is an answer to a speculative question (R 70/76).

Kant, then, does not refer to grace as an external element that enables moral improvement independently of freedom. Nevertheless, because we cannot know that we have changed our moral disposition, and our acquired habits still tempt us to act in accordance with the old disposition, "the accuser within us would be more likely to propose a judgment of condemnation" (R 70/76). Here Kant situates humanity in a condition of radical ignorance regarding its own salvation. Indeed, here, with this denial of knowledge, Kant obtains room for faith as an unavoidable demand of the human condition. Kant then regards grace as serving the function of reminding everyone to "continually test himself as though summoned to account before a judge" (R 135/145). The process requires the positing of an omnipotent moral being as a really existing judge. To the extent that persons present this judge as God (MMV 105/439) and find themselves acquitted before God (MMV 105/440), they are justified in being encouraged in the progress to virtue and the expectation of happiness. Thus "through unquenchable respect" for the moral law, the person "finds in himself justification for confidence in [his] good spirit" (R 135/144). The problem in Kant's account of religion is whether this confidence can be justified simply by reference to the free choice to have a good will.[3]

The role of grace in Kant is clear. Grace is needed to provide acknowledgment of fundamental moral improvement. However, the difficulty in Kant's account of grace arises because the role of grace is often associated with another element in moral improvement. This is the conceptual issue of whether human persons can through their own power rid themselves of their character and the resulting guilt stemming from their initial predisposition to evil. Kant himself confuses the issue when he supposes that the claim that a heavenly grace "shall free some but not others from natural depravity . . . is an absolute mystery"

(R 134/143). Strictly, Kant does not include any appeal to grace as external help producing moral improvement in his account of religion within the limits of reason alone.

In the following, I want to examine this problem in Kant: can Kant consistently demonstrate that no intervention of supernatural power is necessary for expiation? Can religion be kept within the limits of reason alone? In the context of this paper, the question is whether providence is necessary for an individual to undergo the radical moral improvement that is involved in expiation, or whether freedom is both necessary and sufficient.

In this examination, I will first attempt to explain the structure of Kant's account of freedom and its relation to the problem of moral improvement. I shall try to show how Kant's treatment of the question is a significant addition to his moral philosophy. Especially, I shall try to show how Kant's treatment contains implicitly an original account of the human self and the human condition. Central to Kant's account is the treatment of radical choice and the absence of any ordinary relation of radical choice to time. I shall bring out how for Kant radical choice is never of a particular thing but of a whole "ensemble" of possible actions, indeed a whole practical world, and how radical choice for Kant commits the agent permanently to the world chosen. In part it will be this feature of the account of radical choice that prevents Kant from providing an account of religion within the limits of reason alone. In conclusion I shall argue that Kant's contention that providence cannot, so far as reason is able to determine, be necessary for expiation rests on a mistake. This is the mistake of supposing that external influence must always be determining and may not be liberating. I shall show that the moral function of providence can be seen as liberating and in this way as necessary for radical moral improvement.

1.

Before proceeding to the main discussion of Kant's account of expiation, I will clarify some of the concepts he uses. What does Kant mean by "providence?"[4] The direction of Kant's account of providence is to exclude the possibility of a God who acts spontaneously in history through revelation in relation to a particular individual or people. In "Perpetual Peace," Kant characterizes providence as "a necessity working according to laws we do not know . . . inasmuch as we discern in it the profound wisdom of a higher cause which predetermines the course of nature and directs it to the objective final end of the human race" (PP 106/362). Providence for Kant has the following features: (1) causality; (2) a causality that is teleological, working toward a final end; (3) the use of the mechanical order of natural laws as means to achieve the final end; (4) predeterminism of the natural order as means to the final end; (5) wisdom in the predeterminism, i.e., foresight of the effects and a good will governing the choice of means and the final end; (6) a wisdom that cannot be understood or seen into by human faculties. Furthermore, in a footnote, Kant states that he does not allow special acts of providence as distinct from general. Hence, he does not allow that God acts as a free being in response to specific acts of others. He argues that there cannot be a reasonable distinction between general and particular or special providence. "Providence," Kant writes, "is called universal in its purpose, and therefore no single thing can be excluded from it" (PP 106–107n/361n).

Providence as the sustainer of the order of nature is not separated from the main teleological function of providence. Providence cares both for the preservation of the species and for the preservation of the individual. But it does so through the mechanical ordering of sensible nature (PP 106–107n/361n). Furthermore, Kant appears to regard all miraculous occurrences as dependent on providence (cf. R 80n/85n). In effect whatever takes place in time would depend on providence. Thus even divine revelation, so long as this is understood as a historical occurrence, would be seen by Kant as falling under providence, and as taking place in accordance with the laws of sensible nature, even though these particular laws must remain unknown to us (R 81/86). Kant's treatment of providence does not allow anything to interfere with the organization of nature under causal laws.

Kant defines "religion" as the "recognition of all duties as divine commands" (R 142/153). His claim that providence is not necessary for religion (R 143–44/155–56) depends on this characterization of religion as a moral order. However, Kant makes it clear that it is only in its formal aspect that religion is a purely moral order. In content religion always contains teachings of history and revelation (MdST 162–63/487–88). For

Kant, morality is comprehensible only through reference to autonomy and the categorical imperative. But since the categorical imperative[5] is a pure idea of reason, the basic features of the moral commands of any religion must be discoverable by pure reason. Moreover, moral commands apply universally, while revelation is always a particular occurrence at a specific time for particular people. For this reason, revelation lacks the universality required by morality even though what is revealed may be universal. The "prime essential of the true church" does not depend on revelation, for the condition for the true church is "the qualification for universality, so far as one understands by that a validity for everyone, i.e., universal unanimity" (R 145/157).

Kant acknowledges that there might be a contingent relation of providence to religion. By a contingent relation, I mean a relation that is not conceptually required by religion. This would be so in the case of revelations that introduced moral ideas. But Kant remarks that although these are useful in introducing moral ideas, "the occurrence of such a supernatural revelation might subsequently be entirely forgotten without the slightest loss to that religion" (R 144/156).

In relation to the individual, Kant's account of religion gives us a doctrine of how expiation is conceivable within the limits of reason alone. Kant writes, "all religions have involved expiation, on whatever basis they put it" (R 111/120). The central question in expiation is how providence functions in the process whereby a person progresses from having a fundamentally bad character to having a fundamentally good character.

Kant's account of expiation, however, contains a problem that cannot be easily comprehended within his account of the individual's character. The problem is this: How are we to understand the difference between expiating subjects in their first wrongful choice and in their second righteous choice? As a result of the fact that when we look at the matter according to laws of freedom, i.e., according to the "supersensible order of things," "time drops out" (R 111–12n/121n), we are not allowed to consider the contingencies of life and the education of the individual as necessary conditions for the rightful choice. We are not, therefore, allowed to consider providence as having an effect on the personal lives of individuals that leads them to a condition where there is a reason for them to want to change.

Finally, we are not allowed to regard God as acting spontaneously in history as a result of a conception of humanity's present needs. Strictly, Kant does not allow God to be an agent.

In the following, then, I want to consider these two problems: first, whether freedom alone is sufficient to comprehend the alteration from a person who is bad to a person who is, at least in intention, good; second, whether Kant can effectively demonstrate that reason alone can provide an adequate structure and content for religion.

2.

Before proceeding, we must observe that the problem of moral improvement is not only a problem for Kant's philosophy of religion. It is a central problem for Kant's ethics in general. The need for expiation is not something forced on the consideration of ethical matters from the outside, through demands made by historical religions. It is inherent in Kant's ethical views. Hence, elucidation of the problem and its solution in *Religion* will elucidate features of Kant's ethics in general. Most important in the treatment in *Religion* is the way in which it reveals the need for an account of the self as it functions in Kant's ethical thought. Kant's presentation involves an implicit position on the structure of the self and the way in which it functions in relations involving responsibility in ethics. Much of the following will depend on developing an analysis of Kant's implicit doctrine of the moral self and the nature of moral relations.

In his account of the main problem of expiation, Kant develops his concept of the good will further than in his earlier works on ethics. He does this by explaining how humanity in its entire character is situated with regard to good and evil and how, as a result, humanity falls into evil.

To develop his account of the basic human moral situation, Kant uses the idea of the choice of a supreme maxim. Kant claims that so long as one is capable of responsible action, one must have a fundamental maxim of character that is either good or evil, but which cannot be both (R 20/24). Kant's point is that I cannot have the basic character of being morally good without making it my maxim to be good in all respects. If I make it my maxim to be good in only this or that respect, I will not be good. If, for example, I resolve to keep my promises but do not resolve to further the happiness of others, the following problem arises: I allow selfishness to excuse me from fulfilling the law with regard to others' happiness, while I do not allow it as an excuse in the case of promises. In this case, what is the principle whereby I am able to combine my behavior regarding promises with my behavior regarding others' happiness? If the principle of keeping promises is based on the moral law, then it commits me to further others' happiness as well. If the principle on which I decide not to further others' happiness for my own selfish advantage is a general principle, then it is inconsistent with the principle on which I resolve to keep promises. There cannot be compartmentalized specific principles of action. There must be a general principle. We might, however, wonder why Kant thinks that the need for a general principle of behavior must be grasped immediately. Why might we not suppose that the unity of the self through a rational principle is a consequence of learning and reflection? The answer lies in Kant's treatment of the relation of freedom to time.

Most (if not all) commentators have not appreciated the full import of Kant's claim that there must be a supreme maxim.[6] Every specific maxim concerning a specific action must cohere with the agent's supreme maxim. Thus Kant insists that all unlawful conduct is a consequence of the evil maxim (R 26/31). Should human persons subsequently adopt the good maxim, they then can no longer do evil.

Some of Kant's comments, however, suggest that he believes that even after a person has adopted the good supreme maxim, she may act wrongly. He speaks of one who has adopted the good maxim as having "to guard against a relapse" (R 71/77). This does not mean that the agent can change from a good to an evil supreme maxim. For the new maxim is "unchangeable" (R 43/47). The problem is twofold. First, there is the problem of overcoming the habits formed in accordance with the old disposition, i.e., the problem of increasing the strength of the new disposition (R 71/77). But second, Kant's account of the problem of a relapse depends on his view that the individual can never know whether she has really changed her disposition. Kant remarks: *if only one were absolutely assured of the unchangeableness of a disposition of this sort*, the constant 'seeking for the kingdom of God' would be equivalent to knowing oneself to be already in possession of this kingdom" (R 61/

68). The import of this lack of knowledge is that everyone must approach every circumstance as if presented anew with the problem of rejecting the evil maxim in favor of the good maxim. If the good maxim has been chosen, there is no new choice possible. But since no one knows whether the good maxim has been chosen, each must act as if he or she has not yet become good.

Moreover, a central feature of the initial evil maxim is that it is adopted through awareness of the imperative to choose good (PrR 29/29). The moral law always presents an alternative to the evil maxim. Thus Kant contends that since every fundamental disposition "must have been adopted by free choice" (R 20/25), everyone is responsible for the evil principle as well as the good.

Now the basic problem of expiation emerges from the analysis of the way the adoption of a supreme maxim that is evil determines the self by producing an intrinsically guilty character. Kant distinguishes between two kinds of guilt. I shall call these "general" and "specific" guilt. Specific guilt is the guilt ensuing on a particular wrong action. General guilt is the guilt ensuing on the choice of a principle as supreme maxim. General guilt commits the individual to all sorts of possible guilty acts. Kant remarks that the initial adoption of the evil maxim:

> brings with it endless violations of the law and so *infinite* guilt. The extent of this guilt is due . . . to the fact that this moral evil lies in the *disposition* and the maxims in general, in universal basic *principles* rather than in particular transgressions. . . . ([A] human court of justice . . . attends merely to single offenses . . . and not to the general disposition.) It would seem to follow, then, that because of this infinite guilt all mankind must look forward to *endless punishment*. . . . (R 66/72)

This is the main problem. Once the act of adoption of the evil maxim is taken, there is no way out of the moral effects of it. Because the evil maxim now forms the fundamental principle of the subject, i.e., it now forms his or her essence, it would also be a changeless condition of the individual's character and behavior (PrR 103/100). It would, moreover, commit the individual to an infinite number of potential evil actions and to no good actions. From this point of view no avoidance of endless punishment is possible through the labor of the guilty person. The human condition is one of unavoidable "exclusion from the kingdom of God" (R 66/72).

There are then two central issues connected with moral improvement: How can anyone pass from the condition of an evil character to that of a good character? How can anyone even after this transition (by virtue of being in some sense "the same person") avoid the punishment produced by the initial character? In order to investigate the main problem of whether providence is needed to enable radical moral improvement, I shall now examine these questions.

3.

To explain Kant's treatment of radical moral improvement and find the difficulties that it contains, we must understand Kant's concept of moral rebirth. For this, we need to refer to two elements of Kant's doctrine of morality: the conception of the self that it presupposes, and the relation of morality and moral choice to time.

We have, first of all, the fundamental view, in Kant, that humanity is subject to the moral law and is free in being subject to this law. Secondly, as a consequence of the last point, we have the claim that any moral evil in human persons must be a result of their own free choice. Now Kant claims that human persons innately possess a character that, while not being wholly evil, nevertheless presents adherence to the moral law as secondary to the pursuit of selfish interests. Because human persons are free, this natural character must be regarded as a product of free choice and not something produced by nature (R 27/31). Guilt in relation to God is called "sin." This natural character contains what might be called "original sin." Original sin is universal (but because of freedom it cannot be *strictly universal* [cf. *Kritik der reinen Vernunft* B 3–4]). Now Kant maintains that through an act of free will, human persons can make a second fundamental act of choice and alter their character by altering the fundamental principle of their behavior. This second act involves "a revolution in his cast of mind." Kant describes this revolution as "a kind of rebirth, as it were a new creation . . . and a change of heart" (R 43/47).

Rebirth is an alteration of the very essence of the person. It cannot be understood simply as a process in which a human being changes the rules that she acts on. To understand Kant's meaning, it is important to distinguish the two elements: the noumenal and the phenomenal. Kant writes:

> Although the man (regarded from the point of view of his empirical nature as a sentient being) is *physically* the selfsame guilty person as before and must be judged as such before a moral tribunal and hence by himself; yet, because of his new disposition, he is (regarded as an intelligible being) *morally* another in the eyes of a divine judge for whom this disposition takes the place of action. (R 68/74)

Thus Kant affirms that persons with a change of heart are in their nature as noumenal beings absolutely different persons, even though they are physically the same as before.

To understand the nature of rebirth, we must strive further to understand the structure of the self of the finite rational being that Kant's account presupposes. His treatment of rebirth involves an analysis of the self into three features. First, there is an intelligible, moral subject with a determinate character set by the supreme maxim ("the intelligible character," A 551/B 579). Second, there is the subject as a physical being with all the habits resulting from the supreme maxim ("the empirical character," ibid.). However, underlying the moral change, there must also be a third subject, the presence of which is obscured in Kant's analysis. This is the subject that chooses and thus can make the change from the bad to the good character (see MdST 81/418). The chief difficulty in the understanding of the process of change of character is in understanding how this third most basic subject is able to make the transition from the bad to the good character. One of the deepest (although obscure) insights of Kant into human nature is into the existence of this ultimate ontological basis of choice in that nature.

Our next problem is whether the analysis of the structure of the self is sufficient to enable us to comprehend rebirth. In Kant's treatment, we have first an initial act whereby individuals adopt the evil, prudential principle as the principle of their character. Then we have the second act whereby the good person adopts the moral law as the principle of action. Certainly, it would be natural to regard the act of change of heart as affected by the original evil maxim or to suppose that the individual can grow and learn that good is better than evil. But if we suppose this, the first act would have to be regarded as a condition of the second. Kant denies this, however. The denial is implicit in Kant's account of the relation of freedom to time. To understand why Kant insists that freedom is necessary and sufficient for expiation, it is essential to investigate the problem of freedom and time.

4.

It is evident from Kant's comments about the relation of reason to time that past behavior cannot determine or even be a necessary condition for future (radical) choice. Kant insists that a free action is "cognizable by means of pure reason alone, apart from every temporal condition" (R 27/31). Furthermore, "the causality of reason in its intelligible character does not, in producing an effect, *arise* or begin to be at a certain time" (A 552/B 580). Also, "reason is present in all the actions of men at all times and in all circumstances, and is always the same; but it is not itself in time, and does not fall into any new state in which it was not before. In respect to new states, it is *determining*, not *determinable*" (A 556/B 584). This presentation of reason expresses free action as entirely undetermined by what goes before in time. Kant has here in mind the use of reason in the derivation of an action from an already determined supreme maxim. The adoption of a supreme maxim itself, while performed with rational awareness of morality, must be an act performed only by the faculty of choice (*Willkür*). But it too must be outside of time. Hence, his account can make no room for the previous act or any consequence of it as providing the external grounds for a change of heart. The innateness of the character must be a result of the timelessness of the choice of the supreme maxim.

We must be careful to observe that in this account, persons choosing a supreme maxim would be in all relevant respects exactly the same when they chose the good principle as when they initially chose the evil. Notice that not even the development of reason and the greater ability to exercise it can make any difference with regard to the choice of the supreme maxim. When Kant considers the question of original sin, he expresses a difference between Adam and all other human beings. Adam falls into sin from a state of innocence. All other humans are innately wicked. This difference is highlighted by the fact that Adam is "depicted as already in full command of the use of his reason," though evil in all other humans is presented as stemming from a deliberate transgression in a period of our lives "wherein the use of reason had not yet developed" (R 38/43). Nevertheless, there is no difference between the guilt of Adam and that of everyone else. In the same way, although the responsibility for the second act of choosing a supreme maxim is the same as for the first, the free act of change of heart is presented as an act occurring in a person at a later stage, when reason has developed.

His account of the timelessness of free actions is a problem for Kant because it forces him to insist that freedom is both necessary and sufficient for a change of heart and allows him no room for providence. Kant is not entirely unaware of the problem however. He writes: "The lapse from good into evil (when one remembers that this originates in freedom) is no more comprehensible than the reascent from evil into good" (R 40/45; see also 40/44). Kant thinks that any help a human person gets in changing from an evil to a good purpose would have the effect of determining the moral change of heart. Thus anyone contemplating moral improvement must recognize that no outside help can be expected in throwing off the bad self and accepting the good.

In his discussion of religious "mysteries," Kant does give himself a way out by suggesting that the process of a grace that externally determined a change of heart, and the apparent injustice that it would involve if not based on freedom, "must be referred to a wisdom whose rule is for us an absolute mystery" (R 134/143). However, he cautions against such suggestions and indicates that they would lead to "the *salto mortale* [death leap] of human reason" (R 111/121).

Kant's problem is that he thinks that in his own account, the change from evil to good is no more comprehensible than the initial fall into evil. However, the initial act presupposes only the consciousness of the moral law, not a commitment to it (cf. R 31/36). The difficulty with understanding Kant's account of rebirth is not in understanding how there can be a recovery of the initial good maxim but in understanding how there can be a recovery of the state of innocence from which the initial bad choice was made.

Two logical difficulties arise from the problem of rebirth. First of all, since the time intervening between the first choice and the second, and everything that happens in that time, is irrelevant to the second choice, the person at the point of making the second choice is numerically and conceptually indistinguishable from the same person at the point of making the first choice. There is no reason whatsoever for the person to make a different choice on the second occasion than on the first. It is as if one person at one occasion made two choices of incompatible supreme maxims. Only if we allow past experience to have an influence on the present decision can this be avoided. As I shall try to show, this does not mean that past actions are determining of the present decision.

There is, however, a more important logical difficulty, one which leads to a Kantian antinomy (R 107/116). How can the individual recover her initial innocence considering: (1) Since guilt is "infinite," no one is morally in a position to atone for her own guilt. Hence, if atonement is possible, only another person with no guilt can atone for my guilt. (2) But if there can be no atonement by the individual himself or herself, how can there be a vicarious atonement? For according to the concept of the morally good, moral improvement must always be by free action on the part of the individual. It seems rather that vicarious atonement would be analytically impossible. (3) Finally, even if there is moral improvement, how can the endless punishment due to the individual be wiped out?

Kant's solution to the antinomy is unsatisfactory, for it does not explain how the initial responsibility can be removed, i.e., how the old self can be "cast off." His treatment of the issue is nevertheless original. What he does is make the vicarious atonement an atonement carried out not by another person or by the evil self but by the character, with its pure self, into which one changes with the adoption of the supreme maxim. In part, Kant uses the Christian idea of the son of God to express the notion of the pure self. Here the son of God can be the vicarious substitute for the individual's sin, but not strictly as another person. Rather, it is the person's new self, i.e., the new disposition, that vicariously atones for the old. In Christianity, Christ serves as the personification of this moral disposition (R 69/74). But for Kant it is not faith in Christ as a historical individual that leads to release from sin.[7] Rather, such a release requires acceptance of the pure moral principle, exemplified in Christ, as the supreme maxim of one's behavior. This acceptance is entirely from within. It is then the new self—purified—that atones for the sin of the old self, although now the punishments are grasped as means "for the testing and exercising of his disposition to goodness" (R 69n/75n).

While Kant is consistent in requiring that the new self can only be adopted by an act of freedom, he cannot explain how the old self can be cast off. He can allow the act of changing the supreme maxim only if he regards the individual as *not completely determined* by the initial act and as able to adopt a stance from which a choice could be made independently of the evil maxim. The ploy of using the "new self" as the person atoning for the old still assumes that the old self can choose to be good. Kant's view depends on distinguishing the self as structured by the evil maxim from the self as fundamental choosing agent and in explaining how the former can pass into the latter and avoid the commitment of the original act. For the atonement is possible only if there is some element of the self that can act independently of the supreme maxim and, as it were, put the initial bad character into suspension and then destroy it. But Kant fails to supply an account of how the agent can recover the use of the choosing self.

Thus the antinomy in Kant's treatment of rebirth remains. In effect, the problem for Kant is: How can one recover the initial situation from which a choice is made? To pursue this question, I shall first try to elucidate further what the original commitment to the supreme maxim involves and why Kant needs to expand his idea of the self in order to explain radical moral improvement.

5.

In defense of Kant, it might be objected that all that is necessary for a change of heart is the choice to be good. Since man is free, he can make this choice. To understand why freedom is insufficient for expiation, it is necessary to understand why, in Kant's treatment, acts of freedom produce permanent properties of the self. This depends on Kant's account of how free acts are independent of time. Several commentators have observed the problem, but not much has been supplied as an interpretation of it.[8] Kant's comments on the problem elucidate features of morality as well as of the nature of the self in religion.

In Kant's account of nature, the basic structural features through which things are and through which they change are supplied by space, time, and pure concepts. These supply what might be called the "constitutive structure" of change in nature. However, Kant finds human action to belong to a different constitutive structure (see PrR 140/135). In his discussion of promising and contract in the *Rechtslehre*, Kant tries to show why we have to appeal to a different structure to understand human interrelations. He makes the following comment:

> now the [united will of contracting persons] is not possible through empirical acts of declaration which must follow one another necessarily in time and are never simultaneous. For if I have promised and the other now wills acceptance, I can regret it during the time in between (no matter how short it may be), because before the acceptance I am still free; just as on the other side, the acceptant, for the same reason may not be held bound for his counter declaration that follows on the promise. (MdSR 272, my translation)

Kant emphasizes his point: the problem is that "they are always only acts that follow one another in time, where, if the one act is, the other either is not yet or is no more" (MdSR 272, my translation). Thus, although events in time are transitory, the act of promising must persist as a commitment. Only in this way does the acceptance of the offer produce an obligation. He goes on to contend that we can show that promising is possible only through appeal to the idea of an intellectual relation of the two persons in which there is "abstraction of those empirical conditions of rights." Again, Kant comments that pure practical reason abstracts "from all sensible conditions of space and time that concern the concept of rights" (MdSR 273, my translation).

Kant's comments apply to all actions whereby a person may be regarded as committed by or as responsible for an act that he or she performs. An act for which a person can be held responsible cannot be simply something that as an event in time has happened and is no more. Somehow the action must still be a property of the person; otherwise, if it has entirely ceased to exist with the person remaining, there could be no praise or blame for its performance. It would not now be a property of the person, so blame would be inappropriate. Furthermore, if a person could discard the previous act by a new act, he or she could not be responsible at all; there would be no commitment.

So, in the *Critique of Practical Reason*, Kant comments that although to fatalists such as Priestley, repentence for an action long past was absurd, nevertheless,

> as a pain, repentance is entirely legitimate, because reason, when it is a question of the law of our intelligible existence (the moral law), acknowledges no temporal distinctions and only asks whether the event belongs to me as my act, and then morally connects with it the same feeling, whether the event occurs now or is long since past. For the sensuous life is but a single phenomenon in the view of an intelligible consciousness of its existence. (PrR 102/99)

Kant brings out here that morality demands the abstraction of sensible conditions of space and time from consideration of the action. From the moral point of view, the relation of an individual to an action is always, as it were, present and never merely a past relation. As a result, blame and repentance for a past ill deed are justified, for the original act is still present. For this reason, the act of adopting a supreme maxim for action must be an act that occurs outside time and must commit the agent irrevocably.

Kant must be correct. Anyone who participates in moral practices, that is, practices that involve commitment and responsibility, such as the practice of promising, must accept that actions which are intentional and subject to rules in the practice are to be treated as permanent properties of the subject rather than transitory events. To be a moral being, a person, is to participate in this nontemporal moral order (A 548/B 576).

In relation to the problem of a fundamental choice of a supreme maxim that is outside time, Kant is suggesting something like this: at the point of adopting a supreme maxim for behavior, a person must have a kind of picture of two alternative kinds of life. On the one hand is a life aimed at the satisfaction of pleasures and avoidance of pains. On the other hand is a life aimed at being morally good. In each case, the agent would be choosing for all possible situations and must know that both possible kinds of life are available. This does not mean that the agent is conscious of every detail and every contingency in his or her future life. So while there is "a veil of ignorance"[9] preventing knowledge of particular events, one chooses a way of relating to all possible events.

At the moment of choosing, the chooser chooses a whole life. That is, while every contingency in that life cannot be foreseen, the supreme maxim supplies the principle for interpreting the significance of any contingency in relation to the agent and thus whether and how it is a reason to act. It is as if a person were offered the choice of one of two positions in a game. Choosing to be a referee would commit one to a variety of possible situations and problems. Choosing to be a player would commit one to different ones. Notice that in the basic choice, the external conditions, while the same for both the player and referee, do not produce the same actions. The way in which these external conditions serve as reason to act, or whether they are reason to act, depends on the basic choice.

We find so far that Kant's view that fundamental moral choices are timeless makes some sense.[10] However, why would Kant think that the development of the use of reason is irrelevant to the quality of the choice that a person might make in the decision between kinds of lives? The answer to this question is that such choices are entirely independent of abilities and knowledge of self and the external world. If we allow that reason can develop as the basis of choice, we would be compelled to regard individual choices as to some extent affected by past considerations. Although we can agree that reason develops as a consequence of a chosen character, the development does not affect a new choice. For there is nothing in the previous character and the development of reason that can supply the ground of selection of a different character. There is nothing more to understand than good and evil. Once this can be understood, all other achievements (or the lack of them) cannot make any difference by giving guidance to a fundamental choice.

Finally, note that in promise making and in the case of specific wrong actions, there can be counter actions that remove specific obligations incurred, e.g., keeping the promise, being punished for a crime, etc. Here the responsibility and guilt are cancelled even though the acts are properties of the self. Note too that this cancellation is not strictly a causal consequence of the counter actions. The cancellation does not depend on the time factor but on the rules for interpreting the meaning of the action in relation to other actions.

Kant's characterization of the relation of a person to the evil maxim, however, commits him to regard it as a permanent property of the self which is so fundamental that there can be no act by the agent that can simply cancel it. It is not a specific act, produced from a person's character or inclinations, but the inextirpable basis of the character itself (R 32/37) and it must determine one's awareness of one's self as sinful. How then can expiation occur?

In order to explain the problem further, I should like to compare Kant's position with that of a more recent philosopher, Jean-Paul Sartre.

6.

Kant's position might seem to be proto-existentialist—i.e., to be affirming that one's values are a product of radical choice with no objective basis. To exclude this possibility, and further elucidate Kant's position, I want briefly to compare Kant and Jean-Paul Sartre. While Kant speaks of the act of adopting the supreme maxim, Sartre speaks of the choice of one's "being" in a project.[11] Insofar as the project involves ends, it, as it were, provides a supreme maxim from which other subsidiary maxims dealing with specific matters can be discovered. Both agree that the basic choice itself has no end and is indeterminate. Sartre's position helps us to understand Kant's through his central remark that in relation to action, "Causes and motives have meaning only inside a projected ensemble."[12]

Sartre's claim, I take it, is that simple facts, states of affairs in the world, even states of one's own past and character, have as such no causal significance in relation to action. Before these states of affairs can have causal significance, they must be characterized as possible causes (i.e., motives) by the project one has adopted. They must fit into the projected ensemble, even though they are not explicitly identified in the project. Thus if my aim is a life of happiness, and if my way of achieving a life of happiness is the accumulation of wealth, nothing will be able to serve as a motive for my action save insofar as it can be linked to my main ends, happiness and the accumulation of wealth. The fact that buying a rising stock is a likely means to further wealth can be a cause of my action. But the fact that selling a stock might lead to unemployment and the unhappiness of certain other people is not by itself a motive, for the project does not allow it as such.

First of all, this analysis indicates that a project systematically determines what can and what cannot be causes and motives; second, it brings out that the relation of free actions to time is different from that relation in the case of events in nature. In nature events have causes that precede them in time. In the case of free actions, in Sartre's analysis, the past event has causal significance only insofar as I now have a project that presents the past event as a cause or motive for action. Inasmuch as the project is free, moreover, and, in Sartre's case, changeable, at no point is any past event objectively a motive. Its status as a motive entirely depends on the present prevailing project.

The case is similar in Kant's treatment of the supreme maxim. There is nothing that has happened before the first adoption of the supreme maxim that can be a cause of the adoption of that maxim. For any state of affairs is a cause of action only insofar as the supreme maxim allows it as a cause.[13]

Furthermore, until there is a "change of heart" in the adoption of the moral law as the supreme maxim, no state of affairs can be a cause for the adoption of that maxim, because, until the change, all states of affairs have meaning as means to ends and as motives of action only in relation to the prevailing supreme maxim. After the change of heart, what has happened and been done can serve as a motive for certain actions, e.g., making good past wrongs within the new ensemble allowed by the supreme maxim.

Hence, there is in principle nothing in a person's past experience that can lead to the change of heart. At best, experience can lead a person to adopt more realistic or more enlightened prudential rules. The fundamental choice of the moral law as a supreme maxim must be made "outside of time," i.e., independently of anything that has gone before.

In relation to the main problem of moral improvement, there cannot be any specific cause or motive within the world as presented by the evil maxim for the change of heart or any motive derived from that maxim sufficient for the recovery of the initial stance from which a new choice can be made.

The essential difference between Kant and Sartre is that

Sartre's account allows no permanent objective principle that makes individuals eternally responsible for the fundamental choice (of project or supreme maxim). For Kant, the moral law both reveals choice and provides the permanent principle that makes individuals responsible for their choices. Responsibility prevents individuals from reassuming the initial position of pure freedom. It permanently binds individuals to their guilt. Despite his comments to the contrary, Kant, unlike Sartre, does not have the option of appealing to freedom as the means to reassume innocence.

To understand radical moral change, we are presented with the need to look to an external factor as the means for expiation. But notice that this presents two problems. How are individuals led to *want* to change their supreme maxim? After all, there are no motives within the prevailing project permitting this, and the motive supplied by the moral law is the same now as it was when the original choice was made. Since nothing can be said to have changed regarding the original condition, there is no reason for the subject to decide differently. There is also the problem of how the fundamental commitment to the evil maxim can be removed.

Concerning the first problem, we have the following life-schema. First, there is some general feature of the evil world (i.e., the world chosen by the agent in the initial choice of supreme maxim) that, unforeseeable by the chooser, nullifies the agent's maxim and leads him or her to be alienated from that world. Second, this general factor, external to chosen values, affects the agent in such a way that there is no means within the ensemble allowed by the evil maxim to encounter and handle this factor. Thus the agent is compelled to rethink the original choice.

Concerning the second problem, we have the possibility that the agent can be liberated by some external means from responsibility for the evil maxim. In both these matters, it seems that we are compelled to look toward providence as the outer condition for the possibility of an inner change. But how is this conceptually possible?

7.

To recapitulate, in the philosophy of religion, Kant presents us with an account of two acts: the initial act, universally performed, of adoption of the evil maxim, which commits the agent to infinite guilt, and the act of rebirth, through the adoption of the moral law as the supreme maxim of actions. Kant argues that rebirth must be produced by a free act and, hence, that the initial act is paradoxically not totally binding.

My main objection to Kant is that he errs in his understanding of the nature of moral improvement. Kant wrongly supposes that all external conditions of action must be determining. He does not see that there can be an external condition of moral improvement even though it is not determining of the action produced. Kant recognizes this possibility in his treatment of history and its relation to perpetual peace.[14]

There are two respects in which providence can be a condition of moral improvement without being determining: first, providence can produce the condition that enables the individual to recover the original stance from which a new choice of a supreme maxim can be made; second, providence can, through the practical experience of the nullification of the supreme maxim supply the means to teach the individual that it is necessary to change. Both conditions would be required for the change of heart. Something is required to move persons to a position where they recognize the need to make a new choice. Since there is nothing in the choice of the original maxim that can supply this, it must come from without, for there is no logical basis for the claim that the evil maxim cannot be a principle of action.[15]

The prime and standard candidate for an experience that can lead to the nullification of the supreme maxim is fear of death. Although Kant gives this hardly any attention, he nevertheless recognizes its significance (CB 58–59/114–15). And we must remember that the evil maxim determines a world that cannot provide a justification for the claim that the soul is immortal. Although Kant argues for the immortality of the soul as a postulate of pure practical reason (PrR 126/121), we cannot appeal to that postulate to resolve the problem of death. As Allen Wood has shown,[16] the postulate of immortality is made from a standpoint of consciousness of the moral law as binding on oneself. Now we cannot claim that a person who adopts the evil maxim will fear death. For that humans are mortal is a contingent truth of human nature. But a person who has made pleasure the overriding value would, on discovering mortality, be expected to fear death because death must appear to involve the loss of all pleasure. So while adoption of the evil maxim does not alone determine that a person will fear death, in accompaniment with the knowledge of unavoidable death, it would do so. Death can, then, be regarded as an external (providential) obstacle to the end (pleasure) contained in the supreme maxim. The fear of death nullifies the supreme maxim and thus the self determined by that maxim without releasing the agent from guilt.

However, the individual must also be liberated from the responsibility arising from the commitment to the evil maxim. To understand how this is possible, we must refer to Kant's principle expressed in the *Rechtslehre:* "That action that counteracts the hindrance of an effect promotes the effect and is consistent with it" (MMJ 35/231). This principle refers to the removal of a hindrance of an effect. The removal of the hindrance would merely make the effect a possibility without thereby determining it to happen. In relation to humanity, the external removal of the hindrance to the adoption of a good maxim (forgiveness for general guilt) would be liberating, not determining.

It might still seem that in forgiveness we are allowing a person to receive a radical moral improvement without deserving it. But notice that if a person is freed from the effects of her bad character but once more chooses a bad character, nothing is achieved. The only positive consequence of the external act of forgiveness (how it would appear in history would depend on the particular religion) is to provide a condition for the choice of a good character as a permanent possibility. So contrary to Kant, faith in some sort of external power able to release one from the original supreme maxim is essential for radical moral improvement. Also grace must precede the moral improvement, for this release from guilt only repositions the individual in the initial situation and enables the new choice. So it is not that the choice for the moral law must precede grace; rather, it is that grace is of no effect save for the person who is prepared to make a commitment to moral improvement. Through grace the bad person is at every moment able to choose to be good.

Furthermore, we should note that no problem of relative injustice arises in release from the guilt incurred by the initial choice. With regard to general guilt, all are equally guilty for the choice of the evil maxim. There is no moral difference between persons at this point. Furthermore, there is no moral difference between choosing the good maxim earlier than later. Because general guilt is infinite, there is no greater accumulation of guilt resulting from a later choice.

Finally, there is no reason why Kant cannot admit forgiveness into his account of religion.[17] Although at times Kant suggests that he cannot allow forgiveness into his treatment of the human being's relation to sin (MMV 166/490), the reason for this is that we cannot understand how human beings can wrong God. In the *Rechtslehre*, Kant makes it clear that insofar as an action is a wrong against the sovereign alone, the sovereign has the right to pardon the agent (cf. MMJ 108/337). But God is the sovereign in the kingdom of ends (F 52/434). If we then consider sin to be a wrong against God, who has only rights and no duties, God can pardon sin. It is only wrongs against others that God cannot pardon. But from the point of view of religion, all duties are duties to God. Here we should observe that Kant implicitly associates God with pure practical reason itself, as when he writes that the moral command is "seek ye first the kingdom of pure practical reason" (PP 125/378) and when he takes Christ's commandment to love God to mean make duty the incentive of action (R 148/160). God, however, cannot be identified with pure practical reason, for in addition to being sovereign in the kingdom of ends, God is the omnipotent creator (PrR 115/110 and 104/100).

We should also note Kant's final view of the matter of forgiveness. He holds that if forgiveness is not possible, "the creator would have had to avoid a creation that could have produced a result so contrary to his intention, which can have only love as its ground" (MMV 166/491). Justice, Kant remarks, is only the limiting condition of benevolence. Benevolence is the motive for creation, so far as we can conceive of God's motive (MMV 166/491).

Nevertheless Kant points out that it is not possible to regard duties as actually duties to God without a revelation that provides reason for faith in the reality of God (MdST 162–63/487–88) as a "Being existing outside our idea." We cannot regard ourselves as having duties to a mere idea. Revealed religion is thus necessary for us to regard ourselves as having duties to God. But we can represent ourselves as forgiven only if we present all duties as duties to God as a real Being, for only then can God actually forgive. Since we can regard ourselves as forgiven only within revealed religion, Kant's attempt to bring religion within the limits of reason alone fails.

We must give providence and time a necessary place in moral improvement. Without reference to an external influence, it is not possible to understand how the individual can pass from the evil maxim to a position from which a new choice can be made. And also, once we recognize that providence is not determining but only liberating, the moral obstacle to allowing it is overcome.

Furthermore, although in our idea of God we must represent Him as benevolent, we may not assume that God has forgiven, because we have no *right* to God's pardon. We cannot assume that we have received pardon just because we need it, for this would make us entitled to it. Hence, we can know God's pardon exists only through evidence of its having been given. The actuality of pardon depends on a direct act of God, not on the mere thought of that act. As a result, for evidence of pardon, revelation would be necessary. Apart from revelation, we could only hope that there is a God who will pardon, not know that he has pardoned. Access to external liberating influence must be made known to us externally, through revelation.

In conclusion, without altering the place of freedom in Kant's account of morality, providence serves as a necessary condition for the change from a bad to a good character. On the one hand, it is necessary for the education needed to change; on the other hand, it is necessary for the knowledge of the act which is a logical requirement for the negation of the initial evil choice.

NOTES

1. D. M. MacKinnon wonders whether we can attach any sense to Kant's treatment of grace in "Kant's Philosophy of Religion," *Philosophy* 50 (1975): 136. John Silber claims that in admitting grace Kant contradicts his theory of expiation. See "The Ethical Significance of Kant's *Religion*," included in the Introduction to *Religion within the Limits of Religion Alone*, cxxxii.

2. Silber, cxxxiii.

3. *Prima facie* Kant's position seems to be in conflict with some elements of New Testament theology. See, for instance, John 6:65.

4. For a discussion of the problem of providence, see M. J. Langford, *Providence* (London: SCM Press, 1980).

5. For a discussion of the relationship of morality to autonomy and the categorical imperative, see my *Kant's System of Rights* (New York: Columbia University Press, 1990), chs. 1–4.

6. E.g., John Silber seems to regard Kant as claiming that the choice of particular maxims of action is made independently of the choice of supreme maxims. See Silber, cxviii: "Specific acts of *Willkür* have in themselves no direct interrelation. Each is a free decision of *Willkür*."

7. "So far as reason can see," Kant believes, vicarious atonement is impossible (R 134/143). Also, to appeal to vicarious atonement in order to avoid rigorously testing oneself by one's own reason would be to go from grace to virtue rather than to take "the right course" which is "to progress from virtue to pardoning grace" (R 190/202).

8. See Silber, ci; see also Allen Wood, "Kant's Compatibilism," in *Self and Nature in Kant's Philosophy*, Allen Wood, ed. (Ithaca, N.Y.: Cornell University Press, 1984), 97.

9. The expression is from John Rawls, *A Theory of Justice* (Cambridge, Mass.: Belknap Press, 1971), 136ff.

10. See Jonathan Bennett, "Kant's Theory of Freedom," in Wood, ed., 110. Despite grounds for skepticism concerning a pure morality, I do not see how we can avoid understanding time in a Kantian way when we examine the problem of commitment and responsibility. See, however, W. H. Walsh, "Kant's Moral Theology," *Proceedings of the British Academy* 49 (1963): 288.

11. Jean-Paul Sartre, *Being and Nothingness* (New York: Washington Square Press, 1966), 542. For an account that effectively brings out the existentialist elements of Kant's treatment of radical evil, see Emil L. Fackenheim, "Kant and Radical Evil," *University of Toronto Quarterly* 23 (1953–54): 339–53.

12. Sartre, 534.

13. See MMV 54/394; see also R 19–24.

14. See my "Kant on War and International Justice," in *Kant-Studien* 78 (January 1987): 40. Note that the position of the later essay "Perpetual Peace" (1795) might show a development in Kant's thinking on the problem. See Michel Despland, *Kant on History and Religion* (London: McGill-Queens University Press, 1973), 171–72.

15. See my "Egoism and Morality," *Journal of Philosophy* 86 (1989): 542–550. In this paper I argue both that morality cannot be based on egoism and that the egoist would be happier abandoning egoism for morality.

16. See Allen Wood, *Kant's Moral Religion* (Ithaca, N.Y.: Cornell University Press, 1970), 29ff.

17. See Silber, cxxxiii.

Kant's Doctrine of Atonement as a Theory of Subjectivity

Walter Sparn

It is well known that Immanuel Kant, in *Die Religion innerhalb der Grenzen der bloßen Vernunft* of 1793, sets for himself the task of rationally reconstructing the moral-practical substance of biblical revelation, i.e., of traditional Christian dogmatics. Obviously a revision of positive religion according to the "pure religion of reason" cannot be expected to verify directly any dogmatic proposition, or to "rescue" Christian faith by philosophical means, as so many contemporary authors had in mind. For Kant, the philosophical linkage between moral autonomy and religious belief does not result from a lack of a rational foundation of morality and a need for a religious foundation; the competence of practical reason in this respect is fully sufficient. Rather, it is the imperative demand of practical reason itself for the realization of morality under finite, empirical conditions which establishes religion as an authentically philosophical subject. And thus it is the clarifying of the relation between practical reason as such and empirical subjectivity which obliges Kant's philosophy of religion not only to criticize the dogmatic tradition but also to reconstruct a rational analogon of Christian dogmatics.

Such a reconstruction clearly must be based on a philosophical concept of the human being, namely of a free being obliging herself to absolute laws just by her reason: it is an anthropological task. Christian theology, however, has to consider serious reasons for speaking of religion not only in anthropological terms but, in categorical differentiation, also in Christological terms: in this life the difference between empirical self-consciousness and true self-consciousness is, in Christian faith, irreducible. Now it is just this difference, in terms of empirical and transcendental subjectivity and its irreducibility, that is a crucial problem for Kant's philosophy of religion. Kant's discussion of dogmatic Christology, therefore, does not indicate a compromise with dogmatic theology or even an accommodation to it but arises from a genuine motif of Christological argument. In particular, it is the doctrine of Atonement to which Kant turns his philosophical attention.

Christology, however, represents the *topos* where the counterdistinction between revelation and rational religion, as Kant characterizes it, is an essential presupposition of Christian dogmatics itself. Without history (just what the pure religion of reason does not embody), no Christology can be formulated. How, then, should Kant use Christological arguments in defining the relation between practical reason and empirical morality? Does Kant's theory of subjectivity include a Christological difference?

In the following I want to point out, on the one hand, that Kant's concept of the Atonement indeed verifies important elements of dogmatic Christology. To be sure, it does so better than the modern theology of his time, known to him most probably through J. J. Spalding (1748, 1772), J. S. Semler (1774), the Wolfenbüttel Fragments (1774–78), or even C. F. Bahrdt (1781). On the other hand, I want to show that Kant's concept of Atonement does not do justice to classical Christology, although it argues in some sense more traditionally than the conservative theology of his time, known to him through J. F. Stapfer (1746), J. D. Heilmann (1761), or J. D. Michaelis (1760, 1779). To be sure, just in its surprising traditionalism, Kant's concept represents an abstract theory of subjectivity.

Kant speaks of Jesus Christ as the personification of the Good, the Ideal of moral perfection—in religious language, humanity in which God is well-pleased. The Ideal presented to the senses in Jesus Christ dwells in an incomprehensible fashion in practical reason, which gives the moral law. There, independently of experience, it is objectively real. In it, therefore, inheres not only the claim to be the model of moral behavior but also the requisite power to be such.

Its realization, of course, is difficult: we cannot cancel out the indebtedness that accompanies our exodus from an evil attitude and its accompanying evil behavior, even if we adopt a good attitude and the good behavior that goes with it. The debt cannot be removed by good works; they are simply duties, and when they are done nothing is left over. Nor can it be taken over or wiped out by another person—Jesus Christ for example—since the debt of sin, the most personal liability of all, is nontransferable. Punishment, required by the notion of righteousness, must be administered. It may not be visited, however, on that person who once was evil but who has in the meantime become another person. In view of her good attitude, she has become an object of divine goodwill.

The dilemma can be resolved only as follows: because a human being suffers the pain that accompanies the exodus from evil (and which occurs only as a result of entry into the good), he bears the punishment he deserved as Old Man but now as a new, moral person. Indeed, in terms of his empirical character he still is the Old Man. In the very putting on of the New Man, the Old Man is put to death. Before the most high, divine righteousness, therefore, on the basis of his new attitude, this person as intelligible being is therefore his own representative, savior, and intercessor (R 67ff. / 72ff.).

This solution, however, is not good enough; Kant himself admits it does not theoretically resolve the antinomy produced by the connection which is claimed between faith in a vicarious satisfaction or cancellation of punishment and the confidence that through subsequent good behavior one can be well-pleasing to God. A theoretical resolution through insight into the causal determination of human freedom is not possible, although a practical resolution may well be.

If there is to be a moral sense to the belief that the insufficiency of one's own action requires a justifying complement through an actor or judge other than the self, then it is clear that self's own action must be and remain the point of departure for the moral exercise of free will. In Christological terms, the proper object of saving faith is the principle of a life pleasing to God as ideal in our reason, not its possible or real appearance, and consequently not Jesus Christ, either, as an example of it (R 156ff. / 168ff.).

Kant's philosophical reconstruction of the Christian faith and the Atonement between God and man in Jesus Christ is more closely related to the then-contemporary enlightened Protestantism and its theology, the so-called Neology, than it may seem, when read under the heading "reason and / or revelation."

Kant is in full agreement with the Neologians especially with regard to the axiom, contradictory to the traditional doctrine of Atonement, that no person as moral subject can be vicariously represented; under no circumstances, consequently, can guilt and merit be transferred from one agent to another, because that would abolish the agent's subjectivity itself along with her own responsibility. This is the neological criticism of dogma, especially of the doctrine of original sin and of vicarious satisfaction. In 1771, a reviewer in F. Nicolai's *Allgemeine Deutsche Bibliothek* characterized the metamorphosis of the Reformation's religion of conscience in the critique of Christology with the rhetorical question, "How can God grant me obedience, which is not mine? Does an alien virtue give me peace and contentment or make me morally better? And without this inner consciousness that the Good in me results from my own decision, virtue cannot exist, still less the sentiments necessary for salvation."

The key words, "consciousness" (*Bewußtsein*) and "sentiments" (*Empfindungen*), represent a further aspect of the close connection between Kant's philosophical-religious doctrine and the neological theology. For, characteristic for the latter, too, was the basic decision to establish itself not as the exposition of Christian viewpoints but rather as a critique and reconstruction of them. That had been so ever since the transition from traditional natural theology to a rational philosophy of religion as the "horizon of plausibility" of Christian theology, the theology which expounds the Christian tradition (J. J. Spalding, 1748).

The neological principle, of course, is independent empirical subjectivity, which is to say, experienced inner perception. The critique and the construction which proceed from this point could accordingly affirm only the experience of the pious, enlightened individual. Against that, Kant's transcendental reduction of empirical subjectivity permits analyzing it from the perspective of the philosophy of religion. Kant is therefore able also to reconstruct the content of Christian concepts which Neology could only criticize, or—better said—amputate. In the context of the doctrine of Atonement this reconstruction bears especially upon the assumption (emphasized so strongly by Reformation theology) that a Christian is and remains wholly just and wholly a sinner at the same time. In anthropological terms, this is the assumption that a human being as person is neither primarily nor ever constituted through her actions but is constituted as person prior to them. The Kantian formula of radical evil, the spectacular exponent of this anthropology, does not represent a fallback to a pre-enlightenment level, however, but progress toward an enhanced (self-)critical and constructive competence of reason against the contents of the Christian revelation.

With a view toward the supposed rehabilitation of pre-enlightenment theologoumena which imply heteronomy, Kant has not been the object of criticism only; even theologians have praised his overcoming of Neology's flat moralism and eudae-monism. How questionable this praise is, however, can be demonstrated by a theological-historical analysis of Kant's apparent traditionalism. The punitive righteousness of God—which corresponds to Kant's thesis of radical evil—is the thesis especially at issue in the doctrine of the Atonement. It is true, of course, that Kant on this point consciously contradicts Neology, which based its critique of the Anselmian satisfaction theory on the notion (derived from Arminianism) that punishment cannot aim at revenge or expiation but at betterment alone and, in accord with the axiom of the untransferability of morality, at the improvement only of the one punished (J. G. Töllner, 1768; J. J. Spalding, 1772; J. A. Eberhard, 1772; J. S. Semler, 1774; G. S. Steinbart, 1778; C. F. Bahrdt, 1781; F. Chr. Löffler, 1796). It is also true that the theologians who opposed Neology (G. F. Seiler, 1775, 1778; J. D. Michaelis, 1779; G. Chr. Storr, 1789, 1793; see also, on this point, G. E. Lessing, 1773, and J. Chr. Döderlein, 1780) were not able to offer a basis for their opposition, because for them, too, the external punishment had to serve the purpose of deterrence or of divine training. In other words, they more or less clearly repeated Grotius's concept of punishment as example. Against them all Kant defined the sanction for moral guilt as well-grounded precisely as requital and thereby reconstructed the strict concept of the divine punitive righteousness. If one desires to pin things down historically, one might say that he renewed the Anselmian approach—albeit on the basis of practical autonomy, as the discussion of the right of punishment in *Die Metaphysik der Sitten* shows (MMJ 99ff. / 331).

There can be no question of repristination here, even when we take into account Kant's contradiction of the Anselmian theory from the point of view of epistemology, that is, the assumption that God is (infinitely) subject to affront and is wrathful. Here, with the Neologians (since W. A. Teller, 1772), Kant falls in with the rejection of the notion of the wrath of God that was made, especially by the Socinians, on the basis of natural law: humanity, not God, must be reconciled with God. But, contrary to first impressions, his concept of punitive righteousness corresponds to the modern concept of God, which is characterized by natural law. By putting the moral individualism of Socinian practice into the forensic horizon of the Anselmian satisfaction theory (which on this point is similar to the Arminian one), he identifies the divine claim to restoration of wounded honor as a claim of transcendental subjectivity (MMJ 103–04/333–34). Atonement then is a requirement of subjectivity to itself and in itself. The doctrine of the Atonement, therefore, when reconstructed from the salient features inherent in reason as such, raises exclusively the question—despite experience to the contrary—of the "unreasonable demand for self-improvement" (R 47/51). This includes, to be sure, the surplus of good reckoned by grace, both as it is necessary due to the discrepancy between the empirical and the intelligible subject and as it is possible without further conditions, in the other direction (R 70/75–76, cf. 60/66–67).

If one does not want to introduce the distinction between intelligible and empirical subjectivity here (and, in my judgment, one cannot), Kant's doctrine of Atonement remains an abstract theory of subjectivity. In the theory, the self sits yet unmediated, avoids the pain of the otherness of another, and holds tightly to itself without a detour over the failure of direct self-determination. It was just this detour, however, that gave theoretical substance to the traditional (Western) Atonement doctrine, which admittedly was formulated under far simpler theological circumstances. But Kant's reconstruction is also deficient against neological Christology. To judge by the commotion attending the publication of the Wolfenbüttel Fragments (especially *Vom dem Zweck Jesu und seiner Jünger,* 1778), and in view of the ensuing challenge by G. E. Lessing (1780), Neology attempted to adjust its own, justly admonished Christological deficiency in two directions. One was through the development of a historical-psychological hermeneutic (among others, J. G. Herder, 1796, 1797); the other was through the transformation of the problem of reason and revelation into that of revelation and history (J.F.W. Jerusalem, 1768, 1792; J. J. Heß, 1768; J. G. Herder, 1784). Convinced as he was that the historical could contribute nothing to improve human beings, and was therefore "completely insignificant" (R 102/111), Kant was unable to profit from these steps forward. To be sure, he had sharpened anew the theoretical conditions; his epistemological proof of the impossibility of the Christological knowledge that had formerly been affirmed was, of course, an exoneration of historical positivism against the naturalistic denial of any revelation at all; this exoneration, however, still did not mean the solution of the Christological task, as was shown by the arbitrary juxtaposition of its rationalistic, its supernaturalistic, and its combined formulations (e.g., J. H. Tieftrunk, 1789, 1797; K. Chr. Flatt, 1797; C. F. Stäudlin, 1794). If the announcement, "the historical faith is 'dead by its own hand'" (R 102/111) is therefore the last word, even for the theoretical claim implicit in dogmatic Christology, then a Christology in a strict sense is unattainable.

The Christologies of Hegel on the one hand and of Schleiermacher on the other (which, of course, continue the neological approach in a transcendental fashion) were not the first to justify a certain scepticism toward Kant's Christology. It was rather Kant's Christology itself, with its premise of theoretical subjectivity and its antinomy of reason in the problem of Atonement (admitted by Kant himself), that did so; attempts to harmonize this antinomy, among others that of T. Krug (1802), were not successful. Already the faithful Kantian, J. H. Tieftrunk (1797), against the Storr pupil F. G. Süskind (1796), could only defend his master, and argue that the forgiveness of sin is a postulate of practical reason (obviously under the condition of betterment), by assuming that the universality of the moral law could be realized in the empirically particular, that is, it could include Atonement. In other words, Atonement not only demanded adherence to the law but made possible unrestrained love of the law.

SELECTED BIBLIOGRAPHY

Primary Texts

Carl Friedrich Bahrdt 1749–1792
   Apologie der gesunden Vernunft durch die Gründe der Schrift unterstützt, in Bezug auf die christliche Versöhnungslehre. Basel 1781.

Johann Christoph Döderlein 1746-1792

Fragmente und Antifragmente [Zwei Fragmente von H. S. Reimarus aus Lessings Beyträgen zur Litteratur abgedruckt mit Betrachtungen darüber von J. C. Döderlein]. Nürnberg 1778-1779.

Institutio theologi Christiani in capitibus religionis theoreticis, nostris temporibus accomodata. Nürnberg 1780/*Christlicher Religionsunterricht nach den Bedürfnissen unserer Zeit.* Nürnberg 1785.

Johann August Eberhard 1739-1809

Neue Apologie der Sokrates, oder Untersuchung der Lehre von der Seligkeit der Heiden. Berlin 1772-1778.

Karl Christian Flatt 1772-1843

Philosophisch-exegetische Untersuchungen über die Lehre von der Versöhnung der Menschen mit Gott als ein neuer Beytrag zur endlichen Entscheidung der dogmatischen Streitfragen, welche sich auf diese Lehre beziehen. Göttingen 1797/Stuttgart 1798.

Johann David Heilmann 1727-1764

Compendium theologiae dogmaticae. Gottingae 1761.

Johann Gottfried Herder 1744-1803

Ideen zur Philosophie der Geschichte der Menschheit. Riga/Leipzig 1784-1791.

Vom Erlöser der Menschen, nach den ersten drei Evangelien. Riga 1796.

Von Gottes Sohn, der Welt Heiland, nach Johannes' Evangelium. Riga 1797.

Johann Jakob Heß 1741-1828

Geschichte der drey letzten Lebensjahre Jesu. Zurich 1768-1773.

Johann Friedrich Wilhelm Jerusalem 1709-1789

Betrachtungen über die vornehmsten Wahrheiten der Religion. Braunschweig 1768-1772.

Nachgelassene Schriften, Erster Theil. Braunschweig 1792.

Wilhelm Traugott Krug 1770-1842

Der Widerstreit der Vernunft mit sich selbst in der Versöhnungslehre dargestellt und aufgelöst. Zurich/Freistadt 1802.

Gotthold Ephraim Lessing 1729-1781

Leibniz von den ewigen Strafen. Wolfenbüttel 1773.

Die Erziehung des Menschensgeschlechts. Berlin 1780.

Vom dem Zweck Jesu und seiner Jünger. Noch ein Fragment des Wolfenbüttelschen Ungenannten (Hermann Samuel Reimarus). Braunschweig 1778.

Friedrich Christian Löffler 1752-1816.

Über die kirchliche Genugthuungslehre. Züllichau/Freistadt 1796.

Johann David Michaelis 1717-1791

Gedanken über die Lehre der heiligen Schrift von der Sünde und Genugthuung, als eine der Vernunft gemäße Lehre. Göttingen/Bremen 1779.

Compendium theologiae dogmaticae. Gottingae 1760/*Dogmatik.* Göttingen 1784.

Georg Friedrich Seiler 1733-1807

Über die gottheit Jesu Christi, bedes für Glaübige und Zweifler. Leipzig 1775.

Über den Versöhnungstod Jesu Christi. Erlangen 1778–79.

Johann Salomo Semler 1725–1791
Institutio ad doctrinam Christianam liberaliter discendam. Halae 1774 / *Versuch einer freiern theologischen Lehrart.* Halle 1777.

Johann Joachim Spalding 1714–1804
Über die Nutzbarkeit des Predigtamtes und deren Beförderung. Berlin 1772.
(Gedanken über) Die Bestimmung des Menschen. Griefswald 1748.

Carl Friedrich Stäudlin 1761–1826
De mortis Jesu consilio et gravitate. Gottingae 1794 / *Über den Zweck und die Wirkung des Todes Jesu.* Göttingen 1794–1795.

Johann Friedrich Stapfer 1680–1756
Grundlegung zur wahren Religion. Zürich 1746–1753.

Gotthilf Samuel Steinbart 1738–1809
System der reinen Philosophie oder Glückseligkeitslehre des Christentums für die Bedürfnisse seiner aufgeklärten Landsleute und anderer, die nach Weisheit fragen eingerichtet. Züllichau 1778.

Gottlob Christian Storr 1746–1805
Pauli brief an die Hebräer, Zweiter Theil: Über den eigentlichen Zweck des Todes Jesu. Tübingen 1789.
Annotationes quaedam theologicae ad philosophicam Kantii de religione doctrinam. Tubingae 1793. / *Bemerkungen über Kant's philosophische Religionslehre.* Tübingen 1794.
Doctrinae Christianae pars theoretica e sacris literis repetita. Stuttgardi 1793 / *Lehrbuch der christlichen Dogmatik.* Stuttgart 1803.

Friedrich Gottlieb Süskind 1767–1829
Über die Möglichkeit der Strafenaufhebung oder der Sündenvergebung, nach Principien der practischen Vernunft. Tübingen 1796.

Wilhelm Abraham Teller 1734–1804
Wörterbuch des Neuen Testments zur Erklärung der christlichen Lehre. Berlin 1772.
Die Religion der Vollkommnern. Berlin 1792.

Johann Heinrich Tieftrunk 1759–1837
Einzigmöglicher zweck Jesu, aus dem Grundgesetze der Religion entwickelt. Berlin 1789.
Ist die Sündenvergebung ein Postulat der praktischen Vernunft? Lübeck 1797.
Die Religion der Mündigen. Berlin 1800.

Johann Gottlieb Töllner 1724–1774
Die Leiden des Erlösers. Frankfurt / Oder 1757.
Der thätge Gehorsam Jesu Christi. Breslau 1768.

Secondary Literature

Joseph Bohatec
Die Religionsphilosophie Kants in der "Religion innerhalb der Grenzen der bloßen Vernunft." Mit besonderer Berücksichtigung irher theologisch-dogmatischen Quellen. Hamburg 1938.

Hans Jahnson
  *Kants Lehre von der Subjektivität. Eine systematische Analyse des Ver-
    hältnisses transzendentaler und empirischer Subjektivität in seiner
    theoretischen Philosophie.* Bonn 1969.
Walter Sparn
  "Jesus Christus V: Vom Tridentinum bis zur Aufklärung," in *Theolo-
    gische Realenzyklopädie Bd. XVII.* Berlin/New York 1988: 1–16.
Gunther Wenz
  *Geschichte der Versöhnungslehre in der evangelischen Theologie der
    Neuzeit, Bd. 1.* München 1984.

God and Community: An Inquiry into the Religious Implications of the Highest Good

Sharon Anderson-Gold

1.

In a recent article entitled "Moral Actions, Moral Lives," Terry Godlove, Jr., asks, "In what sense, if any, does Kant's moral theory 'belong in a religious setting?'"[1] Godlove notes that this question continues to command attention because, although moral philosophers take the Kantian approach to ethics seriously, the specific role that Kant assigns to religious belief as an essential component of moral activity remains subject to contention. That religious belief may play an important motivational role in the moral life of an individual or culture is not generally deemed to be sufficient to entitle such a belief to be designated as "objective" or "practically necessary," for any number of other kinds of beliefs could in principle play such a role. Godlove terms the motivational theory concerning the relationship between religious belief and moral action the "ignition theory" and notes the following problem:

> Not only a supreme being, but many objects will suffice to tip the motivational balance ... why settle exclusively on God? Why not substitute the memory of a cherished ancestor? After all, he would have wanted us to act morally.[2]

Although references to a motivational relationship between religious belief and moral action occur in Kant's precritical writings and reappear in some passages of the *Critique of Pure*

Reason, a decisive break with this approach is introduced in the *Groundwork.* In the *Groundwork* Kant develops a theory of motivational "autonomy" derived from his characterization of the moral law as both the sole criterion and *sufficient incentive* for morally good action. When the postulate of the existence of God is reintroduced in the *Critique of Practical Reason,* its function shifts from that of a motivational supplement to that of a logical condition of a particular kind of commitment, viz., the adoption of the highest good. Thus the question of the religious "orientation" of Kant's ethics depends upon the demonstration of an intrinsic connection between the highest good and moral volition.

Now the highest good is a "complex" object composed of two apparently separable components, happiness and virtue. Many commentators have rejected Kant's claim that the moral law requires the adoption of this object. The common core of their reasoning seems to be that for this claim to hold, each component of this composite must be independently certifiable as "objectively necessary" or valid for all rational beings.[3] Virtue or respect for the moral law is an obligation pertaining to all rational beings; however, happiness is conceived as a merely "subjectively necessary" end pertaining to human agents qua human. Therefore, Kant's claims concerning this intrinsic connection are construed as an attempt to convert a "subjective limitation" into an objective constraint on the application of the moral law. It is argued that the admission of such a constraint on moral volition would destroy its requisite "purity." Thus Kant has been accused of smuggling in "extra-moral" considerations which are really remnants of the "reward" psychology of his precritical period. Steven Smith, however, takes a more sanguine view of this problem. He argues:

> The merely formal moral law does not hang in the air, enjoining universality of practical judgments in the abstract; it appears to us as a condition of our already-ongoing quest for happiness. Human morality is structured a priori by the fact that we are human beings and not angels. Therefore, if we cannot be moral human beings—if the highest good is demonstrably unattainable because its component parts are irreconcilable—then we cannot be moral at all.[4]

It is true that in the Preface to the *Groundwork* Kant proposes a rather grand and, by his own admission, ambitious plan "to prepare a pure moral philosophy which has been thoroughly cleared of all that is empirical only and belongs to anthropology" (FP3; referred to in the text as *Groundwork*). But it is also true that Kant did not consider the *Groundwork* to be in itself a complete system of moral philosophy and had in view at least two further stages of its development, a critique of practical reason and a metaphysics of morals. The above debate then, on the admission of "human limitations," appears to be geared toward the question: At what stage and with respect to what considerations was Kant justified in "going beyond the law" and in tracing the implications of the applicability of the moral law to humanity, reinscribing those elements into his account of the nature of moral volition?

In the Preface to *Religion*, Kant once again takes up the idea of the highest good as the end which "arises out of morality." In a lengthy footnote he carefully delineates the specific characteristic of volition which generates this object:

> And yet it is one of the inescapable limitations of man and of his faculty of practical reason (a limitation, perhaps, of all other worldly beings as well) to have regard, in every action, to the consequence thereof, in order to discover therein what could serve him as an end and also prove the purity of his intention—which consequence, though last in practice is yet first in representation and intention. (R 6n)

Now since this "limitation" pertains to any finite, purposive, causal agent, I do not think that it can be fairly described as an "anthropological" and therefore an empirical consideration. As Smith noted, the moral law cannot enjoin universality-in-the-abstract. In order to prove the purity of intention, it must be possible to demonstrate that a maxim is "fit" to stand as a universal law, and this requires that the "effects" of morality be traced or exhibited in one's chosen ends. If there is to be a morally causal volition, there must be an objective or necessary end which "represents" the effects of the moral law in all such ends as are in harmony with duty; the subjectively necessary ends conditioned by obedience equal the morally final end. While the claim that happiness is the subjectively necessary end of human beings may be a judgment in some sense conditioned by experience, the notion that there must be some "final end" appears to be a consequence of the application of the moral law to any finite, purposive causal agent. The moral law extends itself to include the moral goal of reason "among its determining grounds" because only in this way can the "concept of morality as causal in the world" be rendered practically significant (R 7n). Thus Kant claims that it is through the idea of the highest good that "man gives evidence of the need, morally effected in him, of also conceiving a final end for his duties, as their consequence" (R 5).

Godlove maintains that, in *Religion*, Kant has moved to a "two tiered" analysis of moral volition, where one level is concerned with the immediate end (duty) of particular acts and does not require reference to the highest good, while simultaneously the same act can be viewed as the product of a more general intending, i.e., the intention to promote the highest good.[5] It is only with respect to the second or more general level of intending that one can speak of a "continuous endeavor," since the requisite internal unity can only be derived from the representation of a final end, "harmony with which, while not multiplying men's duties, yet provides them with a special focus for the unification of all ends" (R 5). Since our volition is exerted for the sake of a "union of the purposiveness arising from freedom with the purposiveness arising from nature" (R 5), the highest good is clearly intended to be realized in this world. However, since "the world" is not of the agent's own creation, the sought-after concurrence must be conceived as arising from the "care" of an omnipotent moral governor. Thus the adoption of the highest good requires a certain "assent" or admission of the "possibility of God's existence."

Godlove concludes that the upshot of Kant's analysis of the relation of the highest good to moral volition is that a non-theist cannot "intend" to lead a moral life "where by the term 'moral life' we mean more than a brute concatenation of otherwise independent moral actions. We mean an action distinguished by its own final end."[6] However, Godlove maintains that this argument demonstrates not that the non-theist cannot act consistently from the moral law, but that such an agent "cannot regard these actions as furthering anything but immediate ends."[7] Godlove hopes to have solved the "puzzle" involved in the thesis that a non-theist can act morally well by distinguishing moral action aimed at the fulfillment of duty in each instance from the deliberate commitment to a "moral life" which properly includes a religious component.

But this juxtaposition, moral actions/moral lives, raises the further question: What is the proper subject of moral evaluation? I do not think that it can be maintained *as Kant's view* that particular actions are ever the subject of moral evaluation, at least not in Godlove's sense in which particular actions aimed at immediate ends are viewed as separable from a continuous endeavor or general pattern of intending. For it is not the act in its particularity that is subject to evaluation but the maxim or subjective principle which it "expresses." But even with the identification of a maxim (which is a general policy or rule), our judgment only reaches to the "conformity" of the will to law and not to the determining ground or motive from which its moral worth derives.

There is a necessary "logical" gap between motive and act which derives from their different ontological status (intelligible/sensible) and renders any inference from ground to consequence "uncertain." However, the skepticism which inhabits this "gap" and pervades Kant's entire analysis of moral volition in the *Groundwork* arises from Kant's view that there are other incentives, generally classifiable under the heading of "self-love," that are capable of determining the will to "conformity with law." Kant writes:

> Out of love for humanity I am willing to admit that even most of our actions are in conformance with duty. But when one examines their intentions more closely the "dear self" everywhere comes to light upon which these intentions are directed. . . . To be sure, it is true at times that, with the keenest self-examination, we can discover nothing that could have been strong enough to induce us to this or that good act and to so great a sacrifice, except the moral basis of duty. However, that is not at all sufficient reason for concluding . . . that no hidden motive of self-love was the actual determining cause of our will. (FP 23)

The definition of an imperfectly rational being underlying Kant's analysis of duty/constraint, a will whose nature does not immediately accord with the moral law, already suggests the existence of a "counterincentive." In addition, Kant postulates that a desire for happiness can be universally ascribed to all human agents and continually points to this desire as a possible determining ground of each and every act that could also be classified as a "duty." But then there appear to be two possible incentives, each of which could be viewed as fundamental in that each could consistently regulate volition in a lawful manner. Since the will is for Kant a causal faculty operating according to fundamental laws, volition must be viewed as a unitary function arising from some supreme determining ground or motive. This implies that only one incentive could be fundamental. In the *Groundwork* Kant has laid out the terms of this problem but has not explained how two such incentives could be viewed as influencing or contributing to volition.

The question "How do competing incentives influence volition?" is basic to the specification of the nature and meaning of moral evil. For if the hindrances to morality are viewed as arising from sources external to the will, the "evil" which results is not attributable to the agent. It is not until Kant introduces the notion of the "disposition"—the intelligible act which determines the significance and order of incentives—that a definition of moral evil compatible with the freedom necessary for accountability can be provided. This procedure, which "internalizes" all resistance, leads to the "postulate" of an "inherent" propensity to evil (R 31). It seems to me that the introduction of this propensity effects a rather profound shift in Kant's overall moral philosophy which I shall subsequently attempt to trace in the following four "stages": (1) as a shift away from the analysis of particular acts to the quality of the moral life "as a whole"; (2) as a shift away from the "individual-in-isolation" to a "focus" on the social dimensions of vice / virtue and the interpersonal context of volition; (3) as a recasting of the final end or highest good as a social goal with the resulting reorientation of the individual toward a common good; and (4) as a recasting of the moral life in terms of ethical community rooted in a moral governor resulting in a more internal constitutive connection between moral striving and religious belief. As a result of this multileveled analysis, I hope to demonstrate that the "minority opinion" in this debate, i.e., that Kant's ethics "belongs in a religious setting," has more power to illumine the nature and meaning of a "moral life."

2.

Kant introduces the notion of the "disposition" in Book I of *Religion* in the context of an inquiry concerning the meaning and possibility of moral evil. This problem has been prefigured but not adequately addressed in the *Groundwork*. As previously noted, Kant's definition of an imperfectly rational being as one whose will does not accord with the moral law "of its own nature" suggests the existence of a "counterincentive." By contrast, a "holy" will is defined as a being without any incentive other than the moral law.[8] I have also noted Kant's view that a desire for happiness can be universally ascribed to all human agents as "given by nature." While nature may "hinder" the realization of morality in its external manifestation, it is unclear how anything external to volition can gain the status of a determining incentive and thus render the will accountable for its failure. Further specification is needed.

In Book I of *Religion*, Kant states that as a result of an entirely "innocent" predisposition (the predisposition to humanity), the will "naturally adopts" self-love as an incentive (R 31). But if this were the only incentive available to the will, human agents would be entirely natural beings and their actions would lack moral significance. Thus the mere adoption of this incentive is not *in itself* a moral act. However, Kant maintains that the moral law is also an incentive for the human will (likewise arising from a predisposition—personality) which is in its own right capable of being an adequate ground of determination. Only with the recognition of both incentives is the stage set for the first and fully significant moral act of the will. Since these two incentives cannot remain on the same level of value for the will, one must be accorded precedence and become the dominant or determinative motive. Thus Kant concludes that the fundamental disposition or "intelligible character" of such a will can only be either good or evil depending upon its dominant incentive.[9] Any preference accorded to self-love then, renders the moral law a subordinate principle and tilts the will off its original axis, creating an enduring "propensity to evil."

Now while this propensity makes us "liable" to transgression and is a necessary presupposition of particular acts which are contrary to the moral law, it does not necessarily follow that the empirical character (resulting conduct) will be bad. Although such a propensity renders one's commitment to morality conditional and thus "contingent" (and this is the genuine "offense"), Kant denies that the human will can entirely eliminate the claims of the moral law. Even the self-interested individual can identify the act that conforms to the "ought" and can reason that in most circumstances the "best means" to happiness may be the performance of "duty." A rather "parasitic" view of the relationship between self-love and the moral law emerges in the following passage:

> This happens when reason employs the unity of maxims in general, a unity which is inherent in the moral law, merely to bestow upon the incentives of inclination, under the name of *happiness*, a unity of maxims which otherwise they cannot have. (For example, truthfulness, if adopted as a basic principle, delivers us from the anxiety of making our lies agree with one another. . . .) (R 32)

While our ability to identify / classify an act as an instance of duty and our ability to act in accordance with law do indicate that the moral law has the status of an "incentive" for us, we cannot conclude from these characteristics of our judgments / actions that the moral law is the supreme or determinative motive for our actions.

Thus, it appears that human beings never have adequate evidence that, in acting consistently in accordance with law, they have acted "morally well" in the sense required by the idea of a *good disposition*. But if an individual cannot appeal directly to her "own" empirical character for evidence of her "own" disposition, what attitude ought she to take and why?

The limits inherent in the analysis of the particular actions of individuals, arising from a combination of epistemological and moral considerations, require Kant to begin his examination of the intelligible disposition in *Religion* at a different level. Allen Wood refers to Kant's procedure as "the critique of man's moral nature":

> Kant attempts to answer these questions through an investigation which is *critical* in character, in that it aims at human self-knowledge obtained systematically by means of an examination of the "sources, extent and limits" of human capacities.[10]

From the outset, Kant explicitly maintains that the subject of this discourse is not the particular individual but the entire species (R 21). He repeatedly notes that in analyzing the fundamental attributes of human volition, he is describing the human condition and is not thereby inferring his concepts from particular actions or deducing anything concerning a particular individual.

Kant begins Book I (as he did Part I of the *Groundwork*) by considering the implications of "ordinary moral judgment." And there appears to be resounding agreement; evil exists. Although one cannot, with respect to the judgment of particular cases, move from *either* "rightness" or "wrongness" to intelligible grounds, the *general evidential* status of these two phenomena are not on the same footing. The former induction is blocked by Kant's view that "rightness" (conformity to law) can, in all cases, admit of derivation from a nonmoral incentive, whereas the connection between "wrongness" (failure to conform) and a "counterincentive" is direct. For if evil can in "any" case be *attributable* to a free being, it can be so *imputed* only by virtue of a characteristic inherent to that freedom. Thus it appears that moral evil is not an "illusion" in the sense that, if evil is *possible* for any free being, it must be *possible* for every free being. Kant defends the nonempirical character of this "universal" judgment in the following passage:

> because this character concerns a relation of the will, which is free (and the concept of which is therefore not empirical), to the moral law as an incentive (the concept of which, likewise, is purely intellectual), it must be apprehended a priori through the concept of evil, so far as evil is possible under the laws of freedom (of obligation and accountability). (R 31)

If then, the individual's "right to assume" the possession of a good will (disposition) is always questionable, moral self-certainty is not a "recommendable" moral attitude and for Kant, is akin to self-deception.

We have seen that from the perspective of a "systematic" and "critical" investigation of the human disposition, Kant has adduced good reasons for the admission or "postulation" of a propensity to evil. But what *difference* does the admission of such a "propensity" make to the moral life of the individual? Does not the individual retain the same set of duties/obligations regardless of the existence of an innate tendency to transgression? Kant's explanation of the function of this postulate in our moral reasoning involves his familiar appeal to "two standpoints."

From the "standpoint" of moral dogmatics, the assumption of such a propensity makes no difference. It does not invalidate the moral law nor eliminate our receptivity to it. We cannot "lose" the moral incentive, for if we did it could never be regained (and the conditions for moral accountability would not obtain). But Kant maintains that from the "standpoint" of moral discipline, this assumption makes a marked difference. For it tells us:

> we cannot start from an innocence natural to us but . . . we must begin with the incessant counteraction against it. Since this leads only to a progress, endlessly continuing . . . it follows that the conversion of the disposition . . . is to be found in the change of the highest inward ground. . . . (R 46)

The "standpoint" of moral discipline is rooted in the empirical character and as such is necessarily "temporal" (as opposed to the "timeless" horizon of the "ought"). But as chastened by the consciousness of our liability to transgression, the "object" of our moral judgment is transformed. Our actions are regarded under the idea of a "progress" which has the following consequences: (1) our concern shifts from the "face value" of independent actions to the principle of their *connectedness* and (2) we are concerned with a "quality of the whole" in terms of which the whole can be regarded as an "act of restoration." The "object" of this endeavor is a "revolution" or what Kant has called "the change of the highest inward ground." Since it is our life "as a whole" that is the subject of this revolution, the transformation that is attributed to the disposition does not entail any sudden or abrupt change in the empirical character. For no part "stands for" the whole, each drawing its moral quality from a course of development. From *within* the temporal perspective, we must view the abandonment of evil and the entrance into goodness as *simultaneously and continuously* occurring and as therefore never complete in time.[11]

Kant concludes that his "two standpoints" are not contradictory, the postulate of this propensity being not opposed "to the possibility of this restoration." Yet there remains a troublesome residue of difference. For would a simple *reversal* of these incentives be adequate to the *original claim* of the moral law to be the "sole" as well as the "sufficient" incentive for our will? Did not the propensity to evil enter as our own "fault"? If this original offense can never be removed, can anything less than its eradication (not merely its subordination) count as "restitution"? By Kant's own admission that is not within our power.

In discussing the issue of irremediable guilt, Kant makes use of concepts drawn from the practical postulates of the immortality of the soul and the existence of God. Nonetheless, the "hope" thus generated is always qualified as *conditioned* by our "own" efforts.[12] But insofar as our "own" efforts are necessarily limited by the continued existence of this propensity (even where the reversal of incentives is granted!) because it is not within our "own" power to break its hold, the "perilousness" of the human condition remains unchanged.

Now Kant does not and cannot leave his analysis of the nature of vice and virtue with the "individual's" predicament. The struggle in which the moral life is engaged is with "principalities and powers" (R 52), and the individual is not as it were the "ultimate frontier" in this story but a participant in a larger drama which concerns the human destiny. In Book III of *Religion*, Kant presses on to investigate the social context of this struggle (life); and what this reveals about the nature of vice and virtue significantly recasts the terms in which we must think about the "moral life" and the nature of the "highest good."

Although we have been analyzing this propensity as it might inhere in a particular subject, we must remember that Kant maintains that the reasons we have for attributing such a propensity to any given subject are the same reasons for ascribing this to all human agents. And this extension has important consequences for the way in which the individual must conceive of the possibility of the "moral revolution" for, as I shall now attempt to demonstrate, the idea of a "moral life" must include not only the unification of all of one's "own" acts/maxims but also an essential referencing of these to the acts/maxims of other moral subjects. In other words, given the universality of the ascription of this propensity, the "moral life" must be represented as a social or collective undertaking, variously referred to as the "kingdom of ends," the "highest good," and the "ethical commonwealth." In the course of clarifying the meaning of this necessary object or final end, the moral force of the theistic postulate will gradually become apparent.

In Book III of *Religion*, subtitled "The Victory of the Good Principle over the Evil Principle, and the Founding of a Kingdom of God on Earth," Kant notes that the "highest prize" that morally well-disposed individuals can attain by virtue of their continuous struggles to reform their own natures is to "be free from bondage"—a negative form of freedom which cannot offer protection from moral backsliding (R 85). When individuals reflect upon the circumstances that expose them to this danger, they must include in these reflections the quality of their relationships with others. Kant then launches into a rather Rousseauean analysis of the human condition in which he notes that it is not because of our individual nature and "original needs" that we become *inclined toward evil*. The passions which disturb our original predisposition to the good are evoked by the *presence of others*. Kant states:

> Envy, the lust for power, greed, and the malignant inclinations bound up with these, besiege his nature, contented within itself, *as soon as he is among men*. And it is not even necessary to assume that these are men sunk in evil and examples to lead him astray; it suffices that they are at hand, that they surround him, and that they are men, for them mutally to corrupt each other's predispositions and make one another evil. (R 85)

These provocative remarks have, however, been prepared for by Kant's presentation of the predisposition to humanity in Book I, where he noted that our original and apparently "innocent" self-love is rooted in a "reason which compares," a predisposition to humanity which inclines us to human society and is intended by nature to be our "spur" to culture. Even our ideas of happiness (which provide the driving contents of self-love) are rooted in this comparative reason, for "we judge ourselves happy or unhappy only by making comparisons with others."[13] Thus what we received from nature as a self-love originally limited to "need" becomes through the exercise of freedom (in the context of human culture) an expanding system of desires referenced to others.

The preference we display for these "acquired desires" is the very formula of the propensity to evil which apparently then includes our entire sociocultural being and is in this sense "entwined with" and "rooted in" our humanity.[14] The propensity to evil, then, is not something that is simply "within me" and "within you" but something that operates *between us*. Thus Kant maintains that our hope to effect a revolution "within" rests upon the transformation of the social conditions of our existence. Models of moral perfection which view the achievement of virtue as a result of "individual" decision making concerned only with the "purity" of intention, detached from all "purposes," are rendered futile by Kant's view of the human condition in *Religion*. To maintain such a posture is to remain in an "ethical state of nature" which Kant defines as "one in which the good principle, which resides in each man, is continually attacked by the evil which is found in him and also in everyone else" (R 88). The social significance of the propensity to evil is not often noted even though Kant takes up this theme quite explicitly and draws from this predicament the conclusion that unless individuals deliberately unite into a society "for the sake of the laws of virtue" they cannot hope to *remain free* from bondage. Kant states:

> If no means could be discovered for the forming of an alliance uniquely designed as a protection against this evil . . . this association with others would keep man, however much, as a single individual, he may have done to throw off the sovereignty of evil, incessantly in danger of falling back under its dominion. (R 85–86)

This is a very challenging statement, for it reaffirms the limited and negative character of the "freedom from" which is all that the unaided individual can attain. Such is not yet freedom in its positive signification of a *power* to live in righteousness. The latter depends upon the individual's submission to *common* principles of virtue which unite the dispositions. One could reduce the twists and turns in Kant's analysis to the following: since the commitment to virtue requires the abandonment of the ethical state of nature, one has an *obligation* to promote the ethical commonwealth.

The idea of a social union is of course not an entirely new development, for in the *Groundwork* Kant links the idea of universal legislation to the status of the legislator as a member of a "realm of ends." Kant states: "Reason then relates every maxim of the will as legislating universally to every other will. . . . Morality consists in the reference of all actions to the making of laws by which alone a realm of ends is possible" (FP

52). At the heart of this "realm" is the idea of a co-legislation from which a harmony of maxims or "whole of ends" is expected to result. Although the realization of such a system is conditional on everyone's adhering to "common laws," these laws are conceived as arising from our "disregarding the personal differences of rational beings and all particular contents of their private ends" (FP 51). The underlying paradigm is one of individual moral self-sufficiency, i.e., if each individual "reformed" her "own" nature (abstracting from the particular and private), a systematic harmony of maxims (dispositions) would result. Good dispositions are naturally in harmony; there can be no conflict between them. There is also a notable lack of reference to the role of theistic belief in realizing such a realm. Kant states that even if such a realm were thought of "as united under a sovereign" (FP 57), this would not add anything essential since he considers the sovereign under the attribute of a divine judge whose relationship to each member is "external," mediated only by the recognition of that virtue which is in and for itself "complete" in each individual. The idea of the sovereign appears primarily useful as a limiting concept: he is that member who is "without wants and of unlimited capabilities" (FP 52). The internal essence of the realm, however, does not appear to require that there be such a being.

In *Religion* one finds a different (and a clearly constitutive) relationship between the idea of God and the ethical commonwealth; the unity of the latter and the purity of its principles are seen as derived from the holiness of the will which serves as its "foundation." Prior to *Religion,* the primary role of God was to allocate happiness (proportioned to virtue) either directly in the next life or indirectly by coaxing nature into agreement with moral volition. This purely supplementary role is a consequence of two suppositions which are surpassed in *Religion:* (1) that individuals can adequately achieve virtue by the exertion of their own moral capacities and (2) that the desire for happiness has independent roots in nature, which necessarily limits the achievement of the complete or highest good.

The introduction of a propensity to evil in Book I of *Religion* alters both assumptions. By rooting desire in volition, all particular desires become expressions of a highest maxim orienting the individual toward happiness and this orientation is interpersonal, the desire for happiness drawing its meaning and significance from our sociocultural context. Nature per se is no longer the targeted culprit and the hindrances to the realization of the highest good are located in the nexus of human relationships. The centrality of the theme of mutual engagement leads Kant to the explicit formulation of the highest good as a social goal. In referring to this "social good," Kant stipulates that it cannot be achieved by the "exertions of the single individual toward his own perfection" (R 89). Now it obviously follows from the characterization of the goal as social that it refers to more than the single individual. But equal emphasis must be placed on the nature of the "perfection" sought, for neither is this a mere *aggregate* of private perfections (as a paradigm of individual moral self-sufficiency would suggest), "but," as Kant writes, "requires rather a union of such individuals into a whole toward the same goal—into a system of well-disposed men, in which *and through whose unity alone* the highest moral good can come to pass" (R 89, italics mine).

Furthermore, this union cannot even be properly represented as arising from the "good will" (as the kingdom of ends is represented) since it is the will that strives to become good which falls under this obligation and morally "needs" this union. While the obligation to enter into such a union is of a totally unique kind, it has the force of duty, for the moral life literally hinges upon it. The obligation to promote this goal in effect subsumes the individual's striving toward personal perfection and fills it with moral content. The commitment to the "highest good" then provides the disposition with the unique "focus" it requires. It is with respect to this commitment that the moral meaning of the postulate of God's existence is finally fully clarified. Kant writes:

> this duty will require the presupposition of another idea, namely, that of a higher moral Being, through whose universal dispensation *the forces of separate individuals, insufficient in themselves, are united* for a common end. (R 89, italics mine)

In "Evil and the Moral Power of God," Philip Rossi argues that in developing an account of the highest good in terms of the social destiny of the human race, Kant is required to provide a more complex account of the relationship between good and evil than that found in the *Groundwork*. He notes that "Actions must now be classified in terms of their bearing on the attainment of this social and historical destiny of the human species as well as in terms of their marking out the good will of agents."[15] Clearly, Kant does not regard the attainment of this social goal to be a straightforward function of the "conscientiousness" of agents. As Rossi notes, the "intended good" can "misfire" or fail to have effects that succeed in promoting the highest good. If we review very carefully what Kant actually says concerning this perplexing possibility, we find that he does not make any reference to the intractability of nature (as he was earlier inclined to do). In *Religion*, Kant's concern is consistently focused on what goes on "inside" volition that thwarts this ideal, or more properly, given what I take to be Kant's expanded understanding of what counts as "internal," what goes on between moral agents. Intending the good is accompanied by a residual reservation that weakens mutual commitment. Kant writes:

> Despite the good will of each individual, yet, because they lack a principle which unites them, they recede, through their dissensions, from the common goal of goodness and, just as though they were *instruments of evil*, expose one another to the risk of falling once again under the sovereignty of the evil principle. (R 88)

By use of a spatial metaphor, this passage indicates a form of "moral distance" between moral subjects which must be overcome. The essentially "private" sphere of intention must take on a public form of communication, a public pledge of "common allegiance" to principles derived from an unchangeable or "holy" will. That is to say, "moral laws" (whose contents do not thereby change) are viewed as "divine commands" constitutive of a particular form of community, namely, an ethical commonwealth.

It appears to be Kant's view that when the moral life is conscientiously pursued, the "moral need" for such a union is undeniable. Moreover, this need reveals itself to be a need we "share" with others. But each being insufficient to stand assurance for his pledge must think or presuppose the existence of a perfect moral being *through whom* we are bound each to each. The idea of a moral governor is the correlate of the "we" which the human community requires as the condition of individual moral perfection. In "Autonomy and Community," Rossi comments: "Although the attainment of an abiding 'we' is the end to which our freedom is ordered, the very exercise of our freedom makes manifest the inability of our freedom to give us surety of the attainment of this end."[16] Rossi concludes that it is through the endeavor of this utterance that we "become open to be touched by the power of God's transcendence." I would add that it is by way of tracking our mutual engagement in the very condition of moral failure from which we all begin (a tracking that it has been the purpose of this paper to reveal) that Kant roots the "moral need for shared faith." And from shared faith arises the "mutual empowerment" which makes the highest good possible.

3.

This conception of God is not derived from the function of a World Designer, not even from the function of a Judge. Rather it is closer to the function attributed in Christian theology to the sanctifying activity of the Holy Spirit, incarnate in the living social organization of the Church. It is an activity which cannot be thought of in terms used to describe an external substance. Clement Webb argues that in the *Opus Postumum*, the fragmentary work of Kant's "last days," Kant was moving away from the deism of his earlier years to a form of religious "immanentism" in which the Moral Law is viewed as the direct revelation of Divine Personality. He cites Kant's statements in support of this interpretation:

> God is thus no substance discoverable outside of me but merely a moral relation within me.
>
> . . . .
>
> In the world considered as a totality of rational beings, there is also a totality of morally practical Reason, and consequently of an imperative Right and therewith also a God.[17]

The Moral Law, which is a relation within the individual, simultaneously directs the individual to a common ground of personal relationships. It appears to be Kant's mature view that this "command" which issues in "reverence" must be a personal force, an activity directed to the wills of beings standing in moral relation to their fellows. The "existential" import of this form of moral-religious experience does not lead to Kierkegaard's religious mysticism but to Buber's ethical communalism. We know God only through his command to create ethical community as the abode of relationships between moral persons. And as this command can only be represented as issuing from a Moral Person, I conclude that Kant's ethics "belongs in a religious setting."

NOTES

1. Terry F. Godlove, Jr., "Moral Actions, Moral Lives: Kant on Intending the Highest Good," *The Southern Journal of Philosophy* 25 (1987): 49. Godlove himself is quoting Alan Donagan, "Comments on Dan Brock and Terrence Reynolds," *Ethics* 95 (July 1985): 875.

2. Godlove, 51.

3. Lewis White Beck and Thomas Auxter are among the more noted critics of Kant's idea of the highest good.

4. Steven Smith, "Worthiness to Be Happy and Kant's Concept of the Highest Good," *Kant-Studien* 75 (1984): 172.

5. Godlove, 56–57.

6. Ibid., 55.

7. Ibid.

8. "Therefore no imperatives hold for the Divine Will or in general for a holy will . . . because already the 'I will' is necessarily of itself in harmony with the law" (FP 30).

9. "Hence the distinction between a good man and one who is evil cannot lie in the difference between the incentives . . . but rather must depend upon *subordination . . . which of the two incentives he makes the condition of the other*" (R 31).

10. Allen Wood, *Kant's Moral Religion* (Ithaca, N.Y.: Cornell University Press, 1970), 219.

11. "But in this change . . . there are not two moral acts . . . but only a single act, . . . the good principle is present quite as much in the desertion of evil as in the adoption of the good disposition" (R 68).

12. "Yet he must be able to *hope* through his *own* efforts to reach the road which leads thither . . ." (R 46).

13. "The predisposition to humanity can be brought under the general title of a self-love which is physical and yet *compares* (for reason is required) . . . " (R 22).

14. "Further, for the sake of freedom these maxims must in themselves be considered contingent, a circumstance which, on the other hand, will not tally with the universality of this evil *unless* the ultimate subjective ground of all maxims somehow or other is entwined with and, as it were, rooted in humanity itself" (R 27–28).

15. Philip Rossi, S. J., "Evil and the Moral Power of God," in

Proceedings of the Sixth International Kant Congress, vol. 2: 2 (Lanham, Md.: Center for Advanced Research in Phenomenology and University Press of America, 1989), 376.

16. Philip Rossi, S. J., "Autonomy and Community: The Social Character of Kant's 'Moral Faith,'" *The Modern Schoolman* 61 (1984), 185.

17. Clement Webb, *Kant's Philosophy of Religion* (Oxford: Oxford University Press, 1926; Kraus Reprint Co., 1970), 198 and 191.

The Final End of All Things: The Highest Good as the Unity of Nature and Freedom

Philip J. Rossi

1. Preliminary Consideration: The Relation between Nature and Freedom as Focus of the Critical Project

In this paper I shall elucidate and defend a thesis about the systematic role that the notion of "the highest good" comes to play within Kant's critical project. This thesis is as follows: The notion of the "highest good," particularly as it is elaborated in *Religion within the Limits of Reason Alone,* serves as the most complete resolution that Kant gives within his critical project to the issue of the mutual relation between the exercise of human (moral) freedom and the nexus of causal relationships that constitute nature.

Before I proceed to the detailed elaboration and defense of this thesis, let me state two sets of preliminary considerations which I think will prove helpful, first, for locating this thesis within a larger interpretive framework and, second, for delimiting with greater precision the specific focus of this thesis.

The first set of preliminary considerations consists of four central interpretive assumptions which provide the context within which I have formulated this thesis. These are assumptions for which I shall not explicitly argue in the course of this essay, though some of the reasons why I consider them appropriate will emerge in the course of my elucidation and defense of the thesis.

My first assumption is that the distinctive feature of Kant's account of the highest good in *Religion* is its explicitly social character, marked out under the image of the "ethical commonwealth" (R 85–127 passim). Kant makes a clear statement of this in Book III:

> Now here we have a duty which is *sui generis*, not of men toward men, but of the human race toward itself. For the species of rational beings is objectively, in the idea of reason, destined for a social goal, namely, the promotion of the highest as a social good. But because the highest moral good cannot be achieved merely by the exertion of a single individual toward his own moral perfection, but requires rather a union of such individuals into a whole toward the same goal—into a system of well-disposed men, in which and through whose unity alone the highest moral good can come to pass—the idea of such a whole, as a universal republic based on laws of virtue, is an idea completely distinguished from all moral laws (which concern what we know to lie in our own power); since it involves working toward a whole regarding which we do not know whether it lies in our power or not. (R 89)

There is evidence that Kant's attribution of this social character to the highest good is neither new nor unique to *Religion*. In consequence, I am also assuming that in making it an explicit focus Kant does not thereby intend to deny the more general function he consistently has given the highest good in earlier stages of the critical project: to represent the hoped-for unity toward which the theoretical and practical uses of reason are ordered and thereby to affirm reason as itself the fundamental ground of the unity of nature and freedom.[1]

My second assumption is that there is an overarching issue that serves as the central focus of Kant's whole critical project: the question of how the exercise of human moral freedom stands in relation to the nexus of necessary causal connections that constitute "nature"—and vice versa.

My third assumption is that, while this issue remains a constant preoccupation throughout Kant's critical philosophy, both the configuration of the issue and Kant's proposed resolution of it undergo development in the course of Kant's execution of his critical project.

My fourth assumption is that it is at least as appropriate to read Kant's earlier efforts at resolution—e.g., the third antinomy in the *Critique of Pure Reason*—from the perspective of his later efforts—e.g., §§86–89 of the *Critique of Judgment,* or Book III of *Religion within the Limits of Reason Alone*—as it is to read these later efforts from the perspective of the earlier ones.

The second set of preliminary considerations consists of two qualifications that I wish to place in the scope and interpretive import of my main thesis.

The first qualification concerns the scope of the claim made in the thesis about the "completeness" of the resolution that the notion of "highest good," as found in *Religion,* provides for the central critical issue of the relationship between human freedom and nature. This "completeness" is to be understood relative to the prior resolutions that Kant had himself proposed at earlier stages of the critical project. In particular, the notion of the highest good found in *Religion* is more "complete" inasmuch as it acknowledges more clearly than any earlier critical discussion that the resolution of the issue of the relation between freedom and nature needs to address the role that the good and evil at work in human society and history play in that relation. I do not propose, however, to defend within this paper Kant's most "mature" critical resolution of this issue as the most complete or most satisfactory relative to different resolutions that have been advanced by philosophers—or theologians—other than Kant.

The second qualification concerns the interpretive import of my thesis in relation to the coherence and continuity of Kant's critical project. I shall certainly stress, in the course of this essay, that the account of the highest good found in *Religion* makes Kant's resolution of the issue of the relation between nature and freedom quite different from that found, for instance, in either the *Critique of Pure Reason* or in the *Foundations of the Metaphysics of Morals;* nonetheless, I also wish to maintain that such difference is a genuine development that derives from Kant's most fundamental critical principles. In other words, it is my hypothesis that Kant's resolution of the issue in *Religion* is different from his resolution in the *Critique of Pure Reason* in consequence of some deep continuities within the critical project—particularly his fundamental confidence in the unity that reason manifests even in the multiplicity of the uses of finite human reason. As I shall shortly point out, the need to reconsider the resolution proposed in the *Critique of Pure Reason* begins to emerge in function of the maturation of Kant's insight, first, into freedom as itself the self-governance of reason and, second, into the manner in which evil takes root within the exercise of human freedom.

2. The Reconsideration of Freedom in Relation to Nature: From Spontaneity to Autonomy

As I noted above, one of my operative interpretive assumptions is that the very configuration of the issue of the relationship between freedom and nature undergoes development in the course of Kant's execution of his critical project. In this section, I shall examine what I consider to be some of the important indications of such development, particularly in the elucidation Kant gives of the notion of freedom. My treatment of these indications makes no pretense to being exhaustive; given the way in which Kant weaves his discussions of freedom closely into the texture of his other central critical concepts, it would be possible to trace other strands along which this development becomes evident. Although I shall take note of some of these other strands of development below, the only ones I propose to follow closely are those that lead to Kant's introduction of the notion of autonomy and his refinement of it into the notion of the self-governance of pure practical reason, both of which then serve as appropriate representations of the "positive" character of freedom. I shall then note the consequences that finding such appropriate representations for "positive" freedom has for the way in which Kant then construes the relationship between nature and freedom in the closing stages of the critical project.

We can set the context in which the development of Kant's elucidation of freedom takes place by consideration of the following three texts, cited in the order of their publication:

> Transcendental freedom is thus, as it would seem, contrary to the law of nature, and therefore to all possible experience; and so remains a problem. But this problem does not come within the province of reason in its practical employment; and we have therefore, in a canon of pure reason to deal only with two questions, which relate to the practical interest of pure reason, and in regard to which a canon of its employment must be possible— Is there a God? and Is there a future life? The question of transcendental freedom is a matter for speculative knowledge only, and when we are dealing with the practical, we can leave it aside as being an issue with which we have no concern. Moreover, a

quite sufficient discussion of it is to be found in the antinomy of pure reason. (A 803–804 / B 831–32)

As a preliminary to a metaphysics of morals which I intend some day to publish, I issue these *Foundations.* There is, to be sure, no other foundation for such a metaphysics than a critical examination of pure practical reason, just as there is no other foundation for metaphysics than the already published critical examination of pure speculative reason. But, in the first place, a critical examination of pure practical reason is not of such extreme importance as that of speculative reason, because human reason, even in the commonest mind, can easily be brought to a high degree of correctness and completeness in moral matters, while, on the other hand, in its theoretical but pure use it is entirely dialectical. In the second place, I require of a critical examination of pure practical reason, if it is to be complete, that its unity with the speculative be subject to presentation under a common principle, because in the final analysis there can be but one and the same reason which must be differentiated only in application. But I could not bring this to such a completeness without bringing in observations of an altogether different kind and without thereby confusing the reader. (F 7–8)

For if pure reason is actually practical, it will show its reality and that of its concepts in actions and all disputations which aim to prove its impossibility will be in vain.

With the pure practical faculty of reason, the reality of transcendental freedom is also confirmed. Indeed, it is substantiated in the absolute sense needed by speculative reason in its use of the concept of causality, for this freedom is required if reason is to rescue itself from the antinomy in which it is inevitably entangled when attempting to think the unconditioned in a causal series. For speculative reason, the concept of freedom was problematic but not impossible; that is to say, speculative reason could think of freedom without contradiction, but it could not assure objective reality to it. Reason showed freedom to be conceivable only in order that its supposed impossibility might not endanger reason's very being and plunge it into an abyss of skepticism.

The concept of freedom, insofar as its reality is proved by an apodictic law of practical reason, is the keystone of the whole architecture of the system of pure reason and even of speculative reason. All other concepts (those of God and immortality) which, as mere ideas, are unsupported by anything in speculative reason now attach themselves to the concept of freedom and gain, with it and through it, stability and objective reality. That is, their possibility is proved by the fact that there really is freedom, for this idea is revealed by the moral law. (PrR 3-4)

I have selected these texts as indicative of the development that takes place in Kant's elucidation of freedom inasmuch as they each explicitly take note of the systematic and even architectonic role that freedom is given to play in the critical project. There are differences, however, in the way each passage characterizes that role; for our purposes, the difference of most interest concerns the extent to which (transcendental) freedom stands in need of its own proper critical establishment. These passages indicate that Kant moved from a view that considered the discussion of the third antinomy adequate for the critical establishment of freedom to a view that required the elaboration of a separate critique, not only for an adequate critical establishment of freedom but also to provide the "keystone" for the whole critical project.

This movement toward an explicit "critique" of practical reason to "confirm" the reality of transcendental freedom signals, in my judgment, that Kant has seen some additional considerations that bear on the configuration and resolution of the issue of the relationship between freedom and nature. These additional considerations will eventually lead to three developments that are important for giving the critical project its mature shape: first, to the introduction of the notion of autonomy to characterize freedom as the moral self-governance of reason;[2] second, to a significant breach of the barrier that the *Critique of Pure Reason* had initially set between the "world" governed by the causal connections of nature and the "world" constituted by the self-governance of reason; and third, to the elucidation of a notion of the highest good in which the moral self-governance of reason functions as a necessary condition for the attainment of the historical and social destiny of the human race.

I consider it of no small importance that Kant had not yet made in the *Critique of Pure Reason* an explicit identification of the exercise of (moral) freedom with "autonomy." The discussion of freedom in the first *Critique* is cast, instead, in terms of the notion of "spontaneity" (A 444–51/B 472–79; A 533/B 561). This is quite in keeping with the general role that the notion of spontaneity plays in Kant's characterization of the function of reason as the synthesizing power operative in human consciousness's cognizing of objects; in this context it serves well as an appropriate term to characterize initially the function of reason, as transcendental causality, in human consciousness's determining of action. Thus, to the extent that Kant understands the notion of spontaneity to be a fundamental characteristic of reason, it allows him to identify human willing, insofar as it can be a spontaneously determining source of action, as an exercise of reason. As long as this simple identification of willing with the practical exercise of the spontaneity of reason suffices, Kant is able consistently to maintain that there is no need for a separate critique of practical reason. The analysis Kant proposes in the *Foundations*, however, indicates that he eventually found this identification with spontaneity inadequate, by virtue of its generality, for specifying the properly practical character that pure reason exhibits as a determining source of human action, viz., the character of self-governance. "Autonomy" will prove to be an apt term for marking out this properly practical character of the exercise of reason in the determination of human action.

Kant's introduction of the notion of autonomy to characterize the function of reason in the human determination of action is thus by no means intended to deny his previous characterization of willing as an exercise of reason in virtue of its spontaneity. It serves, rather, to mark out more clearly a characteristic of the spontaneity of reason that, even though it is proper to the entire exercise of reason, is exhibited most clearly in the practical use of reason: the spontaneity of reason has an ordering principle—its ordering principle is that of its own self-governance. The need for reason to exercise governance of its own spontaneity lies at the very root of "critique": it is not a project to place external constraints upon claims that have been made on behalf of reason but to place human reason under an internal self-discipline by which it acknowledges the limits that its finitude places on its use. In consequence, Kant's formulation of the notion of autonomy to characterize the manner in which reason exercises self-governance in its practical use will prove important not only for the critical examination of the practical use of reason but also for the final systematic shape of the entire critical project.

Among the most significant consequences that I perceive the introduction of the notion of autonomy to have had upon the systematic shape of the critical project is that it leads to a recasting of the distinction between the sensible "world" and the intelligible "world." This recasting is one that breaches the apparently impenetrable barrier set between them in the first *Critique* under the heading of the distinction between phenomena and noumena (A 254–56/B 310–12). It is my hypothesis that this recasting of the distinction between the sensible "world" and the intelligible "world" occurs in function of Kant's turning of the critical project to an explicit examination of the practical use of reason. The critical examination of the practical use of reason begins to show that this distinction, initially posed in its critical form for the purpose of establishing limits to the speculative use of transcendent ideas by reason, cannot subsequently be posed in precisely the same manner for a different purpose: exhibiting the immanent, yet nonetheless objective, practical reality of one of those ideas, freedom, for use by the self-same reason. This critical establishment of freedom as the mode of the objective exercise of pure reason as practical broaches precisely the question of how we might appropriately represent a link between the "worlds" that Kant has distinguished as intelligible and sensible inasmuch as the principle of the unity of reason requires the intelligible world to have an influence on the sensible. Kant's statement in the *Critique of Judgment* notes this requirement:

> Now even if an immeasurable gulf is fixed between the sensible realm of the concept of nature and the supersensible realm of the concept of freedom, so that no transition is possible from the first to the second (by means of the theoretical use of reason), just as if they were two different worlds of which the first could have no influence upon the second, yet the second is *meant* to have an influence on the first. The concept of freedom is meant to actualize in the world of sense the purpose proposed by its laws, and consequently nature must be so thought that the conformity to law of its form at least harmonizes with the possibility of the purposes to be effected in it according to the laws of freedom. (CJ–B 12)

This claim stands in contrast to the cautious expression of the possibility of such influence affirmed in the first *Critique*:

Thus in our judgments in regard to the causality of free actions, we can get as far as the intelligible cause, but not beyond it. We can know that it is free, that is, that it is determined independent of sensibility, and that in this way it may be the sensibly unconditioned condition of appearances, but to explain why in the given circumstances the intelligible character should give just these appearances and this empirical character transcends all the powers of our reason, indeed its rights of questioning, just as if we were to ask why the transcendental object of our outer sensible intuition gives intuition in *space* only and not some other mode of intuition. But the problem we have to solve does not require us to raise any such questions. Our problem was this only: whether freedom and natural necessity can exist without conflict in one and the same action; and this we have sufficiently answered. (A 557/B 585)

A useful way of characterizing this development is to see it as a shift in the function of related contrasts—"sensible/intelligible," "phenomenon/noumenon," "appearance/thing-in-itself"—from principally a negative one of marking a limit to the theoretical use of reason to a positive one of marking out the proper character of the practical use of the self-same reason. In Kant's critique of the speculative use of reason the distinction between the sensible and the intelligible worlds, especially as it is expressed by the contrast between phenomena and noumena, principally serves to systematize Kant's development of Hume's insight that the source of the necessity we attribute to causal connections cannot be located in the immediate presentation that objects make of themselves to our senses. The notion of noumenon is thus negative; it serves to bar us from making claims that objects have, in themselves, "intelligible" grounds, i.e., grounds whose exhibition in concepts bears no reference to an ordering of time or in space. The notion of "noumenon" thus serves as a reminder that human reason, properly aware of its own limitations in its theoretical use, has no right there to make a positive characterization of whatever might link a realm of objects to their "intelligible ground." Reason has no right here because even the suggestion of such a link might lead us to embark on the very search for "intelligible grounds" that this negatively functioning concept of noumenon is designed to block.

Even in the first edition of the first *Critique*, however, Kant gives indications of a positive function to the notion of the "noumenon" and its parallel concepts. These indications bring these notions to bear upon the practical employment of reason (A 542–57/B 570–85). Reason, with reference to its governance of human willing, represents itself as the source of intelligible causality:

> No matter how many natural grounds or how many sensuous impulses may impel me to *will*, they can never give rise to the "ought," but only to a willing which, while very far from being necessary, is always conditioned; and the "ought" pronounced by reason confronts such willing with a limit and an end—nay more, forbids or authorizes it. Whether what is willed be an object of mere sensibility (the pleasant) or of pure reason (the good), reason will not give way to any ground which is empirically given. Reason does not here follow the order of things as they present themselves in appearance, but frames for itself with perfect spontaneity an order of its own according to ideas, to which it adapts the empirical conditions, and according to which it declares actions to be necessary, even though they have never taken place, and perhaps never will take place. And at the same time reason also presupposes that it can have causality in regard to all these actions, since otherwise no empirical effects could be expected from its ideas. (A 548/B 576)

It is important to note that reason's representation of itself as intelligible cause here is not the forbidden one of serving as representation of the metaphysical "ground" of objects in that totality of connections called "nature." It is, instead, a representation of the spontaneous, self-governing activity by which human agents mutually constitute the totality of connections that make them, each and all, members of that intelligible realm that Kant calls a *"corpus mysticum* of . . . rational beings," or, following Leibniz, "a kingdom of grace" (A 808/B 836; A 812/B 840). One passage from Kant's discussion is especially worth noting now, since it contains a significant anticipation of the issue that gives focus to the elaboration of the highest good that finally emerges in *Religion:*

> I entitle the world a *moral world*, insofar as it may be in accordance with all moral laws; and this is what by means of the freedom of the rational being it *can be*, and what according to the necessary laws of morality it *ought to be*. Owing to our here

leaving out of account all conditions (ends) and even all the special difficulties to which morality is exposed (weakness or depravity of human nature), this world is so far thought of as an intelligible world only. To this extent, therefore, it is a mere idea, though at the same time a practical idea, which really can have, as it also ought to have, an influence upon the sensible world, to bring that world, so far as may be possible, into conformity with the idea. The idea of a moral world has, therefore, objective reality, not as referring to an object of intelligible intuition (we are quite unable to think any such object), but as referring to the sensible world, viewed, however, as being an object of pure reason in its practical employment, that is, as a *corpus mysticum* of the rational beings in it, so far as the free will of each being is, under moral laws, in complete systematic unity with itself and with the freedom of every other. (A 808/B 836)

These preliminary indications of the systematic importance of the contrast between the sensible and the intelligible worlds for a critical elucidation or establishment of the practical use of reason do not, however, mark out the contrast with either the clarity or vigor expressed in passages such as the following from, respectively, *The Foundations of the Metaphysics of Morals*, the *Critique of Practical Reason*, and the *Critique of Judgment*. These passages will provide a context for discussion of the next element involved in Kant's reconsideration of the relation between nature and freedom, namely the role of autonomy in the ordering of the world:

Without this use of sensibility it [understanding] would not think at all, while, on the other hand, reason shows such a pure spontaneity in the case of ideas that it far transcends anything that sensibility can give to consciousness and shows its chief occupation in distinguishing the world of sense from the world of understanding, thereby prescribing limits to the understanding itself.

For this reason a rational being must regard himself as intelligence (and not from the side of his lower powers), as belonging to the world of understanding and not to that of the senses. Thus he has two standpoints from which he can consider himself and recognize the laws of the employment of his powers and consequently of all his actions: first, as belonging to the world of sense under laws of nature (heteronomy), and, second, as belonging to the intelligible world under laws which, independent of nature, are not empirical but founded only on reason. (F 71)

So far from being incoherent, the highly consistent structure of the *Critique of Pure Reason* is very satisfyingly revealed here. For in that work the objects of experience as such, including even our own subject, were explained only as *appearances*, though as based upon things-in-themselves; consequently, even in that *Critique* it was emphasized that the supersensible was not mere fancy and that its concepts were not empty. Now practical reason itself, without any collusion with the speculative, provides reality to a supersensible object of the category of causality, i.e., to freedom. This is a practical concept and as such is subject only to practical use; but what in the speculative critique could only be thought is now confirmed by fact. (PrR 6)

These two different realms [that of natural concepts and that of the concept of freedom], then, do not limit each other in their legislation, though they perpetually do so in the world of sense. That they do not constitute *one* realm arises from this that the natural concept represents its objects in intuition, not as things in themselves, but as mere phenomena; the concept of freedom, on the other hand, represents in its object a thing in itself, but not in intuition. Hence neither of them can furnish a theoretical knowledge of its object (or even of the thinking subject) as a thing in itself; this would be the supersensible, the idea of which we must indeed make the basis of the possibility of all these objects of experience, but which we never can extend or elevate into a cognition. (CJ-B 11)

3. The Reconsideration of Freedom in Relation to Nature: Autonomy and the Ordering of the World

My discussion of autonomy in the previous section was concerned with showing that, with its introduction, Kant has an apt term for characterizing the self-governance by which reason orders its own spontaneity. My concern in this section will be to show how Kant's continuing elucidation of the self-governance of reason, as it develops from the *Foundations* to *Religion*, initiates a reconsideration of the proper way to characterize the relationship between freedom and nature. This reconsideration emerges as Kant moves his elucidation of the self-governance of reason from a focus on its role in the constitution of moral agency to a focus on the role it can—and, indeed, must—play in shaping the sensible "world" into the configuration called for by the intelligible, i.e., moral, "world."

The passage from the *Critique of Pure Reason* (A 808/B 836) cited above makes it clear that the question of the role pure practical reason plays in shaping even the sensible world does not arise only in the later works of the critical project. It is, however, a question to which Kant is required to provide a more complex answer after he has formulated and developed some of the social and historical ramifications of the notion of autonomy. That answer, in turn, requires further modification once the question of the source of human evil is posed in the context of his account of autonomy.

A useful place from which to start an examination of the impact Kant's development of the notion of autonomy has upon his account of the relation between freedom and nature is the account he gives in the *Critique of Pure Reason* (A 812–16/B 840–44), from which I shall here cite one interesting paragraph:

> But this systematic unity of ends in this world of intelligences—a world which is indeed, as mere nature, a sensible world only, but which, as a system of freedom, can be entitled an intelligible, that is, a moral world (*regnum gratiae*)—leads inevitably also to the purposive unity of all things, which constitute this great whole, in accordance with the universal laws of nature (just as the former unity is in accordance with universal and necessary laws of morality), and thus unites the practical with the speculative reason. This world must be represented as having originated from an idea if it is to be in harmony with that employment of reason without which we should indeed hold ourselves to be unworthy of reason, namely, with the moral employment—which is founded entirely on the idea of the supreme good. In this way all investigation of nature tends to take the form of a system of ends, and in its widest extension becomes a physico-theology. But this, as it has its source in the moral order, as a unity grounded in freedom's own essential nature, and not accidentally instituted through external commands, connects the purposiveness of nature with grounds that must be inseparably connected *a priori* with the inner possibility of things, and so leads to a *transcendental theology*—a theology which takes the ideal of a supreme ontological perfection as a principle of systematic unity. And since all things have their origin in the absolute necessity of the one primordial being, that principle connects them in accordance with universal and necessary laws of nature. (A 815–16/B 843–44)

There are two observations I wish to make about this account.

First, I think it can be appropriately understood as an account of the unity of the "world" that, though still strongly Leibnizian in its "harmony," has had the unifying principle for such harmony transposed onto moral grounds that temper Leibnizian optimism. Second, it is an account that seems not to be remarkably modified by the discussion of autonomy initiated in the *Foundations of the Metaphysics of Morals*, to the extent, that is, that an account of the matter of the relation between freedom and nature can be discerned in that work.

I do not propose here to develop the implications of my first observation; I offer it merely to signal what I think is the relatively unproblematic status in which the first *Critique* seems to leave the relation between freedom and nature. It is relatively unproblematic in that Kant's perspective on the relation seems to take shape in consequence of the central, but not yet explicitly examined, critical principle of the unity of reason. In connection with this I think it worthwhile to note, moreover, that in the triad of citations found on pages 135–37, an explicit focus on the unity of reason emerges in conjunction with the development of a specific critical examination of the practical use of reason. It is unproblematic also to the extent that Kant's affirmation of the principle of ordering as fundamentally moral—an affirmation that will be maintained throughout his critical project— has yet to specify the manner of such ordering as the self-governance of reason.

I shall explore the implications of my second observation, however, inasmuch as I think it sets us on the track of a development in Kant's elaboration of autonomy that initiates a reconsideration of the relatively unproblematic view of the relation between freedom and nature expressed in the first *Critique*, a reconsideration culminating in the notion of the "highest good" that is formulated in *Religion*. There is, I believe, a simple way to explain why the account of autonomy given in the *Foundations* does not fundamentally disturb the resolution of the relation between freedom and nature found in the first *Critique*: the account of autonomy given in the *Foundations* treats it principally as the exercise of pure reason in the moral agency of individual finite rational beings. From this perspective, the question of the relationship between freedom and nature, particularly as it undergoes the kind of moral transposition Kant provides at the end of the first *Critique*, comes to focus on the appropriate apportionment of happiness—and next-worldly happiness at that—to individual moral agents in virtue of their moral worthiness.[3] Crucial developments that take place in Kant's account of autonomy, subsequent to its initial enunciation in the *Foundations*, bring about a shift from an exclusive or even primary focus on the apportionment of happiness to individual moral agents. These developments are, first, a clearer articulation of the social character of autonomy itself and of the social and historical context of its exercise and, second, an attempt to confront the question of how evil gains its footing both within the individual moral agent and the social and historical activity of human persons. This second development provides the final catalyst for the account of the "highest good" that is formulated in *Religion*.

I have argued elsewhere for interpreting Kant's account of autonomy in terms of a commitment to mutuality that manifests the essentially social character of human freedom.[4] I do not propose to repeat those arguments here: I wish instead to focus on what appears to be the gradual and sometimes even halting emergence of the social character of autonomy as Kant traces the lineaments of the practical use of reason. I think it undeniable that the treatment given to autonomy in the *Foundations* does not make it all that evident—save in images such as the kingdom of ends—that autonomy can, let alone should, be appropriately rendered as an account of the social character of human freedom. Nonetheless, the presence of such images suggestive of a social dimension to the practical use of reason is well in keeping even with Kant's initial critical discussion of the practical use of reason, "The Canon of Pure Reason." In that section of the first *Critique*,[5] his discussion of the issues that will later preoccupy the second and third *Critiques*, such as the unity and purposes of the various uses of reason, is cast in terms and images such as "world" and "kingdom" that, to the extent that they signal an essential interrelatedness of rational beings, mark out the social character of reason and its uses. The presence, in this earliest presentation of the critical project, both of these images and of a concern to affirm the unity of reason and the (at least hoped-for) final unity of the sensible and intelligible worlds can serve to alert us to the possibility that the eventual placement of autonomy in an essentially social context—which develops in the second and third *Critiques* and is fully emergent in *Religion*—is in keeping with a most fundamental principle of Kant's project.

The emergence of the social character of autonomy complicates Kant's initial resolution of the issue of the relationship between freedom and nature in terms of appropriate moral apportionment of (next-worldly) happiness to individual moral agents to the extent that it suggests that such apportionment, designated as the "highest good," may not simply be the aggregate sum total of the happiness apportioned singly to individuals. This complication, however, seems one of degree rather than of kind: the calculation of appropriate apportionment must now take into account not only the worthiness of individuals considered singly but also the final "harmony" of the totality of the moral "world" that such individuals constitute. In fact, I think that one could justly argue that this turns out to be no complication at all: Kant's account would just require us to place "moral faith" in a God who, as moral ruler of the world, has a "view" of such a harmonious totality and of the requisite "calculation" for bringing about the morally appropriate apportionment that is, of necessity, "timeless." To the extent, therefore, that autonomy is conceived of as an agency that, even in its social character, stands "outside" the ordering of time—and thus "outside" the sensible "world"—the moral power of God functions simply as a calculative agency to apportion appropriate moral desert to individuals.[6]

Yet even in his treatment of autonomy as the exercise of practical reason in the moral agency of individual rational beings, Kant is not able to keep it standing totally "outside" the sensible world, inasmuch as this is the "world" in which human moral conduct and character take their concrete shape. The specific way in which Kant first acknowledges this kind of breach in the "barrier" between the intelligible and sensible worlds is in his discussion of the feeling of respect: the feeling of respect marks out the one sensible effect that Kant is willing to affirm as having its origin in the intelligible causality that we represent as autonomy (PrR 78–79, 81–82). Kant's account of respect suggests the possibility, moreover, that autonomy can be appropriately understood as the power that the exercise of human freedom has to give abiding shape to the moral conduct and character of individual human persons. This possibility is significant for his account of the relation between freedom and nature to the extent that it brings that relation to bear not only on the final harmony of the two "worlds" envisioned in the first *Critique*, nor just on the final apportionment of happiness as moral desert, but also on the continuing, "this worldly" process of the formation of moral agency as a "good will."

Kant's discussion of respect in the second *Critique* is an advance over his discussion of that feeling in the *Foundations* inasmuch as it identifies the particular form that the effect of intelligible causality takes in the sensible world. Still, it is not much of an advance over the bare affirmation made in the *Foundations* that there must be such causality: it does not show how this power of freedom actually gives concrete shape to the agency and conduct of human persons, nor does it make evident the bearing that the social character of autonomy has upon our understanding of this power and the mode of its exercise. These limitations will become most evident once the question of evil becomes the focus of Kant's discussion. The final two sections of this essay will thus consider, first, how that question pushes Kant toward a significant reconfiguration of his account of moral freedom/autonomy and, second, how that reconfiguration leads to the account of the highest good presented in *Religion*.

4. The Reconsideration of Freedom in Relation to Nature: The Roots of Evil

In this penultimate section I shall suggest how Kant's treatment of the question of evil brings two lines of development in his account of autonomy—autonomy as the self-governance of reason and autonomy as the exhibition of the social character of human freedom—close to convergence. The near convergence, in my judgment, allows Kant to articulate the issue of the relation between freedom and nature in its most comprehensive critical form. The convergence, however, is not complete: although the problem of evil drives each line of development onto the terrain of human temporality, they are unable to effect a juncture. In consequence, as the final section will show, Kant's resolution of the issue does not fully meet the demands that his most comprehensive formulation of the issue articulates.

The first converging line of development is one in which Kant continues to track the implications of autonomy, as the self-governance of reason, for the moral agency of the individual human person. The previous section indicated that, as Kant tracks these implications, he singles out the feeling of respect as that which has power to shape the conduct and character of the person in accord with the self-governance of reason. That section also indicated that the account of respect represents a significant development in the systematic configuration of Kant's critical system, viz., the identification of a specific link between what Kant has separated as the sensible world and the intelligible world. As we shall soon see, Kant does not forge this link strongly enough to show how autonomy, conceived atemporally as once and for all fixed in its ordering to good and evil, can issue in the variegated concrete configuration that a human person's conduct and character take in and through the course of time. Although Kant's account thus opens the possibility of exhibiting in the structure of human moral agency a fundamental relation between freedom and nature, the structure that is so exhibited retains a duality unbridged by the relation. This duality has its source in the ambiguity of Kant's rendering of the temporality and historicity of human moral agency, and it emerges most notably in Kant's efforts, valiant but not fully successful, to account for the possibility of turning from evil to good, and vice versa.

The second converging line of development is the one in which Kant continues to track the implications of the social character of autonomy and, in particular, the way in which this social character takes concrete shape in the institutions of human culture. I have not followed Kant closely along this track in this essay, in large measure because Collins, Despland, and Yovel, among others, have traced well the course he follows and have made it abundantly evident that temporality and history loom large in the terrain through which it runs. They differ in their estimation of how well Kant has mastered this terrain and thus also make it clear that his account of the relation between freedom and nature undergoes a particularly crucial test of its adequacy here.[7]

As I suggested two paragraphs above, Kant seems to move hesitantly toward this feature of the terrain as he tracks the development of autonomy in terms of individual moral agency. It is on this ground that he is, in my judgment, ultimately daunted by the question of evil in its concrete particularity in the agency and conduct of an individual human person. Even though he moves more boldly along the second line, he also fails there to master fully the stretch of terrain athwart which lies the problem of evil. I think it would thus be appropriate to say that these two lines fail to converge fully with one another inasmuch as Kant is unable to elucidate fully along either one of them how the self-governance of reason gains mastery over the historical concreteness of evil, be it in the life of an individual human person or in the historical development of the institutions of human society.

If I am correct about the way Kant moves along these two lines of development, then I think we can discern the following elements which enter into the configuration of the issue of the relation between freedom and nature as it emerges in the discussion of *Religion*.

On the one hand, Kant envisions the relation between freedom and nature as one that has an important bearing upon the total and final outcome of all human moral activity. Inasmuch as Kant consistently envisions this outcome, throughout the critical project, as having an essentially moral ordering, its delimitation requires some account of the overcoming of evil. In the earlier stages of the critical project he seemed content to characterize this outcome as one that finally stands not only at the end of history but in some measure "outside" it as well. As a consequence, there is need only to provide an account of the overcoming of evil as a final result at some atemporal, next-worldly "end" of history. In the later stages of the critical project, however, he begins to characterize the total and final outcome of human moral activity more clearly as a human destiny that is to be attained within history, in the context of the historicity of the human species and its social institutions. In consequence, a proper characterization of the relation between freedom and nature will now need to delimit in some manner the bearing this relation has upon the attainment of human destiny not simply as an end that can be conceived to stand "outside" history but also as a process and a result *within* history. A critical delimitation of this outcome thus now has to include an account not only of the final overcoming of evil at the "end" of history but also of the presence of evil and the process of overcoming it within the course of history.

On the other hand, Kant also envisions the relation between

freedom and nature as having an important bearing on the total and final outcome of an individual's moral conduct. In the earlier stages of the critical project, extending even into the second *Critique*, Kant views this outcome principally, if not exclusively, in "next worldly" terms: the "postulate" of immortality serves to represent the bearing that the relation between freedom and nature has upon the final outcome of an individual's moral life. That outcome is represented as standing "outside" temporality and history. Although the locus of this outcome remains "outside" history, there is one notable shift in the characterization of this outcome that takes place in Kant's discussions of immortality from the first *Critique* to the second *Critique*. In the first *Critique*, immortality functions as a postulate for appropriate moral desert, whereas in the second *Critique* it functions as a guarantee of endless moral progress (A 811–12/B 839–40; PrR 126–28). This shift suggests, first, a sharpening of the model of struggle that is in the fore of Kant's understanding of moral life and, second, the persistence of an essential element of human moral agency's temporality even within the "timeless" outcome of immortality. The view of this outcome found in *Religion*, however, represents a far more decisive turn from an exclusively "next worldly" focus: the outcome on which the relation between freedom and nature has a significant bearing is no longer just the apportionment of desert in the next world but the way in which moral agency and conduct take concrete shape in an individual's moral life in the persistent struggle within that life to overcome evil.

The shifts that I have suggested in Kant's perspective on each of these outcomes are not unrelated. From what I have already noted in the earlier sections of this essay, it should be clear that, while I see these shifts emerging from Kant's increasingly explicit attention to the social character of the self-governance of reason, I also see Kant's effort to deal with the problem of evil as a catalyst that makes these shifts play a central role in giving a final configuration to the critical project. This catalytic effect can be seen most dramatically, in my judgment, through a consideration of how Kant comes to see, in *Religion*, that the roots of evil can be traced back even to the self-governance of reason.

Throughout much of the critical project, Kant seems content to locate the source of evil in a conflict between the sensible and the intelligible determining of human reason in its function as "will." This seems to be the view found in a number of places in the first *Critique*,[8] in the *Foundations* (F 72–74), though modified to the extent that there can be rational as well as empirical sources of heteronomy in the determining of the human will, and in the second *Critique*.[9] The third *Critique* does not clearly suggest either a modification or an abandonment of the view that the source of evil lies in a conflict between the sensible and the intelligible determining of human reason in its function as "will." Yet it, too, contains passages that I think can be fairly interpreted as showing that Kant's descriptive renderings of the presence of evil bring into focus the source of evil that lies within reason's own self-governance in a way that his formal analyses in terms of a conflict between the sensible and intelligible determining of the will had not been able to do.[10]

In *Religion*, Kant finally makes the source of evil that lies within reason's own self-governance his analytic as well as his descriptive focus. I do not propose to examine here whether there might have been any significant external factors leading him to bring this at last into his analytic purview. I am concerned simply to note and examine what I judge to be the point at which the source of evil within reason's own self-governance becomes most evident: in Kant's description and account of the possibility of what I shall term moral "conversion."

Perhaps the passage that captures most directly the terms in which Kant envisions this possibility is the following from the "General Observation" at the end of Book I:

> But if a man is to become not merely, *legally* but *morally*, a good man (pleasing to God), that is, a man endowed with virtue in its intelligible character *(virtus noumenon)* and one who, knowing something to be his duty, requires no incentive other than this representation of duty itself, *this* cannot be brought about by gradual *reformation* so long as the basis of the maxims remains impure, but must be effected through a *revolution* in the man's disposition (a going over to the maxim of holiness in the disposition). He can become a new man only by a kind of rebirth, as it were a new creation (John III,5; compare also Genesis I,2), and a change of heart.
>
> But if a man is corrupt in the very ground of his maxims, how can he possibly bring about this revolution by his own powers

and of himself become a good man? Yet duty bids us do this, and duty demands nothing of us which we cannot do. There is no reconciliation possible here except by saying that man is under the necessity of, and is therefore capable of, a revolution in his cast of mind, but only of a gradual reform in his sensuous nature (which places obstacles in the way of the former). That is, if a man reverses, by a single unchangeable decision, that highest ground of his maxims whereby he was an evil man (and thus puts on the new man), he is, so far as his principle and cast of mind are concerned, a subject susceptible of goodness, but only in continuous labor and growth is he a good man. That is, he can hope that in the light of that purity of the principle which he has adopted as the supreme maxim of his will, and of its stability, to find himself upon the good (though strait) path of continual *progress* from bad to better. For him who penetrates to the intelligible ground of the heart (the ground of all maxims of the will) and for whom this unending progress is a unity, i.e., for God, this amounts to his being actually a good man (pleasing to Him); and thus viewed, this change can be regarded as a revolution. But in the judgment of men, who can appraise themselves and the strength of their maxims only by the ascendency which they win over their sensuous nature in time, this change must be regarded as nothing but an ever-during struggle toward the better, hence as a gradual reformation of the propensity to evil, the perverted cast of mind. (R 42–43)

There are three observations I shall make on this passage which I think will suffice to complete the task set for this section, viz., to show how the problem of evil brings Kant's development of autonomy as the self-governance of reason onto the terrain of the temporality and historicity of human moral agency and, thus, on a line of convergence with his development of autonomy as the exhibition of the social character of human freedom.

My first observation is offered to locate this passage in the context of Kant's extended discussion of "radical evil" in Book I. As I understand that discussion, it shows that Kant moved from a view that locates the most fundamental source of evil in a conflict between the sensible and intelligible determining of the will to one that locates it in the power resident in human will itself—i.e., in the very self-governance of reason—to make the sensible determining of the will a constant principle of choice (R 30–32, 78). This affirmation suggests that even though Kant terms this an account of radical evil, it might equally be called an account of radical freedom: the self-governance of reason is constantly confronted by its own possibility for evil, resident in the human freedom to determine choice as we will. Thus the very possibility of what Kant calls "reversing the moral order of incentives" —i.e., of making sensible determination a principle of choice—is radicated not in the character of any particular "incentive" as "sensible" but in the capacity of human freedom to make that incentive a ground for action.

My second observation is that one would have to have great temerity even to attempt to improve upon the descriptive accuracy of Kant's distillation of what takes place in one who goes through a "moral conversion": "man is under the necessity of, and is therefore capable of, a revolution in his cast of mind, but only of a gradual reform in his sensuous nature." This phrase captures, in its epigrammatic terseness, the "once-for-all-ness" demanded by the decisiveness of conversion yet the constant and even lifelong task it places on one who has made this decisive turn. It is, nonetheless, the very descriptive accuracy of Kant's phrase that helps bring into focus why his final, accurate tracking of evil to its source in the self-governance of reason then goes astray on the terrain of temporality.

This brings me to my third observation: once evil has been traced to a source in the radical freedom of the self-governance of reason, it remains unclear how any "revolution" in one's "cast of mind" can have the kind of "once-for-all-ness" that Kant claims for it in its very origin without thereby destroying the very radical freedom on which its possibility rests. We should note, in fairness to Kant, that the issues about moral agency broached here are ones for which it would be rash to say that any moral philosopher has yet offered a fully satisfactory resolution. One of the major achievements of Kant's *Religion*, in fact, is that it provides a description so unerringly and so uncannily accurate that it shows the deep intractability of these issues.

There is, however, a more specific set of factors that make Kant's particular treatment of these issues less than fully adequate. In large measure, these factors can be identified by distinguishing Kant's description of the presence of evil in human moral agency and of the possibility of moral conversion from his efforts to analyze these descriptions in terms of an account of moral agency that holds fast to a distinction between its "intelligible" and "sensible" aspects, particularly insofar as temporality stands solely on the "sensible" side of the distinction. Two of the consequences of this incongruity between description and analysis are of consequence for my purpose of showing how two lines of Kant's development of autonomy come close to convergence on the ground that marks out the temporality of human moral agency.

First, the analysis affirms the permanence of conversion as a consequence of the atemporality of the intelligible aspect of moral agency.[11] This is not and cannot be affirmed by the description of the radical evil from which one turns in conversion.[12] This description embeds the precariousness of alterations and temporality into the very intelligible character of moral agency.

Second, the description suggests that the reform of conduct has the possibility of giving a shape to the intelligible character of moral agency that could, in fact, lead to the permanency and stability which is hoped for in moral conversion. The analysis, by its reaffirmation of the principle that the sensible does not affect the intelligible, precludes the possibility that concrete conduct in the sensible world can play such a role in shaping moral agency.[13] A brief elucidation of these consequences will prepare the way for discussion, in the final section, of how the account of the highest good, developed in *Religion* on the basis of the social character of freedom expressed by autonomy, also points to an acknowledgment of the fundamental temporality of human moral agency.

Kant's affirmation of the fixity of moral conversion in his analysis seems intended to establish the possibility of an enduring overcoming of evil within the moral agency of an individual human person. Yet, by making such endurance a consequence of the atemporality of the intelligible aspect of moral agency, the analysis provides no way for such an enduring character to become manifest with surety to the person who has made the turn of moral conversion. This "revolution" is not directly accessible to the moral agent insofar as concrete human moral awareness is, like all human finite awareness, always conditioned by temporality (R 56–57, 65). It is, at best, "indirectly" accessible but not with surety, inasmuch as the "reformation" of conduct that is putatively the effect of conversion takes place within the sensible world that is bound in and by time and thus cannot serve as a reliable index that the "revolution" occasioned by conversion has been firmly and permanently fixed within one's "cast of mind."

Yet, most important of all, the possibility of the kind of atemporal permanence envisioned by Kant's analysis is not affirmed by the description he gives of the radical evil from which one turns in conversion. This description of radical evil, as the will's own possibility for alteration, embeds temporality deeply into moral agency; the abiding possibility of making sensible determination of the will a maxim for conduct makes any "revolution" which such moral agency initiates a precarious one. This rooting of evil in radical freedom suggests that temporality, at least as the abiding possibility of alteration and moral reversal, has permanently entered into the "intelligible" world of moral agency. The entrance of temporality into moral agency will become even more evident when Kant turns his attention to the possibility of a permanent overcoming of evil in the social unfolding of human history.

Presupposed in the second incongruity between Kant's description and analysis is a common starting point; his description and analysis both correctly locate that which sets the overcoming of evil on its course—an act of the human freedom to turn away from the evil that stands before it as ever-present possibility. Description and analysis stand in tension, however, over what then makes it possible for the overcoming of evil to become definitive and fixed. As already noted, Kant's analysis affirms such fixity from the very "outset" of the turn from evil, in virtue of the atemporal character of intelligible moral agency. Kant's description of the reform of conduct, on the other hand, very sketchily suggests a different possibility for giving the intelligible character of moral agency the kind of shape that leads to the permanency and stability of moral conversion: such permanency results inasmuch as moral conduct takes shape in accord with the course first set by freedom, but this conduct must, in its turn, then give concrete shape to the moral agency of the particular individual. Continued shaping of moral agency is required inasmuch as evil continues to stand as an ever-present possibility before human freedom even after it has made the turn that sets it on the course of conversion.[14]

His description, in short, suggests the possibility of introducing a thoroughgoing temporality and historicity into human moral agency even in its intelligible dimension inasmuch as the "sensible"—i.e., the concrete history of an individual's moral conduct—enters into the final shaping of moral agency by making conversion permanent through time. Kant's description, of course, can only hint at this possibility, since otherwise it would surely overturn a fundamental principle of the distinction he has constantly made between the sensible and the intelligible: though the intelligible may—and, in the feeling of respect, even must—have an effect upon the sensible, the converse does not hold. Yet, to the extent that such definitive overcoming of moral evil in the moral agency of the individual takes place as a concrete historical process, space for such a possibility has been cleared. Kant will approach this space even more closely in the account of the highest good that he gives in *Religion*, in which the concrete course of human history takes a central role in the process by which reason can hope to work the definitive overcoming of evil both in the individual and in human society. This account, which picks up the line of development along which Kant has been tracking autonomy as the expression of the social character of human freedom, also suggests this most radical possibility for recasting the relation between the sensible and intelligible worlds: the possibility that the sensible world, by virtue of its temporality, has influence upon the intelligible world in the course of the human history that brings us, as a species, to our final destiny.

5. The Final End of All Things: The History That Gives Shape to Moral Agency

An initial reading of *Religion within the Limits of Reason Alone* seems unlikely to suggest that Kant has radically revised his account of the relation between the intelligible and the sensible worlds as he charts the pattern of the establishment of the sovereignty of the good principle on earth. This pattern, in which "pure religious faith" eventually supercedes "ecclesiastical faith," seems to be a straightforward exhibition of Kant's hope that in matters religious as well as moral an intelligible principle will ultimately take full governance of the realm of human activity (R 115). The possibility discussed at the close of the last section, viz., that the sensible might play a role in the final intelligible shaping of the world, seems to be precluded.

Collins, Despland, and Yovel have suggested that such an initial reading of *Religion* may not be entirely accurate. They each would acknowledge as certainly true that Kant steadfastly holds to the principle that the final outcome to which human reason properly directs itself is the (moral) governance of the world in accord with principles whose origin he represents as intelligible. Yet they would also point out that Kant's descriptions and analyses in *Religion* suggest how he has come explicitly to envision this outcome as the concrete historical result of the governance of the human world through time by finite reason.[15] In characterizing Kant's account by terms such as "concrete," "historical," "human," "through time," and "finite," this interpretation marks a "this worldly" dimension to the final outcome of the governance of reason. Such a "this worldly" emphasis was muted, if not lacking, in the earlier critical presentations of this final outcome. To the extent, therefore, that such a final outcome is "this worldly," it will necessarily have a sensible component; yet as long as Kant takes the sensible component to be merely that which can be receptive to the shaping power of the intelligible, the role of the sensible in this final outcome will be entirely passive—it is that to which the intelligible gives shape, but it has no shaping power of its own.

The shift to a "this worldly" perspective upon the outcome of the self-governance of reason has been charted by Collins, Despland, and Yovel as part of their examinations of the increasingly important role that history plays in the denouement of Kant's critical project. Each of them also notes what I think can aptly be characterized as a deep ambiguity in Kant's understanding of history; this ambiguity comes out particularly in efforts, such as the one presented in *Religion,* to exhibit the presence of the self-governance of reason in the concrete course of human history. This ambiguity resides in the limits that Kant effectively places on the role that time can play in such a "history of reason": although there are resources in his account for making time itself fundamental to such history, Kant does not systematically employ them and thus he ordinarily makes the critical "reading" of history one in which time merely unfolds that which has already, as intelligible, been timelessly present.

I do not think it forced to consider the issue confronting Kant here as at least parallel to the issue, sketched out in the previous section, of the extent to which temporality is an essential feature of finite rational moral agency. My suspicion is that these, indeed, are not simply parallel issues but an expression of one and the same issue: the extent to which temporality is an essential mark of the finitude of human reason. In each case Kant seems unable explicitly to consider the possibility that temporality does not at all diminish human reason's claim to be reason; even less does he entertain the more startling possibility that such temporality may very well be essential to the claim of human reason to be reason. Explicit notice of such possibilities might have led Kant to develop the tantalizing hints he makes in *Religion* that the final outcome of human history, precisely as the history of reason, is given its particular shape as the highest good in virtue of the exercise of a human moral agency that is fundamentally bound in and to time.

A brief look at some of those hints will help to show that this possibility of binding the final outcome of reason's activity to time makes notable the account of the highest good that Kant presents in *Religion*. One hint issues as an implication of the image Kant uses to make the social character and context of the exercise of human freedom: the ethical commonwealth. This image is, undoubtedly, a refraction of Kant's earlier image of the temporal moral world shaped by the self-governance of reason, the kingdom of ends. Kant uses the image of the ethical commonwealth, however, not only to represent such an atemporal realm of moral relations but also to characterize the concrete task that the duty to promote the highest good places upon all human persons. Of particular note is the fact that Kant affirms, first, that the task is precisely to make the invisible and atemporal moral world a public and visible one and, second, that the actual shape such public and visible exhibition of the moral world takes in the course of history is concretely determined by human activity (R 86, 96–97). In making both claims Kant has writ in large public and social terms the relation that his discussion of evil and conversion exhibits as so problematic for his account of individual moral agency: the relation between the atemporal intelligible moral world and the concrete human conduct that of necessity takes form in the sensible world that is bound by time.

Kant acknowledges this problematic character, in my judgment, inasmuch as he wisely leaves unspecified what he envisions as the final concrete form the ethical commonwealth will take. I read this lack of specification as more than unwillingness on Kant's part to sketch some kind of utopian or eschatological possibility. It is a specification that he cannot give, inasmuch as the "final" form of the human moral world can emerge only as the consequence of the totality of particular human conduct, of which only that of the past has taken definite shape. This lack of specification suggests that the moral world cannot take its final shape simply in consequence of the activity of an atemporal moral agency that has increasingly freed itself from conditions of sensible determination, for in that case the final shape of the human moral world could be specified no matter what the particular moral conduct of human moral agents in the course of history has been. Of course, to the extent that Kant continues to maintain an atemporal, "next worldly" outcome that is distinct from the concrete "end" of history, he does suggest an outcome that will emerge with the same final shape no matter what the particulars of human conduct have been throughout the course of history. I consider it one measure of the ambiguity of Kant's own views at this stage of the critical project that commentators can legitimately disagree sharply on the extent to which Kant continues to maintain a fully distinct "next worldly" account of the final outcome of human moral conduct.[16] This much, however, is certain: whether the "this worldly" account of the outcome stands alone or in correlation to a "next worldly" account, its presence marks a recognition on Kant's part that the actual course of human history, which takes place in the sensible world bound by time, plays a central role in giving concrete shape to the "highest good," which is the outcome reason requires of human moral conduct. To this extent, the sensible world and its temporality may very well function as active powers for bringing about the final unity of freedom and nature that Kant terms the highest good.

A second hint about a positive role for the sensible world in giving the ethical commonwealth its final shape can be developed by attending to the implications of Kant's claim that the establishment of this commonwealth is a public task and that this task is incumbent upon each generation in the course of human history. To the extent that Kant's making this task historical is meant to affirm that there have been and can be closer concrete approximations to the final form of the ethical commonwealth as human beings move history on its course, it opens the possibility of making another breach in the barrier between the sensible and intelligible worlds. The public character of this task suggests the possibility that temporality will be present even in the final establishment of the ethical commonwealth: the human fashioning of history brings about public, concrete, exterior forms for ordering moral conduct and relationships that, in the course of time, more approximately exhibit the ethical commonwealth and bring it closer to a final establishment that will also have a public, concrete, and exterior form. If the final establishment of the highest good has such a public character, it indicates that Kant can no longer maintain the sharp distinction between the exterior (legal) and the interior (moral) by which he has refracted the contrast between the sensible and intelligible worlds into his moral theory. In affirming an essentially public character to the human task of promoting the highest good through the establishment of an ethical commonwealth, Kant also increases the tension already noted between the "this worldy" and the "next worldly" characterizations of the final outcome of human moral conduct. To the extent that a "next worldly" characterization of this final outcome requires that it be wholly interior and thus atemporal, it stands in tension with the possibility that Kant now opens that the final outcome will itself be exterior and public and thereby bound in time.

A third hint about a positive role for the sensible world in giving the ethical commonwealth its final shape can be found in Kant's own reading of human moral history, particularly in the way he characterizes the movements and persons that have occasioned the governance that reason already exhibits over human moral life. Once again, I read the hint from Kant's ambiguity about the role particular individuals have played in human moral progress: on the one hand, Kant does show confidence that such progress is inevitable. Put perhaps oversimply, if Jesus had not been the personified idea of the good principle, we would have found another personification; on the other hand, elements of Kant's description of the role of Jesus suggest that he does not entirely dismiss the depth of historical contingency that might be at work in such progress. It thus might make sense both to ask whether such progress needed to wait for Jesus and no other and to answer "yes" to this question. Despland thus draws the conclusion that

> In contrast to the views which minimize the originality of what happened in the life of Jesus of Nazareth (merely a historical

illustration or realization of the eternal moral ideal), Kant empha-sized that a genuine existential breakthrough took place then and there. The hope in the growth of good on earth became a really live hope only in the Son of God. Opposing the intellectualistic views which stress that Jesus brought a teaching we could have found elsewhere anyway if we tried harder, Kant began to insist that in his person, through his work in history, Jesus Christ liberated us from an enslavement from which we could not liberate ourselves.[17]

It is not my intent here to criticize Kant for not developing these hints into an explicit consideration of the possibilities I proposed above. My intent has been, rather, to bring to focus the most important basis for my judgment that the notion of the "highest good" elaborated in *Religion* provides the most complete resolution Kant gives to the central critical issue of the relationship between freedom and nature. This resolution is most complete inasmuch as it attempts to address, albeit haltingly, the possibility that the relationship by which freedom and nature are mutually bound to each other rests upon the temporality by which reason takes its finite, human shape. This temporality, moreover, has its fundamental locus in human moral agency. Kant addresses this possibility in his efforts to delimit a this-worldly, public character to the highest good that takes final, concrete shape and is fully established in conse-quence of the moral conduct of particular human persons and human communities in the course of history.

NOTES

1. See for instance A 811–12/B 838–39; PrR 129–31; CJ-B §84, 285–86, §88, 304–309.

2. Lewis White Beck, *A Commentary on Kant's Critique of Prac-tical Reason* (Chicago: University of Chicago Press, 1960), 11; cf. 200.

3. A 814/B 842: "Happiness, therefore, in exact proportion with the morality of the rational beings who are thereby rendered worthy of it, alone constitutes the supreme good of that world wherein, in accordance with the commands of pure but practical reason, we are under obligation to place ourselves."

4. *Together Toward Hope: A Journey to Moral Theology* (Notre Dame, Ind.: University of Notre Dame Press, 1983), 81–107; "Auton-

omy and Community: The Social Character of Kant's 'Moral Faith',"
The Modern Schoolman 61 (1984): 169–86.

5. See especially sections I and II, A 797–819/B 825–47.

6. This point has been developed in my essay "Evil and the Moral Power of God," in *Proceedings of the Sixth International Kant Congress*, vol. 2:2 (Lanham, Md.: Center for Advanced Research in Phenomenology and University Press of America, 1989), 369–81.

7. James Collins, *The Emergence of Philosophy of Religion* (New Haven: Yale University Press, 1967), 170–204; Michel Despland, *Kant on History and Religion* (Montreal: McGill-Queen's University Press, 1973), 263–68; Yirmiahu Yovel, *Kant and the Philosophy of History* (Princeton: Princeton University Press, 1980), 271–306.

8. E.g., B 29; A 547–48/B 575–76; A 809/B 837; though cf. A 554–56/B 582–84, which offers a brief "phenomenology" of evil that seems in more accord with the account Kant later develops in *Religion*.

9. PrR 33–34, though cf. 99, 101, 103 for certain descriptive passages about moral imputation that, like their counterparts in the first *Critique*, suggest a more complex account.

10. §87, especially 14n, 299–300, 302–304.

11. "Since this leads only to a progress, endlessly continuing, from bad to better, it follows that the conversion of the disposition of a bad man into that of a good one is to be found in the change in the highest inward ground of the adoption of all his maxims, conformable to the moral law, so far as this new ground (the new heart) is now itself unchangeable" (R 46).

12. Among the passages in which this tension is evident is the following: "According to our mode of estimation, therefore, conduct itself, as a continual and endless advance from a deficient to a better good, ever remains defective. We must consequently regard the good as it appears in us, that is, in the guise of *an act*, as being *always* inadequate to a holy law. But we may also think of this endless progress of our goodness towards conformity to the law, even if this progress is conceived in terms of actual deeds, or life conduct, as being judged by Him who knows the heart, through a purely intellectual intuition, as a completed whole, because of the *disposition*, supersensible in its nature, from which this progress itself is derived. Thus may man, notwithstanding his permanent deficiency, yet expect to be essentially well-pleasing to God, at whatever instant his existence be terminated" (R 60–61; cf. also 65).

13. "From this it follows that man's moral growth of necessity begins not in the improvement of his practices but rather in the transforming of his cast of mind and in the grounding of a character; though customarily man goes about the matter otherwise and fights against vices one by one, leaving undisturbed their common root" (R 43–44; cf. also 46, 67–69).

14. "It is true, indeed, that the man who, through a sufficiently long course of life, has observed the efficacy of these principles of goodness, from the time of their adoption, in his conduct, that is, in the steady

improvement of his way of life, can only *conjecture* from this that there has been a fundamental improvement in his inner disposition. Yet he has reasonable grounds for *hope* as well. Since such improvements, if only their underlying principle is good, ever increase his *strength* for future advances, he can hope that he will never forsake this course during his life on earth but will press on with ever increasing courage" (R 62; cf. 36–38).

15. Collins, 182–86, 197–204; Despland, 107–109, 223–27; Yovel, 72–77, 170–73, 222–23, 272–74.

16. Yovel sees Kant moving toward an abandonment of a "next worldly" account; Collins and Despland see him continuing to maintain it. A recent study by Gordon E. Michalson, Jr., *Fallen Freedom: Kant on Radical Evil and Moral Regeneration* (Cambridge: Cambridge University Press, 1990), offers an insightful account of the ambiguities in Kant's views on this point and the source of those ambiguities in the tensions between Christian doctrines and the critical demands of Kant's philosophy.

17. Despland, 223–24.

"For reason . . . also has its mysteries": Immortality, *Religion*, and "The End of All Things"

Anthony N. Perovich, Jr.

"No religion can be conceived of which involves no belief in a future life . . ." (R 117/126). Indeed, some commentators go beyond this claim of the mature Kant and regard the establishment of our immortality as the ultimate goal of the entire critical philosophy.[1] Yet while there is no doubt that Kant intends to affirm a belief in immortality, the attempt to determine the content of this belief uncovers conflicting tendencies in his thought. On the one hand, a number of writers note that it would be natural for him to consider the next life to be outside time, given that temporality characterizes merely our phenomenal existence.[2] On the other hand, Kant frequently construes immortality temporally, an interpretation that the second *Critique*, by postulating endless progress, in fact demands. It is sometimes suggested that an inconsistency here would hardly have disturbed Kant, as knowledge of the supersensible exceeds our grasp.[3] In any case, the essay "The End of All Things," where one might be expected to turn for a clarification of the critical position regarding our immortal state, may seem not to address and settle this conflict in any but an inconclusive and perplexing fashion.[4] Nevertheless, Kant was in fact concerned with how best to conceive our future state and did come to accept an atemporal conception of it. However, this acceptance appears to be based less on considerations of consistency than on the conviction that viewing our future existence as eternal turns out to be practically preferable to viewing it as temporal.

Furthermore, discussions within *Religion* can be seen to provide both the context necessary for understanding the intricacies of the atemporal conception found in "The End of All Things" and the tools useful for restructuring our idea of immortality: the notion of a "mystery" enables us to situate this idea, with its attendant complexities, in the critical landscape, and the notion of a "disposition" helps redefine the central object of hope in the light of a revised conception of the life to come.

Kant could not resist musing on our future state. To be sure, a necessary ignorance in this area is officially endorsed: "We know nothing of the future, and we ought not to seek to know more than what is rationally bound up with the incentives of morality and their end" (R 149n / 161–62). Yet while such protestations are in keeping with critical limitations on speculation, Kant is found in practice to ponder quite frequently what awaits us in the after-life. Because the features of that life will be determined (as they are in this one) by how we know, the basic distinction between a discursive and an intuitive intellect leads naturally to a distinc-tion between two possible immortal states, one temporal and the other eternal. Were we to preserve our discursive intellect in our future life, we should then continue to depend on sensibility for our intuition and could thus anticipate that the temporal char-acter of our experience would persist postmortem.[5] It is possible, however, that in the life to come our cognitive apparatus of discursive intellect cum sensibility might be replaced with an intuitive intellect. "In this life we have no concept of such an immediate intuition of the understanding. But it can neither be denied nor demonstrated that a separated soul, as an intelligence, might contain a similar intuition in place of sensibility . . ." (L 87 / 1053). The cognition of such a mind, like God's, would, of course, take place *sub specie aeternitatis*.[6]

Kant's distinction of a discursive intellect from an intuitive one thus encourages the formation of alternative conceptions of the future life, one of a temporal, the other of an eternal exis-tence. Both conceptions can be found in the writings of the critical period, even if attention is restricted to works published prior to 1793.[7] On the one hand, the immortality postulated in the second *Critique* must be understood as temporal. Endless moral progress toward holiness is required, and such progress can occur only in time. To regard the series of stages that constitutes this progress as somehow atemporal would make nonsense of Kant's claim that the "Infinite Being, *to whom the temporal condition is nothing,* sees in this series, which is for us without end, a whole conformable to the moral law" (PrR 127/123; italics mine; cf. 137/132). On the other hand, Kant considers in the first *Critique* the transcendental hypothesis "that separation from the body may . . . be regarded as the end of this sensible employment of our faculty of knowledge" (A 778/B 806), and thus by implication the end of our existence in time. While such hypotheses do not admit of proof, neither do they admit of refutation; consequently, because Kant is quite willing to entertain the possibility of an eternal afterlife, he cannot (at least while contemplating such a hypothesis) consider himself committed to a future state that is temporal. In fact, conceptions of immortality of both a temporal and an atemporal sort are present in the *Critique of Pure Reason* itself.[8]

The persistence of two different accounts of our future life— one viewing it as temporal in character, presumably by expecting the employment of our current cognitive apparatus to continue in some fashion, the other deriving the eternal character of that life either from our participation in the divine mind or from our coming to know in a manner at least similar to God's— explains the significance of the article "The End of All Things," for there Kant seeks to interpret the common saying that death represents a passage from time to eternity. However, criticisms of both conceptions of our immortal state seem at first to frustrate the hope that the essay will demonstrate which conception appears more adequate from the critical vantage. On the one hand, the thought of a passage from time into eternity "revolts our imagination" (ET 78/334), for the standstill of eternity must appear as the annihilation of anything that we can understand as life. On the other hand, a temporally unending process of change (even one making continual progress toward the highest good) dashes any hopes we might have for contentment in the life to come, for such a future offers a prospect only of "an unending series of evils" (ET 79/335). Such a prospect is so unsettling that a person may be inclined to exchange this unsatisfying sequence of evils for annihilation, if not of life then at least of personality: thus the mystic seeks the eternal repose that results from fusion with the Godhead.

This discussion is puzzling because it appears to be so inconclusive. Kant's hostility to mysticism is well attested,[9] and his remarks in this essay are entirely characteristic: the mystical alternative is a "monstrosity" (ET 79/335). But if the experience of reabsorption into the Godhead does not offer a satisfying foretaste of the life to come, it would also appear that Kant here considers the conceptions of a temporal as well as of an atemporal future state to be unsatisfactory. It is possible, however, to see in this discussion an endorsement of the position that our immortal state is best regarded as timeless, once we have distinguished, for conceptions of immortality, theoretical from practical dissatisfaction and have examined Kant's notion of a "mystery." The eternal condition of our future life then emerges as a mystery, theoretically incomprehensible but practically significant, and thus serves for moral guidance while remaining suited to critical strictures concerning the theoretical inaccessibility of the supersensible.

Although he adversely criticizes both conceptions of immortality, Kant's line of attack is importantly different in the two cases. Conceptions such as those we have of our future state may be evaluated both theoretically and practically, and what is comprehensible and acceptable from the former perspective may turn out to be objectionable from the latter, and vice versa.

On the one hand, the idea of a temporal afterlife is theoretically acceptable but practically unsatisfactory. Kant had already seen, in reflecting on our present situation, that moral progress derived from a good disposition could render us well-pleasing to God (R 60–61/67); we may view our immortal state as temporal merely by projecting this condition into the future so as to yield a conception of unending moral progress. Indeed, Kant maintains that only in this way can we conceive our future life (ET 77–78/334). Nevertheless, however well-pleasing that condition may be to God, and (more importantly from our theoretical perspective) however unavoidable such a conception may be to us when we try to render immortality thinkable, the view of our afterlife continuing in time leaves us dissatisfied practically. We can connect no contentment with the prospect of an unending series of evils (ET 78–79/335); immortality, after all, was postulated in response to the need to attain the highest good. The discontent at such a prospect is, as already noted, sufficiently dismal to turn some to mysticism in hopes of reaching the satisfaction that a future life conceived in temporal terms fails to supply. The conception of a future life consisting of a ceaseless sequence of evils, in which contentment is never achieved, is practically pernicious: far from promoting moral behavior, its discouraging depiction encourages none to act in hopes of achieving a state of blessed fulfillment and drives some to extinguish their reason in mystical fantasies.

On the other hand, the idea of an atemporal afterlife confounds us theoretically while yet offering wholesome practical guidance. Such an atemporal state is theoretically incomprehensible: in order to conceive the passage from time to eternity we must represent to ourselves a common moment that serves as both the end of the former and also the beginning of the latter, but this result unintelligibly locates both time and eternity in the same temporal sequence (ET 77/334). Moreover, because we can be conscious of our existence and can represent our mental life only in time, to think ourselves as atemporal exceeds our conceptual capacity (ET 78/334). Nevertheless, the view of a future life that is outside time has positive practical significance. Because that life is timeless, it can no longer be understood as a sequence, neither as a sequence of evils nor as a sequence of anything else; consequently, it no longer offers us an opportunity to improve our moral condition. What it does offer, says Kant, is the prospect of an unchangeable moral state along with our subjection to the manner of eternal existence which is consequent on that ultimate moral condition. In this view, all ethical development must occur in the present, while the revelations of conscience about that development help us to anticipate the character of the timeless future and to respond accordingly: if our conscience reveals a moral life governed by principles of goodness, we have reason to hope for a blessed eternity and shall find the peace that accompanies such a hope; if, however, our conscience reveals the continued workings of evil principles, our fear of eternal misery may have the beneficial moral effect of leading us to reform (R 63/69; ET 73, 78/330, 334).[10] In either case, the thought that our moral condition is settled on leaving this life (because the next one is atemporal) is practically advantageous, whatever its theoretical drawbacks.

Thus both conceptions of immortality seem unsatisfactory in some respects and satisfying in others; yet their comparison hardly results in a deadlock, at least when considered from the Kantian perspective. What we want in our conceptions of the supersensible is help for the moral life of the present, not encouragement for speculation about a sphere about which we can, after all, know nothing.

> In general, if we limited our judgment to *regulative* principles, which content themselves with their own possible application to the moral life, instead of aiming at *constitutive* principles of a knowledge of supersensible objects, insight into which, after all, is forever impossible to us, human wisdom would be better off in a great many ways, and there would be no breeding of a presumptive knowledge of that about which, in the last analysis, we know nothing at all—a groundless sophistry that glitters indeed for a time but only, as in the end becomes apparent, to the detriment of morality. (R 65/71)

The conception of a timeless afterlife clearly benefits human wisdom in precisely the way this passage suggests: by comforting the good and spurring the evil to improvement, the view that situates our immortal state in eternity regulates our moral life, while speculative pretensions are curbed by the recognition that this view exceeds our conceptual grasp. Consequently, Kant distinguishes the natural end of all things from the supernatural end of all things. The former (in which "natural" characterizes merely whatever proceeds according to laws, be those laws physical or moral) refers to our eternal life insofar as it is comprehensible, and it is comprehensible only in a practical sense; the latter refers to our eternal life as an object of speculative knowledge, and of such an object we in fact comprehend nothing (ET 76/333). The conception of a temporal afterlife is thus doubly deleterious: not only does it fail to provide an incentive for moral behavior, its theoretical intelligibility "breeds presumptive knowledge" of an area where we in fact are and must remain ignorant.

Such an attitude toward immortality may seem remarkable. It may be possible to explain how the utterly incomprehensible can serve as a moral guide by arguing that the merely negative concept of the eternal (which is available to us; see ET 77/334) is sufficient for the purpose: what is needed, after all, is only the recognition that the afterlife will provide no opportunity for change and hence for further moral development. On the other hand, there is something perplexing about the acceptance of a belief regarding the supersensible that is acknowledged to be self-contradictory and that is not accompanied by an attempt to explain away its contradictory character. Nevertheless, such a belief is surely Kant's. In fact, he has a category for concepts that function precisely as does the view of immortality as eternal: he calls them "mysteries." I want to suggest that Kant's account of immortality is clarified on recognizing that he regards the afterlife to be, in respect of its atemporality, a "mystery."

Kant's main discussion of mysteries occurs in the "General Observation" appended to Book III of *Religion;* there he sets out the mysteries of faith that concern God. It is helpful, I believe, to consider "The End of All Things" as a discussion parallel to the "General Observation," except that the mystery treated in the essay concerns immortality rather than God.

Kant defines a mystery as "something *holy* which may indeed be *known* by each single individual but cannot be *made known* publicly, that is, shared universally" (R 129/137). That it can be known by the individual Kant immediately glosses by claiming that mysteries are known "from within" to an extent that at least permits them to influence our moral behavior. That a mystery cannot be known generally Kant then glosses by stating that, while admitting of a practical use, mysteries do not admit of a theoretical use. A mystery is thus an article of faith which is hidden from our theoretical yet revealed to our practical reason: "Only that which, in a practical context, can be thoroughly understood and comprehended, but which, taken theoretically (for the determination of the nature of the object in itself), transcends all our concepts, is a mystery (in one respect) and can yet (in another) be revealed" (R 133/142).[11] To seek knowledge of a mystery is consequently misguided; those who attempt it through an illumination of the understanding Kant refers to as "adepts" (R 48/53). They suffer from the illusion of experiencing and (as experience is for Kant a species of knowledge) of knowing what can in fact be the object only of a practical faith.

To view God as triune is to encounter a mystery in the sense just described. God wills to be served, says Kant, under three moral aspects: as holy legislator, as benevolent ruler, and as righteous judge. These conceptions tell us about his laws and connect our beliefs about God to our ethical life, that is, they merely express his moral relation to us. No mystery, then, results from a practical consideration of God as triune, but to try theoretically to comprehend him as such yields very different results:

> But if this faith (in a divine tri-unity) were to be regarded not merely as a representation of a practical idea but as a faith which is to describe what God is in Himself, it would be a mystery transcending all human concepts, and hence a mystery of revelation, unsuited to man's power of comprehension; in this account, therefore, we can declare it to be such. (R 133/142)[12]

To view the afterlife as atemporal is likewise to encounter a mystery in the sense described. While the conception of our immortal state as temporal is theoretically transparent but practically useless, the conception of the next life as eternal is, as we have seen above, a mystery to our understanding, incapable of receiving a "public" explication that is theoretically satisfying, and yet is revealed from within to each individual who comprehends and makes use of it in a practical sense. Moreover, the mystics, who seek consciousness of their own eternal condition, are described by Kant in "The End of All Things" as committing precisely the mistake that adepts generally make in regard to mysteries: they seek to experience, and thus to know, what ought to remain and in fact must remain opaque theoretically. Thus, in pondering immortality,

> the speculative man becomes entangled in mysticism where his reason does not understand itself and what it wants, and rather prefers to dote on the beyond than to confine itself within the bounds of this world, as is fitting for an intellectual inhabitant of a sensible world; *for reason, because it is not easily satisfied with its immanent, that is, its practical use but likes to attempt something in the transcendent, also has its mysteries.* (ET 79/335, italics mine)[13]

We must, then, in considering God and the soul, distinguish between the existence of each and its intrinsic determination in exactly the same way. *That* God exists, *that* we shall continue to exist in a life to come, are, Kant believes, propositions that are certain and capable of (moral) proof. Theoretical reason cannot by itself *attain* even this stage; it cannot *comprehend* anything beyond this stage. Nevertheless, we still ask for further information regarding the characteristics of God and the soul and find that we are led to further ascriptions, of trinity to God and of timeless eternity to the soul, which, however, possess only practical and not theoretical significance. In the sensible realm, theoretical reason can comprehend and demonstrate; in the supersensible realm, theoretical reason can still comprehend existence (the existence of God and the future existence of the soul) but must turn to practical reason for demonstrations of it. But in the supersensible realm, the determination of the nature of these existents may lie beyond even theoretical (although not practical) comprehension, in which case what is a mystery for theoretical reason is a revelation to practical reason. The eternal character of our future life is, for Kant, just such a mystery and just such a revelation: much that is puzzling in "The End of All Things" ceases to be so once it is recognized that Kant, by treating eternity as a mystery, is committed to arguing for both the theoretical incomprehensibility and the practical significance of the conception of a timeless afterlife. Without this recognition, the essay must appear as a curious mixture of opposed tendencies.[14]

On the interpretation just offered, the divine and the human receive like treatment: God's existence and our future existence can be understood theoretically and proven practically, whereas intrinsic determinations of those natures, such as God's triune character or our timeless status, can be understood only practically. However, acceptance of the eternal character of the afterlife demands that this way of formulating Kant's doctrine be reconsidered, for the introduction of eternity calls into question not only the proof of immortality offered in the *Critique of Practical Reason* but indeed the very idea of offering a proof of immortality at all.

The argument for immortality presented in the second *Critique* is certainly incompatible with these latest views of Kant's. There he sought to establish immortality as the necessary condition for the endless progress toward holiness demanded by morality. But as Beck has pointed out, we cannot very well understand the future life postulated there to be timeless if the needs of the argument are satisfied only by assuming that life to be one of ceaseless progress: we may want to say that the future state of the soul is eternal rather than temporal, but "we must be reminded that the premise for the eternity of the soul includes the idea of continuous change, which is a temporal and not an eternal mode."[15] If immortality cannot be viewed both as eternal and as a life of infinite progress (and consequently of continuous temporal development), then a choice must be made, and in "The End of All Things" Kant has made it: immortality is to be conceived as eternal, and thus no argument of the sort offered in the *Critique of Practical Reason* will even be relevant (leaving aside questions of acceptability) because the immortality postulated by the *Critique* is different from the immortality Kant ultimately recognizes, and incompatible with it.

One conclusion that may, of course, be drawn from the foregoing discussion is that a new argument for the immortality of the soul is called for. Kant, however, shows no interest in providing it, and there are good reasons for resisting this call. Concern for immortality typically arises only insofar as we regard ourselves as temporal and worry about a termination of our existence at some future point. For example, the threats to immortality mentioned in the "Refutation of Mendelssohn's Proof of the Permanence of the Soul" (B 413–15), viz., the soul's ceasing to be through dissolution and its passing out of existence through vanishing, clearly require a conception of the soul as a temporal being. If, however, the true mode of existence of the soul is timeless, temporality being a condition to which it is subject only in this life, then, assuming that our soul exists at all, its eternal existence is assured and fear for its extinction is seen to be groundless. As Schopenhauer remarked, "For it is true that everyone is transitory only as phenomenon; on the other hand, as thing-in-itself he is timeless, and so endless."[16] Or as Kant himself writes, "where there is no time, also no end is possible" (ET 77/334).[17] Once we locate ourselves in eternity, the need for an elaborate proof of immortality loses its urgency.

While the response just given—that it is conceptually misguided to search for a new proof guaranteeing that we, as timeless existents, will not pass away—seems to me to be basically correct, it is nevertheless bound to cause uneasiness as it stands. In particular, the critical philosopher may object that the response presupposes a good deal of theoretical knowledge about the soul and its ultimate condition, knowledge that we are denied. In fact, however, this objection is unfounded: all that is required is that we be entitled to conceive ourselves as possessed of an underlying, eternal existence. While such a level of our being may be closed off to theoretical knowledge, it may nevertheless be accessible to us from a practical point of view. The introduction of the idea of a "disposition" (*Gesinnung*) offers precisely such a practical access to our eternal status, a status that renders the search for a new proof of immortality unnecessary.

Kant defines the disposition as "the ultimate subjective ground of the adoption of maxims" (R 20/25), thus as the basis for all our particular decisions. He sometimes refers to it as "the *homo noumenon*" (ET 78/334),[18] thereby revealing its significance and centrality for his conception of human beings. The focus of our moral character can sometimes appear to shift rather markedly from our sensible to our supersensible life once this concept is introduced. It is instructive, for example, to compare two descriptions Kant gives of the intuition by which God recognizes our goodness. In the second *Critique* he writes:

> Only endless progress from lower to higher stages of moral perfection is possible to a rational but finite being. The Infinite Being, to whom the temporal condition is nothing, sees in this series, which is for us without end, a whole conformable to the moral law. . . . (PrR 127/123)

On the other hand, in *Religion*, Kant states:

> But we may also think of this endless progress of our goodness towards conformity to the law, even if this progress is conceived in terms of actual deeds, or life conduct, as being judged by Him who knows the heart, through a purely intellectual intuition, as a completed whole, because of the disposition, supersensible in its nature, from which this progress itself is derived. (R 60–61/67)

The first quotation contrasts the human and the divine points of view on the series of steps that makes up our moral development. The clear suggestion is that this progress is and must be experienced by us temporally and seriatim, whereas to God it is seen as timeless and as a whole. Thus, endless temporal duration seems to be the only sort of immortality a finite, rational being may hope to experience, however that life may be viewed by God. The second quotation revises this conception by distinguishing our underlying disposition from the moral progress derived from it. Kant no longer writes in such a way as to encourage us to regard ourselves as primarily temporal beings whose temporal progress is regarded as timeless only from God's standpoint; rather, his new manner of expression makes it clear that the object of divine intuition is no longer an endless series at all but the underlying disposition, which, as the "noumenal man," offers us a conception of ourselves that is fundamentally atemporal and that regards our temporal characteristics such as our moral progress as apparent and derivative.[19] Such a noumenal focus for the self as morality provides, combined with our previous conclusions regarding the eternal character of the life to come, enables us to answer the questions that arise regarding immortality without any appeal to developed arguments.

The questions regarding immortality are two: (1) whether I shall cease to exist and (2) if not, what the nature of the future life will be. The answers to both are now straightforward. Insofar as ceasing to exist necessarily takes place in time, and insofar as Kant believes that morality compels us to focus ourselves in a timeless disposition, the eternal status of the self, "(the *homo noumenon*, 'whose change takes place in heaven')" (ET 78/334),[20] and the impossibility of its passing away are assured. Insofar as Kant believes that morality prescribes for us (as we saw earlier) a view of the afterlife as atemporal, we must acknowledge that our temporal self and life *will* pass away, although our eternal self and its life remains. Thus morality assures us of our eternal existence without the aid of elaborate argumentation and also assures us that it will be experienced as eternal, again without the aid of elaborate argument (and in defiance of any argument, even Kant's own, that might suggest otherwise). Consequently, it is mistaken to suggest that reflection on the supersensuous state of the soul and its afterlife should be of little concern to Kant: reflection that takes his own moral considerations into account not only guides our thinking about the soul and its destiny but also shows that even his attempt to offer an argument for immortality as part of the critical edifice is misconceived.

Even if we should conclude that the sort of effort made in the second *Critique* to establish the immortality of the soul is unnecessary and even misguided, we should not conclude that hopes and fears regarding a future life no longer occupy us, only that the focus of the hopes and fears is likely to change. Once eternity rather than temporal progress is anticipated, we can expect the concern for the continuation or termination of our existence to be replaced with a concern for the character of our eternal state. While Kant himself may not have completed such a transition of concerns,[21] there is nevertheless some evidence in the writings considered here of a change of emphasis regarding the hopes and fears central to the topic of a future life: a hope for eternal blessedness replaces a mere hope for immortality, just as a fear of eternal damnation takes the place of a fear of extinction. Thus, in *Religion,* Kant points out that reflection on the course of our moral life can reveal steady improvement or decline. We may extrapolate these paths into the life to come, always recognizing that such a future life will be experienced "under other conditions," and foresee an afterlife whose underlying principle is either good or evil. "Now in the first experience we have a glimpse of an *immeasurable* future, yet one which is happy and to be desired; in the second, of as *incalculable a misery*—either of them being for men, so far as they can judge, a blessed or cursed *eternity*" (R 63/69). Similarly, in "the End of All Things" Kant insists that the principles of good or evil that have governed us in this life can be expected to prevail in the afterlife as well; as that afterlife is eternal, so the consequences of the adoption of those principles are eternal (ET 73/330).

> Hence the inhabitants of the other world, according to their dwelling place (heaven or hell), are presented as singing forever and ever the same song, either their hallelujah, or eternally doleful notes (Rev. 19:1–6; 20:15); in this way the total absence of all change is meant to be indicated in their state. (ET 78/334–35)

Although such images are recognized as only imperfectly representing our future state, they nevertheless do succeed in delineating objects of hope and fear. Hence, whereas "blessedness" in the *Critique of Practical Reason* is dispatched in a footnote as an idea never to be attained even by an immortal finite creature (PrR 128/123), a blessed eternity now becomes an object of hope. This, of course, is entirely understandable once mere survival has lost its urgency and our eternal status is assured: it is the condition of that eternal life that now naturally becomes an object of concern.

While *Religion* and "The End of All Things" do not show Kant reconsidering his conviction that our only access to the supersensible is through morality, they do show him reconsidering his view of what morality reveals to us about immortality. In particular, he comes to see that a conception of our future life as eternal is, while a mystery, practically preferable to a conception of it as temporal. Once we are able to locate a moral focus for our timeless existence, a goal achieved by Kant's introduction of our disposition, the eternal existence of our true self is already assured in this life. Hopes and fears for the future are free to pass beyond issues of "continued" existence and the argument for it to issues of the status of that future life. Thus while these later writings do not abandon the Kantian view that beliefs about the supersensible are to have a practical basis, they certainly reveal considerable room for development within it.[22]

NOTES

1. See Friedrich Paulsen, *Immanuel Kant: His Life and Doctrine*, trans. J. E. Creighton and Albert Lefevre (New York: Frederick Ungar, 1963), 252.

2. See, e.g., Lewis White Beck, *A Commentary on Kant's Critique of Practical Reason* (Chicago: University of Chicago Press, 1960), 270; and Emil L. Fackenheim, "Immanuel Kant," in *Nineteenth Century Religious Thought in the West*, Ninian Smart, John Clayton, Steven Katz, and Patrick Sherry, eds. (Cambridge: Cambridge University Press, 1985), vol. 1:22; cf. Karl Ameriks, *Kant's Theory of Mind* (Oxford: Clarendon Press, 1982), 184.

3. Thus Beck, 271: "But I doubt very much that these objections to the conception of life after death would have troubled Kant. He was not concerned with any theoretical determination of the supersensuous, because it would be impossible on theoretical grounds and empty of practical significance."

4. Cf. the remarks of Ameriks, 185–86.

5. Whether our experience might remain sensible but become subject to other forms of sensibility at this juncture is a possibility Kant understandably does not consider. Such a suggestion raises problems for the unity of consciousness, although these problems need to be addressed for the case of the transition to an eternal state as well.

6. Cf. L 89/1054–55. Kant is ambiguous on the question whether such cognition employs an intellect similar to God's or proceeds simply by a participation in the divine mind. See L 86–87/1052.

7. Some authors, e.g., Allen W. Wood, *Kant's Moral Religion* (Ithaca, N. Y.: Cornell University Press, 1970), 123, and Michel Despland, *Kant on History and Religion* (Montreal: McGill-Queen's University Press, 1973), 272, represent the "endless progress" of the afterlife as occurring outside time. Such an interpretation, however, seems to me incompatible both with Kant's text (see below) and with the probable consequences of Kant's indecision about the epistemological status of our future state.

8. See Ameriks, 183–84, and the passages referred to there.

9. See, e.g., PrR 125/120–21; CJ-P 135–36, 205, 351/275, 334, 459; and Kant's essay, VpS 434–47.

10. In *Religion,* where attention is not focused on immortality, Kant writes in a way that suggests he still views the life to come as temporal: "if after this life another life awaits him, he may hope to follow this course [of constant improvement] still . . . " (R 62/68). Nevertheless, he immediately notes that the future life will take place "under other conditions," and these may be presumed to be atemporal conditions. He then proceeds to offer a moral (although not a dogmatic) interpretation of the ideas of a blessed and a cursed eternity. While it would be difficult to base an argument for a view of our immortal condition as atemporal solely on *Religion,* what Kant says there can ultimately be seen to be consistent with the conception of an eternal afterlife I take to be endorsed in the essay "The End of All Things," and in fact can be seen to illuminate the statement of that view in the essay.

11. Greene and Hudson have "theologically" where Kant has "theoretically."

12. Kant's discussion of the trinity is found in R 131–33/139–42.

13. Kant finds mysticism objectionable *only* considered in relation to "an intellectual inhabitant of a sensible world," as he has it here; freed from the limitations of sensibility, the intuition of God and his ideas may occur just as the mystics describe. Their only error, states Kant in the "Danziger Rationaltheologie," lies in not postponing such an intuition until the next life (GS vol. 18, 1256–68).

14. Keith Ward's *The Development of Kant's View of Ethics* (Oxford: Basil Blackwell, 1972), 152, e.g., represents Kant's essay as just such a mixture. While the contradictions to which Kant refers in "The End of All Things" all arise from the attempt to understand eternity theoretically, Ward finds the contradiction in which "reason becomes entangled" to hold between the pictures of the afterlife as temporal and atemporal and finds Kant endorsing both pictures as practically significant, although neither offers theoretical knowledge of the next world. Such an interpretation fails to appreciate both the very different sorts of criticism Kant levels against each conception and also (although Ward immediately treats of holy mysteries in religion) the illumination consequent on recognizing immortality as a mystery.

15. Beck, 271.

16. Arthur Schopenhauer, *The World as Will and Representation,*

trans. E. F. J. Payne (New York: Dover, 1969), vol. 1: 282, *Sämtliche Werke*, Max Frischeisen-Koehler, ed. (Berlin: A. Weichert, n. d.), vol. 2: 323.

17. Thus, insofar as the "true" self lies outside time, we have a negative idea of both its freedom and its immortality; but whereas the moral law gives a positive content to the concept of freedom, any attempt to represent our eternal state positively "revolts our imagination," as we have seen. Hence, immortality, but not freedom, offers us a mystery of reason. See R 129/138.

18. Concepts similar to the idea of a "disposition," at least in part, appear earlier in the critical philosophy; cf. Kant's discussion of "intelligible character" in A 539 ff./B 567 ff. and of "personality" in PrR 89–90/87.

19. Some commentators, e.g., Edward Caird, *The Critical Philosophy of Immanuel Kant* (New York: Kraus Reprint Co., 1968), vol. 2: 303, and Allen Wood, "Kant's Compatibilism," in *Self and Nature in Kant's Philosophy*, Allen W. Wood, ed. (Ithaca, N. Y.: Cornell University Press, 1984), 98, point out that such a view makes it difficult for us to take the ideas of moral striving and moral progress seriously, i.e., literally, whether in this life or in the next. While this may be true, the notion of a noumenal disposition certainly coheres well with Kant's overall views of the self and reality.

20. Kant here states that we must take our maxims "as if" our moral state, with respect to its disposition, were not subject to moral change; earlier (ET 73/330) he counsels us to act "as if" the next life and our moral condition in it were unchangeable. The force of the "as if" in these passages is, I believe, to acknowledge that we cannot know (indeed, we cannot really comprehend), in any theoretical sense, the supersensible states that nevertheless have a function to play in the sphere of practical guidance.

21. Even at a time roughly contemporary with *Religion* and "The End of All Things," Kant can still be found to restate the argument for immortality developed in the *Critique of Practical Reason*. See Immanuel Kant, *What Real Progress Has Metaphysics Made in Germany Since the Time of Leibniz and Wolff?*, trans. Ted Humphrey (New York: Abaris Books, 1983), 153/GS 20:309.

22. Work on this essay was supported by a grant from the Matthew J. and Anne C. Wilson Foundation Faculty Development Fund of Hope College.

Rationis societas: Remarks on Kant and Hegel

Burkhard Tuschling

1.

To call Kant's ethics "monological" or even "solipsistic" as some do is a fundamental misunderstanding. To be a moral agent or, in Kantian terms, to be author and subject of the categorical imperative is to be sovereign as well as subject of a legislation by and for all rational beings. In their search for an "intersubjective" dimension which they are unable to find in Kantian[1] and even in Hegelian practical philosophy[2] they ignore the fact that any legislation, moral, juridical, or whatever, is logically and objectively possible only for a system or totality of agents capable of obliging themselves—and of being obliged—by mutual and thoroughgoing claims and corresponding obligations. Thus, Kantian moral philosophy not only does not lack a "social" dimension nor just accidentally have certain social implications; it is, instead, inextricably intertwined with a basically social conception of the human being as a member of the totality of rational and free agents;[3] in short, of humankind.[4]

This misunderstanding has its roots in the empiricist or nominalistic concept of an individual which dominates twentieth-century philosophy and is even shared by those who are in search of the a priori of human linguistic or scientific community. Eighteenth-century philosophy, on the contrary, even in its more individualistic and pro-empiricist (or sensualist) versions, conceives the individual as a singular being *and* as a representative of its kind, i.e., as singular and general or universal at the same time. The "I" which accompanies "all my representations" or at least necessarily *may* do so, the "I" of "apperception" and "pure reason," speculative as well as practical, moral as well as juridical, is a universal *and* singular term.

That is to say, it is universal not only with respect to the infinity of representations or other acts of the intelligence of an individual human being but also with respect to all human persons who ever lived and ever will live. For it comprises the individual as the rational representative of its kind. Kant or Hegel (as well as Leibniz, Condillac, or even Locke and Hume), therefore, do not even need to *look* for a "social" dimension of their theories and, in particular, of their concept of an individual because *it is there from the outset.*

Thus, Kantian ethics, however "individualistic" it may be, even where it addresses the individual *in foro interno* and therefore addresses the individual in inner self-conversation that excludes relations toward and conversations with any other individual,[5] *at the same time*[6] presupposes and places the individual within that universal relationship toward fellow human and rational beings from which she excludes herself in the process of moral reflection and legislation: the *Fürsichsein* (being-for-oneself) of the moral agent is, for all its apparent absoluteness, nothing but a particular mode of being-for-others.

This follows not only from the fact that the individual—and the concept of an individual—involves and is involved within a totality or even two different totalities of infinite relations involving other such (or different) individuals; these are totalities which might be called "universe," "cosmos," or "nature" on the one hand and "humankind," "history," "freedom," "society," or "spirit" on the other, as was argued above. It follows as well from the *forum internum* situation of *any* ethics, even if it dispenses with explicit reference to any kind of legislation, any talk of rational beings, and any reference to the *concept* of an individual whatsoever. For this very ethical situation is just the converse of other forms of social organization or legislation for free agents, regarded as its "opposites," e.g., "legality"[7] or politics, and is therefore inextricably connected with them.

Thus the "empire of ends" formula (Gr 433–36; see also KpV 86–87) and the idea of an "ethical commonwealth" are not additions trying to annex a social or "intersubjective" dimension to a basically unsocial or even antisocial conceptual scheme. On the contrary, they are nothing but analytical evolutions of implications that are involved in the concepts of an individual, of reason, of a rational being, of freedom, and of a free agent.

Kant's *Critiques* as well as his *Religion within the Limits of Reason Alone* presuppose and address[8] the individual as a member of "universus hic mundus una civitas communis deorum atque hominum"[9] of Augustine's and Leibniz's *Civitas Dei* or *République des Monades.* Moreover, the late formula of Kant's *opus postumum*—"Gott, die *Welt,* universum und ich Selbst, der *Mensch,* als moralisches Wesen"[10]—exposes once again Kant's even more fundamental belief which had been guiding him through his whole lifetime from the early cosmological or physical writings to the late "critical" and postcritical works, summed up in the often quoted statements of the *Beschluß* of the *Critique of Practical Reason* (KpV 161): humanity is part of the universe, to be conceived of as nature and freedom whose laws it finds in itself as a *cosmotheoros*[11] and as a moral agent. The natural world is one single system governed by Newtonian causal laws whose detection and securing against skeptical doubts is the most worthy intellectual enterprise; this enterprise is the aim of the first *Critique,* which founds the system of this cosmos on the intellectual activities of the knowing subject engaged in the process of perceiving phenomena.

The world of freedom is not accessible to theoretical reason (Gr 458, 462–63; KpV 4, 7) but becomes real by persons developing their faculties as rational beings, thereby coming to know what they are and ought to be, and, at the same time, *creating* the world of freedom. At first they are brutally forced to do so by the antagonism caused by that very same freedom they enjoy as rational beings, erecting a legal system of states.[12] Then, after a long and costly process of cultivation and bloodshed,[13] at the end of history, they freely identify themselves with the laws and conditions securing freedom and equality for all, in a system of mere morality or an "ethical commonwealth."[14]

In this perspective the inner systematic structure of Kant's practical philosophy may be summarized as follows: the human being, as a rational being, capable of freedom—in the Kantian sense of being the autonomous[15] author[16] of the law determining her maxims, ends, and actions—is:

(1) A moral agent, reflecting upon or deliberating about her own and others' choices, subject to the moral law, binding or necessitating herself by the very idea of the law without any other incentive (*Triebfeder*) like fear of the physical power of

the legal system. This is the sphere of "inner" freedom where concordance with the law is "morality," not "legality" (KpV 71–89; RGV 98–99, 219–21).

(2) An agent enjoying the freedom of appropriating objects of her free will (MdSR §2, 246ff.) according—or in opposition—to the principles of right which safeguard the freedom of every one to do the same. This is the sphere of "outer" freedom where accordance to the law may exceptionally result from "morality"—the unforced self-restriction of the agent upon the condition of her own freedom's being compatible with the freedom of everyone else—but where it is regularly enforced: in the state of nature, by any other agent acting according to the principles of (juridico) practical reason (MdSR C §§ 41 and 42, 231, 306, 307–308), or under the public law, by the general will and power of the sovereign.

(3) A citizen—or even the sovereign—of a state which is opposed to other such states and their citizens, in a state of mere war, latent or manifest, not subject to any kind of law restricting individual freedom to the condition of its compatibility with everyone else's freedom. This, once again, is "outer freedom," such that as long as the "state of nature" between states persists there is nowhere on earth "peremptory juridical possession," no right in the strict sense, no public law, but property or juridical possession and legal order only in the provisional sense (MdSR 350ff., 354f.).

It is in (3) where the idea of eternal peace as the highest good within the bounds of the law,[17] the idea of an ethical commonwealth (*Religion*, Book III), and the idea of the final coincidence of legality and morality (I 21–31) come into play. The idea of physical force, the legal order and the state, gives way to a situation of free association among rational beings, subject to the moral law alone, acting in accordance with it by mere "respect of the law," i.e., united in an "ethical commonwealth."

Note that there are at least two paradoxical consequences involved: pure reason does not become "practical" in the *strict* sense before eternal peace becomes real and the "state of nature" is turned into a "state of right (or law)" everywhere on earth; and right and law among human persons become strictly real only when they become superfluous.

From this point of view—looking at the entire complex system of legislation by the categorical imperative or Kantian practical philosophy as a whole—one can see why, as has been said above, it is absurd to suppose a "monological" or "solipsistic" ethics even to be possible on Kantian principles. On the contrary, to be free, to be a moral agent, necessarily involves citizenship in the empire of all rational beings, the realm of ends or the city of God. It is on this condition alone that for Kant a "deduction" of categorical imperatives is possible at all.[18] Thus, Kantian practical philosophy does *not merely have* a social dimension, it *is* intrinsically social by its constitutive rationalistic concepts of the human being as a free agent and person.[19]

To be an individual, to think and act freely, is to be and to act as a referent involved in an infinitude of relations toward the world as the totality of what there is (nature) and toward an infinite number of other such intelligences making up one single universal system of intelligent and free agents ("freedom" or "spirit"). The individual is thus conceived as the focus of reflection, involving an infinitude of relations to "the other" as the medium of "being—theoretically and practically—for oneself." Kant and Hegel may differ with respect to the degree of explicitness and elaboration of the constitutive features of this concept and with respect to the basis for deducing this concept as well as to the method of deduction itself. But for all these formal differences, important as they are, their concept of an individual is materially the same: for both of them an individual is a (self-)conscious and free rational being, conceived as a focus of the "identity of identity and non-identity" of the infinitude of relations within which it is theoretically and practically involved.[20]

Religion[21] is involved in all three levels presented above:

(1) The moral law is the rule of a good and holy will; "my" reason as the origin of this law (EF 350, KpV 129) is one and the same in all humans, in all rational beings, in God:[22] reason as the legislator and the executor of the moral law is *divine* reason,[23] realizing itself in and by the "morality" of actions of humans.

(2) To unite oneself with others under a civil constitution is an absolute and supreme duty; the end of such an "external relation" which is a duty in itself and which, in turn, is the highest formal condition of all other "external" duties is to establish "the right of humans under public coercive laws

whereby for everyone, one's own is determined and secured against anyone else's interference" (TP 289). Therefore "the idea of a constitution in general which is, at the same time, an absolute command of practical reason judging by juridical concepts, is holy and irresistible for all peoples" (MdSR 372).

(3) The idea of an "invisible church" or an "ethical commonwealth" represents the final end (*summum bonum*), the highest possible good *in the world*[24] and the telos of history— of humanity's coming to the final point of its perfectibility[25] and rationality. This is the point of coincidence of "legality" and "morality," of "strict right," of reason becoming practical. It marks also the point where humanity *is* or has become what it *ought* to be, where *is* and *ought* coincide. This, however, is the point where humanity becomes not only *gottwohlgefällig* but God.

Leaving aside the difficulties involved here, we may finally state that what has been said of Kant's practical philosophy and ethics holds of his philosophy of religion also: that it conceives of the human being as an originally free and social being, a member of the city of God as a society of rational beings. In particular, the "good principle as a person" is "humankind (the rational being in general) in the state of its utmost ethical perfection" (RGV 60). "Our moral condition which we are to think as originally spoilt" (RGV 58 and context), therefore, does not mean our individual life is a unique process or existential project to be assessed by standards which morally qualify our actions in their individual uniqueness. On the contrary, just as the end of creation is nothing but "humankind in the state of its utmost ethical perfection," the final, absolute end of the individual free agent (which, therefore, cannot in turn be the means to other more eminent ends) is to realize this destination as her own and to contribute in her life, according to her abilities, to the destination of her kind, i.e., the kind of rational beings to which a free will was given and which therefore is capable of a legislation by pure practical reason. The individual fulfills not an existential project to be realized uniquely by this one individual but the one and only universal project of humankind which is to be realized and which alone, for Kant, makes individuality possible at all: the destiny of the human being to be rational and free. Therefore, it is the task of the individual to strive to become one with the ideal of humanity as being agreeable to God (ein "Gott wohlgefälliger Mensch" zu sein), although she knows that this is, strictly speaking, impossible and that she is not worthy of such a unification (RGV 61).

In this way, Kant's *Religion within the Limits of Reason Alone* also puts the individual into a realm of rational beings in which everyone is at the same time the author and subject of a legislation determining the rational free will (cf. RGV 67, 79, and Book III passim). Religion is therefore—in perfect accordance with the definition given in the *Critique of Practical Reason*— conceived as conscious and willed unification with an empire of God which nevertheless is nothing but the idea of human reason and freedom having come to their utmost perfection.

The "invisible church," therefore, which is dealt with in the third chapter of *Religion* is not an accidental metaphor but expresses a deep conviciton of the author: all religion up to the present day culminates in Christian religion, which is, in truth, moral religion: human persons' knowledge of their destination and their conscious identification with this their final destination. If one joins to this systematic idea the conviction arising from the philosophy of history that humankind struggling from primitive beginnings of knowledge and freedom to reach the higher stages of the development of its faculties comes to know its destination with ever growing clearness[26] and to identify itself consciously with this its destination, it then becomes evident that the process of "positive" historical religions becoming more and more morally sublime does not come to an end in Christendom. The Christian religion in turn is going to be "sublated" in a state where human beings do and will the reasonable and rational for its own sake, where the destination of all as rational and free is realized without any further use of religious belief as a vehicle (RGV 106, 107, 118) for the realization of an empire of God thought of as an ethical commonwealth in the Kantian sense.

In Kant's *Religion,* as in Lessing's *Education of Mankind,* therefore, all positive religion, Christian religion not excluded, comes to be treated as a mere means of preparing humankind for its destination to be able to use its own reason and to be free to determine itself.

2.

Precisely this idea is the point of identification and of departure for the young Hegel as a follower of the Kantian philosophical revolution. In a letter to Schelling, dating from January 1795, he writes, "Das Reich Gottes komme, und unsere Hände seien nicht müßig im Schoße ... Vernunft und Freiheit bleiben unsere Lösung, und unser Vereinigungspunkt die unsichtbare Kirche."[27]

Hegel evidently refers to Kant's *Religion*, in particular to Book III and the idea of an empire of God on earth to be prepared (if not realized) by the unification of all adherents to rational religion into an invisible church of reason and freedom. *Vereinigungspunkt* even sounds like a specific reference to RGV 94 (or 101); *unsichtbare Kirche* clearly refers to 101[28] and context.

However this may be, Hegel aims not only and not primarily at some sort of practical *imitatio Kantii* but at a theoretical identification, i.e., at a *philosophical* program, as the context of the letter from which the above is quoted as well as the manuscripts from the Bern and the later Frankfurt period show.

In a certain sense this program of identifying himself with, by diverging from, Kantian philosophy, practical as well as theoretical, remained valid for Hegel throughout his life. He surely did not intend to write mere footnotes to Kant, but what he *did* intend was to give the "*true* critique of the categories and of pure reason"[29] and the *true* "system of pure reason."[30] I cannot even begin to show this here. I can only hint at some basic ideas which gave rise to that development of Hegel which culminated in the science of an idea which contains in itself all reason and all freedom, thus being in itself self-sufficient, and nevertheless condescends to debase itself, to alienate itself from itself by creating finite nature and finite freedom (spirit), but only in order to realize its own concept as absolute and free reason by realizing the destination of humanity as a rational being and free agent.

Nevertheless, at an important point of his development and at an important place in his publications—i.e., at the end of *Glauben und Wissen*—Hegel acknowledges[31] his indebtedness to Kant with respect to the very heart of speculative philosophy; in the famous passage on the "speculative Good Friday" he says:

> [Der reine Begriff ... muß den unendlichen Schmerz ... rein als Moment, aber auch nicht mehr denn als Moment, der höchsten Idee bezeichnen] und so dem, was etwa auch moralische Vorschrift einer Aufopferung des empirischen Wesens oder der Begriff formeller Abstraction war, eine philosophische Existenz geben. ...[32]

Here we have:

(1) The clearly recognizable reference to Book III of *Religion*,[33] in particular to RGV 66 ("The law commands: 'Be holy'") and to 74ff., i.e., to the interpretation of the change of heart as an imitation of the death of Jesus Christ on the cross: the death of the "subject of sin with all its inclinations." Hegel in his turn at GW 4.414, 5 expressly refers to the "empirical character" which is dealt with by Kant in RGV 74 and expressly mentioned in line 18 of that page.

(2) The "speculative interpretation" of the otherwise Kantian (or, perhaps, even pre-Kantian) idea of Christ's death playing a fundamental part in the process of humanity's becoming what it is, which in turn becomes identified with the process of the concept's realizing itself.

(3) Hegel's acknowledgment that his reconstruction of God's death as a "moment of the supreme idea" is intended as a direct philosophical substitute of Kant's interpretation of the role of God's death within the process of human moral improvement.

Keeping in mind this general idea of a close and intimate relationship of the Hegelian to the Kantian program for a rational reconstruction of human freedom, let us now turn to some more specific points of connection between the two systems.

For all its beauty, the Kantian system of practical philosophy for all rational beings has its (obvious and hidden) shortcomings and contradictions. At first, however, Hegel basically identified himself with it. In particular, his earliest philosophical essay[34] shows Kantian lines: he accepts Kant's concept of morality and tries to show how religion—moral or philosophical, not positive Christian religion—can become "totally subjective,"[35] the guiding principle and enlivening motive of a community, determining the beliefs and actions of its members, organizing their lives in all its manifestations into an organic social whole and, at the same time, uniting them as members of the "invisible church" with their God[36] in a spiritual whole, the spirit of a people.[37]

Even such a rough description as this shows how Kantian doctrines, transferred into a conception of a commonwealth which is "ethical" or "religious" and, at the same time, a sociopolitical reality, change their meaning—their "spirit" if not their letter. Kant is seen and accepted by Hegel within a framework of ideas originating from Montesquieu,[38] Rousseau,[39] Lessing,[40]

Fichte,[41] and others. Thus, even by accepting Kantian ideas and results in practical philosophy and natural religion, Hegel diverges from Kant from the outset in at least four important respects which anticipate key notions of the later Hegelian concept of *Sittlichkeit*:

(1) Following Rousseau and Schiller, the young Hegel refuses to accept Kant's assessment of the sensual nature of the human being. Virtue is to be attained not by subduing pleasure and the senses; these cannot be dispensed with, but are accepted as a means to the end of virtue. In particular, attachment to others, feeling, "the heart" are not to be disqualified as immoral incentives: love is expressly called an *analogon rationis*.[42]

(2) The systematic sphere where virtue is realized is the constitution of a people, the living spirit of a nation created by the free constitution of its members, the free expression of its character.[43] Thus, as early as 1792–93, the characteristic conjunction of freedom, virtue, politics, and religion, and of the cultural and material life of a nation which is later called *Sittlichkeit* is present in Hegel's attempt to think how religion may become "wholly subjective," how reason can become practical, or how an ethical commonwealth may become true.

(3) At the center of the idea of a morally qualified action or behavior is love, conceived as constituted by a dialectical structure which is basically the same as "concept" or "freedom" in the later system: (a) relation of the lover to the loved as the other; (b) self-denial of the lover on behalf of the loved; and (c) true realization of the loving self by denying oneself in the process of giving oneself up for the beloved.[44]

(4) The realization of virtue or morality in a commonwealth and ethico-religious unification with God is not postponed, as in Kant, until the end of history, or transferred to a domain separate from actual life. Rather it is actual, present in this life by the individual's becoming a member and active participant in the spiritual and material life of the people, by the individual's life becoming the means of the realization of the spirit of the whole, a subjective-objective unity, or, in short, by becoming objective spirit.

Although it is appropriate to say—as has been done above—that Hegel diverges from Kant even while taking his starting point from Kantian tenets, it is no less adequate to point out how close to Kant constitutive features of the pattern of early

Hegelian practical philosophy really are if compared with what I have sketched under the label of "interior systematic" above. Basic tenets of both are, in fact, identical: e.g., the series of subordinated-superimposed levels of realization of freedom, personal love, spirit of the people, history as a process of production of different levels of "spirits"[45] correspond more or less adequately to the Kantian notions of a sphere of individual morality, of the system of "legality" in a state of "public law," of a permanent state (or, as Kant puts it, a state of "peremptorical" possession) of right and law among nations, and, finally, of the process of development of human reason as a theoretical as well as a practical faculty by ever-rising stages of enlightenment and freedom in the course of human history.[46]

It is easy to overlook how much Hegel could and actually did borrow from Kant. And it is not too much to say that the basic structure of Hegel's system of practical philosophy is already present at least in outline in Kant's "interior systematic." In particular, it is interesting to see from a systematic point of view which includes the whole fabric of Kant's metaphysics of morals and of history that in Kant morality or ethics[47] already tends to be subordinated to the sphere of civil and public law and the state, to the duty[48] to live in the state and to take an active part in the process of making reason practical and real by establishing rational and reasonable forms of organizing social human life. Some of the features for which Hegel is either blamed or praised[49] are Kantian[50] in origin. On the other hand, the non-Kantian features—stemming from Montesquieu, Rousseau, Lessing, and others[51] (mentioned above) should not be overlooked. In particular, the emerging concept of speculative identity of non-identicals,[52] the idea of a spiritual community organizing the physical and cultural life of a people as a nation, and the idea of the actuality of reason as well are basically alien to Kant, although there are corresponding (familiar?) traits in Kant's philosophy.

To sum up: Hegel's conception of *Sittlichkeit* arises from the development, especially in the philosophy of right and the philosophy of history, of genuine Kantian tenets by means of equally genuine Kantian as well as non-Kantian motives—into non-Kantian, genuinely Hegelian results.

I cannot work out here the concept of *Sittlichkeit* as it emerged in the later 1790s in greater detail but must confine myself to general reference to Henry Harris's work. In particular, I cannot comment on the extensive works in the field of logic, politics, political economy, and political history which have been so important for the development of Hegel's theory of "absolute Sittlichkeit."[53] I only want to note the following points:

(1) By 1797–98, Kantian ethics is criticized as substituting inner serfdom and force for outward suppression and dominion: the idea of autonomy in the Kantian sense is rejected as a genuine way of realizing freedom and absolute self-determination of the will. For the time being, Hegel sees primordial Christian love as taught and practiced by Jesus as the only way to the leading of a truly self-determined life. In that period love means for Hegel sublation of "positivity" and force; in particular it means denial of the law by "fulfillment" of the law, transforming "law"—as a means of being determined by an alien power—into the self-determined union of the believer with God.

(2) By 1801, Hegel has developed, at least in outline, basic concepts of his emerging speculative philosophy, e.g., the concept of the absolute, of subject-object, reason versus understanding, etc.,[54] and he has accepted the basic tenet of Hobbes:[55] under the conditions of absolute individual freedom, a meaningful, objectively determined and, therefore, valid distinction between good and evil, right and wrong, is possible if and only if individual freedom is integrated into a *social system* of freedom governed and secured by the state. "Morality," therefore, as a situation of absolute self-determination of the isolated self or individual reason, is unable to supply the conceptual or practical foundation for the distinction of good and evil. On the contrary, taken by itself, in isolation of any social institution or objectivation of a "general" social will, "morality" *is itself*—by that very situation into which it puts the "moral" will as a moral legislator—*the denial of that same possibility, of "good" and "evil", "just" and "unjust," "justice" and "injustice" as meaningfully and referentially distinct concepts.* Because of its emptiness, the concept of a "moral" action and of the "moral law,"[56] therefore, is not only insufficient for the foundation of right and Sittlichkeit, but it is only another expression for being in that "state of nature" which destroys and excludes such a foundation. For, by Hobbes's criterion,[57] being one's own and any other's legislator and judge is nothing but the individual's freedom in that state. Therefore, to live and to remain in a state of mere

"morality" is not, as Kant had thought, the *summum bonum*, the idea of the final state of the development of human reason and freedom. It means, on the contrary, (a) to remain in the state of nature; (b) to refuse the imperative of the *exeundum* which Kant himself had declared to be the absolute, categorical imperative and duty (TP 289; MdSR §§ 41, 305–307); and (c) to prevent freedom and the legislation of reason from becoming objective and possible at all. This is the reason why, in his essay on the different scientific methods of dealing with natural law, Hegel calls Kant's and Fichte's principles of morality "the principle of immorality:"[58] the principle of the individual's being her (and any other's) one and only legislator absolutely excludes[59] any notion and, more important, any possibility of objective freedom, legislation of practical reason, duty, public law, and right.

(3) By 1800,[60] 1801,[61] and 1802,[62] Hegel has developed the idea that a human is rational, free, truly infinite, spiritual, a subject only in so far as one is united with and a self-differentiation of the one universal subject-object, the absolute reason and self. The idea of a *civitas dei*, a commonwealth of all rational beings, created as well as uncreated, the invisible church,[63] has come to be fully integrated into the emerging speculative system.

By 1802, finally, Hegel had worked out his basic tenets concerning the concept and the method of dealing with "natural right" (or "natural law"), negatively, as opposed to Hobbes, Kant, or Fichte. And he began working on that succession of drafts of his "System der Sittlichkeit," beginning with the manuscript bearing that title, followed by the formerly so-called "Real-philosophie I and II,"[64] the Phenomenology of 1807, the Nuremberg manuscripts, and the lectures of 1817–18 and 1818–19,[65] culminating in the different versions of a philosophy of "objective spirit" (1817, 1827, and 1830) and the "philosophy of right" (1820–21), finally ending with the Berlin lectures of which the *Nachschrift v. Griesheim* of 1824–25 probably preserves the last and most mature elaboration.

Can we point to any arguments which make plausible and even cogent this transition from a more or less Kantian starting point to a speculative philosophy of spirit? I think we can; I believe that I have already given the core of the argument which Hegel proffered and which, in my opinion, can with certain qualifications be accepted as cogent. In any case, the essay on natural right of 1802 probably supplies the most succinct elaboration of such arguments or reasons Hegel ever published. Taking the "paradigm" of the school of natural right as the main object of his criticism as well as the point of departure for his own constructions, Hegel there points out:

(1) The "empiricist" version of the argument the school has proffered lacks among other things any acceptable proof for the necessity of what is declared to be necessary: the social organization of freedom by the state of nature—taken as an organization of freedom existing for and by itself, to be left for the legal state in order for freedom under the law to become possible[66]—is empty, leading to an explanation of *idem per idem.* What is called the state of nature presupposes the legal state and sovereign power and is really nothing but an abiding feature of the social order organized by the state and of sovereign power itself. And, finally, how is it possible to derive the principles of duty, of absolute obligation and *Sittlichkeit,* from the principles of freedom if that freedom is something to be given up as being contrary to either "morality" or *Sittlichkeit?*

(2) The formal a priori version of the natural law theory necessarily splits the system of objectified freedom into two distinct, mutually exclusive, even incompatible, systems, called legality and morality respectively, which both fail to supply the foundations of all obligation and right among humanity.

(3) Legality fails because within a system of mere legal force, identity of individual and general freedom and the corresponding wills is impossible. Radicalizing Locke's objection to Hobbes,[67] Hegel objects as follows to Kant's and Fichte's concept of a system of "legality": Even if it is granted that the individuals may be forced to conformity or identity of their wills with the general will, how is the coercive power itself to be forced to that conformity or identity?[68] The attempt to do this leads into a vicious infinite regress.

(4) Morality fails because on Kantian as well as on Fichtean premises the formalizing process of the "law giving" practical reason leaves the content of the will undetermined. It is therefore unable to discriminate either positively or negatively what ends, means, objects of the will, or actions are to be realized, are absolutely "right," "just," or the source of absolute obligation. Consequently it remains absolutely contingent whether we are to respect property, give back a *depositum,* etc. In other words,

the natural rights theory still lacks what it has promised to give: a basis for the deduction of nonempirical, necessary duties and claims.

(5) Taking up the criticism of Kantian practical philosophy published by Gentz, Rehberg, and Garve,[69] Hegel states that Kant's idea of a moral law and a legislation of practical reason is not only insufficient for "practice" but even contradicts it: it supplies only one single formal law where several materially distinct laws and duties are needed. It is not sufficient to lay the foundations of property as a nonempirical or an "absolute" right; and by allowing empirical content to be chosen indiscriminately on behalf of its own merely formal character, it leads to consequences which are rather "amoral" (*unsittlich*) than "moral" or "ethical" (*sittlich*).[70]

(6) The absolute separation of reason and empirical content from each other and their mutually exclusive opposition to each other, therefore, has to be overcome. The problem of exposing the foundations of right, duty, and the state—the central problem of the school of natural right—can be solved only if we suppose that the coercive power of the legal order as well as the inner force of the moral consciousness—as necessary as they are—are not isolated, self-sufficient, and mutually exclusive systems of legislation of freedom but rather are necessary parts to be integrated into an overarching system of subjective-objective reason and freedom. The core of the solution is the idea that the individual is united with absolute sovereignty, not by the coercive power of the legal order nor by the interior pressure of the individual moral consciousness but by unforced, self-determined identification with the "*absolute sittliche Totalität*" of the people[71] of whose constitution and sociocultural organization or of whose *corpus politicum* she is a living part. This self-conscious identification of the individual with the life of the social whole is the realization of reason: the identity of the individual and general will. This cannot come about by force: "force is not able to constitute right and law," Hegel says, following Rousseau.[72] Nor can it be brought about by the process of formalizing our maxims according to the idea of a general law of reason: this is not enough for our practice and even contradicts it, says Hegel, following Gentz, Rehberg, and Garve.[73] There is only one way to the realization of absolute reason: its self-realization in organizing ever higher systems of

freedom or self-determined human life in history which is the same as the conscious identification and unification of individual and "general" or social freedom in the life, institutions, and living customs of a people.

(7) It should not be forgotten that Hegel had to solve, among other things, the problem of showing what, in his eyes, Kant and Fichte had failed to show: the absolute necessity, reasonableness, and right of private property. And he was, indeed, convinced that he had found the true reason and deductive basis for such a right. An unmediated identity of individual and objective reason would not suffice; slavery was the other side of *that* coin. It was the absolute right of the principle of individual freedom and equality which caused the decline and fall of the ancient systems of *Sittlichkeit*.[74] Yet it was an absolute historical necessity that the principle of subjectivity realizing itself in the "system of possession,"[75] of egoism and its destructive *"abgesonderte(n) Energien des Sittlichen,"*[76] got its right; *true* identity of the individual and the universal, or, conversely, self-realization of absolute reason and substance in the individual and collective subjects of a people, therefore, presuppose[77] the development of the system of egoism and property: that system which is contained by coercive power only and, at the same time, by the infinite return of the free agent into itself and its free identification with the logic and reason governing this whole system of—"its"—freedom.

I do not believe that Hegel finally *did* solve the problems of freedom and the state that the natural right tradition (including Kant and Fichte) had failed to solve. I do not think that he more than Kant or anyone else succeeded in showing the non-positive, nonhistorical, a priori necessity and reasonableness of private property and the kind of freedom it establishes. What I *did* want to show was that there *were* cogent reasons for Hegel, intrinsic to the paradigm of practical philosophy, which he was confronted with and accepted as a foundation for his own work, to end up with a speculative theory in which the former paradigm was absorbed.

Hegel *did* succeed in showing—over and above what his predecessors had shown—that *this* freedom, *this* kind of property, and *this* subjective-objective reason and its logic *are* the supreme—and insofar absolute—foundations of any right, any obligation whatsoever as long as the *bürgerliche Gesellschaft*, the *Not- und Verstandesstaat* and its principles, the person and private property, prevail.

The paradigm of the natural right tradition is not the only matrix into which Hegel's emerging philosophy of *Sittlichkeit* can be integrated. The representatives of this tradition, ancient and modern, had constantly connected it with the idea of an empire of reason. Cicero, to whom I referred for this idea of a city of God as a society of reason, is certainly not its author; he sums up what has come down to him from the Heraclitean-Stoic as well as from the Platonic tradition. However, he expresses the idea of a universe of *orthos logos*, uniting God and humanity, in a most pregnant way, pregnant in particular for philosophers who try to combine the ancient idea of reason creating and giving laws to the world so as to make it a cosmos with the modern idea that oneself as individual, conceived of as absolutely free agent, is truly determining oneself only if determined by one's own reason which is the same in all.

This idea, elaborated by the natural law tradition from Hobbes down to Rousseau, is recurrent in Kant, turning up in his philosophy of history of the 1780s as well as in his ethics (Gr, KpV), in his philosophy of religion, in the essays on political philosophy of the 1790s (TP, EF, SF), and in his philosophy of right. It is *the keystone of Kantian practical philosophy* with respect to its overall systematic structure *and* to its content: *only as citizens of an empire of intelligent and free agents are we truly free and truly human beings, fulfilling the plan of nature or God by realizing in theory and practice what we are destined for, reason and freedom.*

It is to this idea that Hegel refers so emphatically in the letter to Schelling, quoted above, and the early manuscripts show that it governed his work from the beginning. Moreover, Hegel remained faithful to this concept throughout his lifetime, constantly working on this classical-modern paradigm. It is not so much that he substituted new terms for traditional concepts: Kant's practical reason, especially in its role as starting point, moving force, and telos in the process of evolution of humankind can, indeed, be easily recognized in Hegel's "absolute" of 1801–1802[78] as well as in the "absolute spirit"—differentiating itself into the infinity of finite spirits—of the later versions of the system from 1803–1804 on. Rather, Hegel contributed far more to the paradigm, giving to it its final elaboration:

(1) By giving a radically un- or even anti-Kantian reinterpretation of these key concepts;

(2) By integrating them into an encyclopedic deductive scheme of Leibniz-Wolffian dimensions;[79]

(3) By exposing the dialectics of evolving involved contradictions, to be solved by integrating the contradictories into conceptual units of greater universality, producing in turn implicit contradictions to be exposed at later stages of the deductive, analytico-synthetic conceptual development;

(4) By integrating ethics and natural law[80] into a systematic whole, interpreting them as mutually exclusive and inclusive systems of acting freely, governed by one universal concept of reason and self-determination which manifests itself conditionally in all these spheres, taken distributively, but which is unconditioned, absolute reason, and freedom only as the concept of the whole, and in the totality of its manifestations; and

(5) By analytically deducing the conceptual wealth of the paradigm's key notions, combined with the synthetic exposition and integration of the wealth of empirical subject matter to be organized by those same concepts or concept. And it is only the concept in *all* its conceptual self-differentiations and empirical manifestations which makes up for Hegel that *one city of God, the absolutely free being, reason, and spirit.*

Most of us today do not believe in this idea, and, I think, no one who knows its implications honestly can anymore. More than 200 years ago Voltaire had good reasons to ridicule this kind of rationalistic optimism. People who live in the last decades of the twentieth century are confronted with many more reasons to come to the same conclusion. Two-thirds of the world's population live below subsistence level; thousands die every day. Earth, water, air, and organic life on earth are constantly and systematically polluted, mutilated, threatened with extinction—all this as a consequence of humanity's freedom to appropriate and exploit the wealth of nature, regardless of the cost.[81] And the most powerful nations of the world as well as many others threaten to extinguish each other mutually by means which threaten to destroy human life altogether.

These are so many reasons to doubt that it is absolute reason which manifests itself in absolute individual freedom and private property, in the *Not- und Verstandesstaat* of bourgeois society— or any other actual society whatever its social constitution may be—or even in Hegel's "political state." One lesson to be learned from this story of a commonwealth of reason, at least in its Hegelian version, is nevertheless still valid: *there is just as much reason, freedom, humanism in human relations, institutions, actions, and productions as we give to them.*

Thus, it is up to us, theoretically and practically, to prove that this was *not* the last word to be said about reason and freedom in history. The destructive *Energien des Sittlichen*[82] are too devastating and endangering for human life to leave it at that.

NOTES

1. J. Habermas, "Moralität und Sittlichkeit. Treffen Hegels Einwände gegen Kant auch auf die Diskursethik zu?" in *Moralität und Sittlichkeit. Das Problem Hegels und die Diskursethik.* (Frankfurt: Suhrkamp, 1986), 24; K. O. Apel, "Kann der postkantische Standpunkt der Moralität noch einmal in substantielle Sittklichkeit > aufgehoben < werden?" ibid., 226.

2. V. Hösle, "Die Stellung von Hegels Philosophie des objektiven Geistes in seinem System und ihre Aporie," in *Anspruch und Leistung von Hegels Rechtsphilosophie.* Hrsg.v. Chr. Jermann, (Stuttgart: Fromman-Holzboog, 1987), 32–42.

3. In order to show how central this idea of an empire of ends or of rational beings (intelligences) is, I give the following list of references from the *Grundlegung:* 408, 413, 415, 425, 426, 429–31, 433–36, 447–48, 453–54, 457–59, 462–63.

4. For this reference to humankind in general, compare also I 17–31 passim; TP 289–90; EF 348, 350; MdSR 246–47; 255–56, and, in particular, 350 and 354f.

5. This, after all, is the basic situation of moral reflection and legislation as it takes place *in foro interno*.

6. See again Gr 403, "als ein allgemeines Gesetz (sowohl für mich als für andere)," and 453f.: the idea of being a member of the intellectual world as the basis for the deduction of the categorical imperative. Perhaps the shortest and most concise expression of this intrinsic reference to the universe of rational beings is to be found in § 1 of the *Critique of Pure Reason:* there a practical principle is called "objective" (or a "law") if the condition it contains is known to be "objectively valid, i.e., valid for the will of any rational being" (KpV 19 and note); see also KpV 27, 32, 36, 42–50, 87, and 133.

7. In the Kantian sense of the term; see MdSR 219.

8. Compare Kant's phrases in Gr 433–34 with Cicero's description of the *rationis societas* in the text below and the following footnote. The idea of one universal rational system or *natura rerum* serves even

as the basis of Kant's deduction of the categorical imperative: Gr 453, 454. Cf. also Montesquieu, *De l'esprit des lois* I:1.

9. "This universe (is to be thought as) one commonwealth, common to gods and men": *De legibus* I:23; see also the statements preceding this phrase: "Est igitur . . . prima homini cum deo rationis societas. Inter quos autem ratio, inter eosdem etiam recta ratio communis est; quae cum sit lex, lege quoque consociati homines cum dis putamus. Inter quos porro est communio legis, inter eos communio iuris est . . . . Parent autem huic caelesti descriptioni mentique divinae et praepotenti deo, ut iam universus hic mundus una civitas communis deorum atque hominum." "There is, therefore . . . a primordial community of reason between god and men. Those who have reason in common also have right reason in common. Right reason, however, is law. We must therefore believe that men are associated to the gods by law. Moreover, between whom there is a community of law, between those there is a community of right reason also . . . but they all obey indeed this heavenly order, this divine mind and most powerful god in such a way that this universe is to be thought as one commonwealth, common to gods and men" (my translation).

10. Under the title "System der Transcendental/Philosophie in drey Abschnitten," GS 21:27; cf. also the following text and comparable formulas elsewhere in the late *Opus postumum*.

11. *Opus postumum* GS 21:31, 43, 101, 553, and KpV 162. According to Adickes the term goes back to a posthumous work of Chr. Huyghens.

12. I Prop. 4:20–22; EF 360–368.

13. Kant is never particularly explicit on the miseries of war and the costs of progress. But for all his optimism he remains a pupil of Rousseau until his end: in EF 334, e.g., one can feel the author's moral indignation on behalf of the final division and political annihilation of Poland, which happened in the year Kant's essay appeared. At the same time, however, Kant's optimism makes him accept even such events as necessary for the overall reasonable outcome of human history, whose function is that of a *Weltgericht*. Hegel (cf. *Philosophy of Right* §§ 340ff.) has developed this idea, like so many others, from Kantian origins; see I 29–30.

14. RGV, Book III, 96–124; see text further below; see also EF 348–49, 355–56, 362: it is an absolute duty to prepare the eternal peace. It is realized in a continuous approach to the idea of eternal peace or of a world federation of states: EF 356, 365–68; see once again MdSR 354f.

15. Gr 432–36, 440, 446, 452; KpV § 8:33, 43, in particular 129; RGV 3.

16. Cf. Hobbes's theory of authorization in *Leviathan* Chapter 16.

17. MdSR, "Beschluß," 354, 355: the "highest political good"; for references to EF, see note 14 above.

18. Gr 453–55, 458; KpV 34, 42–50, although Kant here refuses to talk of a "deduction" of the moral principle.

19. Kant never tires of stressing the fact that it is not the "empire of nature, but of freedom" (RGV 82), the social interdependence of humanity—the mere fact of being related to other human beings—

which is at the root of the problems of good and evil, of ethics and the philosophy of law, and of practical philosophy in general (see e.g., RGV 93–94). Moral duties and the idea of an ethical commonwealth, in particular, are specifically related to humankind, to the "ideal of a whole of all men," engaged in the process of erecting an "absolute ethical whole" (RGV 96). Moreover, the idea of a rational religion or a rational faith, originating from the "moral disposition in us" (RGV 121) get their meaning and reference only with respect to mankind, to the idea of a continuous approach to a "(divine) ethical commonwealth" on earth (RGV 122) in a process of continuous elaboration of the "good principle" (RGV 124).

20. It is precisely because they ignore this rationalistic, dialectic concept of an individual that Habermas and Apel, and their followers, can talk of the "lonesome" I as the subject of the unity of apperception or as subject of the categorical imperative at all. And it is only because they substitute their own empiricist *Vorstellung* of the subject for the Kantian-Hegelian rationalistic concept that their problem of "intersubjectivity" arises at all. Within this perspective of an empirical phenomenology of consciousness, the dialectic of Kant's and Hegel's notions of reason, freedom, abstract law versus morality versus *Sittlichkeit*, etc., is lost.

21. See the definitions in KpV 129, 145–46; RGV 153.

22. Cf. Gr 432–34 with 408–409; KpV 105–106; cf. also KpV 32–33, although, according to Kant, only God's will is holy: the will of a "finite practical reason" (KpV 33) or a finite reasonable being, though "pure," is not "holy" (KpV 32–33); KpV 82, 84, 87, 129–32. But Kant wavers a little on this point of the holiness of our will: the *law* is holy, we are told in *Religion*. But we are told as well: "Be holy!" And although man is infinitely distant from the good, he is nevertheless obliged to strive for the good. Thus, he must be able to integrate "the holy principle into his supreme maxim: a change in his state of mind which must be possible, because it is our duty" (RGV 66–67).

23. Or, more precisely, the concept of God and his divine will is at first made up from "the law of freedom of my own reason": EF 350; cf. KpV 4–5, 105, 124–126, 129, 130.

24. Cf. KpV 33 in the context of 32–33, 43, 107 passim, and, in particular, 124–26, 127–30; KpV 133, 142–46; RGV 5, 6–8; RGV Chapter 3 passim, in particular 96–107 and 109–24.

25. I Prop. 1–3 and 9 (in particular I 30).

26. An idea which Kant had sketched in the "Idee zu einer allgemeinen Geschichte" and in "Mutmaßlicher Anfang der Menschengeschichte."

27. "The Empire of God shall come. We shall not keep our hands lying lazy in our laps . . . 'Reason and freedom' remains our password, and the invisible church the point of unification" (and identification with absolute reason). *Briefe von und an Hegel*, Hrsg. v. Johannes Hoffmeister (Hamburg: Meiner, 1969), I 18; see also Hölderlin's letter, ibid., 9.

28. "Ein ethisches gemeines Wesen unter der göttlichen moralischen

Gesetzgebung ist eine *Kirche,* welche, so fern sie kein Gegenstand möglicher Erfahrung ist, die *unsichtbare Kirche* heißt (eine bloße Idee von der Vereinigung aller Rechtschaffenen unter der görrlichen unmittelbaren . . . Weltregierung, wie sie jeder von Menschen zu stiftenden zum Urbilde dient)."

29. *Science of Logic,* in GW 21.77, 7f. Wherever possible I quote from *G. W. F. Hegels Gesammelte Werke.* Hrsg. v.d. Rhein.-Westf. Akademie der Wissenschaften (Hamburg: Meiner, 1968), hereafter cited as GW followed by indication of volume, page, and line.

30. Ibid., GW 11.21, 17; 21.34, 6f.

31. Although in his usual covert, indirect way; thus it has been widely overlooked.

32. GW 4.413, 34–414, 7.

33. RGV 60ff., 74–75, 79.

34. *Volksreligion und Christentum* (hereafter cited as VR). I quote from the Theorie-Werk-Ausgabe (hereafter cited as TWA), edited by E. Moldenhauer and K. M. Michel, vol. 1 (Frankfurt: Suhrkamp, 1971).

35. TWA 1.16.

36. This expression is not in the text of VR. At TWA 1.29, however, we find "eine allgemeine geistige Kirche . . . ein Ideal der Vernunft."

37. TWA 1.12f., 23 ("lebendige Anerkennung von seiten des Volks"), 24, 33f., 37–44; 45–47; 54ff.

38. TWA 1.60.

39. Not quoted directly, but implicitly referred to passim, e.g., 11, 29 f.

40. TWA 1.19, 20, 21, 28, 51, 54, 86; *Die Positivität der christlichen Religion;* ibid., 109, 131, 148, 158, 201, 224.

41. See TWA 1.60; Fichte is used in this text as the anonymous author of "Kritik aller Offenbarung." See *Hegels theologische Jugendschriften.* Hrsg.v.H. Nohl, Tübingen 1907 (repr. Frankfurt: Minerva, 1966), 355.

42. TWA 1.30.

43. TWA 1.12 and the other passages referred to in note 37.

44. TWA 1.30. In the "Systemfragment" of 1800 the same structure or movement is taken to constitute religion, true infinity, and the reciprocal process of self-differentiation of the infinite into the finite and its converse, unification of the finite with the infinite, of humanity with God; see TWA 1.421–22 (cf. also 419f.).

45. In VR this is already present—although, to be sure, in a rudimentary way—and is going to be elaborated in the course of the later nineties, in particular in the fragments belonging to the manuscript entitled "Spirit of Christianity."

46. For the idea of a development of humankind through different stages in Kant, see again I 30 and MMG 109f., 111–15 (an essay exhibiting a concept of history on Rousseauean lines as exposed in the second *Discours,* although with an optimistic intention).

47. Which is so prominent in Kant and in the present discussion of Kantian philosophy.

48. Which is, even in Kant, *absolute.*

49. Such as the subordination of morality or the predominance and "absolute" character of the state or the idea of progress of freedom in history by a gradation of sociocultural progress.

50. The last mentioned feature obviously goes further back, i.e., to Rousseau.

51. Including authors like Ferguson, Garve, Mendelssohn, and Herder.

52. Or of "identity of identity and nonidentity": GW 4.64, 14; 11.37, 9; 21.60, 29.

53. For the later development of this concept in Jena between 1801 and 1805/1806, see Franz Hespe's Ph.D. thesis "Sittlichkeit als konkrete Allgemeinheit," Diss. Marburg 1991 (forthcoming).

54. See "Differenz des Fichteschen und Schellingschen Systems der Philosophie," GW 4.5–92 passim.

55. See the ninth of the so-called "Habilitationsthesen," TWA 2.533: "Status naturae non est iniustus et ob eam causem ex illo exeundum" ("The state of nature is not unjust and is therefore to be left"); see the translation by N. Waszek, in *Hegel and Modern Philosophy,* edited by David Lamb (London and New York: Croom Helm, 1987), 249–60; for Hegel's relation to Hobbes, see L. Siep, "Der Kampf um Anerkennung. Zu Hegels Auseinandersetzung mit Hobbes in den Jenaer Schriften," *Hegel-Studien* 9 (1974), 155–207.

56. Which results from separating the notion of absolute autonomy or self-determination from the idea of a social system of freedom governed by a "general," politically organized, legislating, and powerful will.

57. *De cive* I 9; repeated by Locke, *Second Treatise* § 125; by Kant MdSR § 44, 312; see also EF 354.

58. "Und daß, weil Sittlichkeit etwas absolutes ist, jener Standpunkt nicht der Standpunkt der Sittlichkeit, sondern daß in ihm keine Sittlichkeit ist . . . jener Standpunkt, welcher, da das Verhältniß für sich isoliert, als an sich seyend, und nicht als Moment gesetzt ist das Princip der Unsittlichkeit ist" (GW 4.434, 17–22).

59. As Hobbes, I 11–15 and footnote to I 10, as well as—among others—Locke and Kant, at the places referred to above, had clearly seen.

60. In the so-called *Systemfragment:* TWA 1.419ff.

61. In the *Differenz* essay.

62. "Glauben und Wissen," esp. ad finem.

63. See Hegel's letter to Schelling 1795; Glauben und Sein; Geist des Christentums v.a. 1.324u.U., *Systemfragment.*

64. Now: "Jenaer Systementwürfe II und III." See GW, vols. 6–8.

65. *Nachschrift Wannenmann:* See G. W. F. Hegel, *Die Philosophie des Rechts.* Die Mitschriften Wannenmann (Heidelberg 1817/18) und Homeyer (Berlin 1818/19), hrsg.v. K. H. Ilting (Stuttgart: Klett-Cotta, 1983); alternatively: G. W. F. Hegel, *Vorlesungen über Naturrecht und Staatswissenschaft.* Heidelberg 1817/1818 mit Nachträgen aus der Vorlesung 1818/1819. *Nachgeschrieben v.P.Wannenmann.* Hrsg.v. C.

Becker et al., mit einem Nachwort v.O. Pöggeler (Hamburg: Meiner, 1983).

66. It is important to keep these qualifications in mind, for Hegel does not at all reject the concept of a state of nature altogether; on the contrary, he accepts it as a necessary ingredient of the "absolute idea of *Sittlichkeit*" in which "state of nature" and "majesty" (i.e., sovereign power) are absolutely identical (GW 4.427, 15ff.). Hegel thus criticizes not the concept of a state of nature as such but the fact that it has been isolated from its context of meaning and reference in order to serve as a basis for the concepts of right and the state.

67. Locke, §§ 90 ff.

68. In proposition 6 of the "Idee zu einer allgemeinen Geschichte," Kant had raised this problem, but only to declare a thoroughgoing solution to be impossible (I 23). Hegel, on the contrary, sees, as Rousseau had done before him (*Contrat Social* I 3, I 6), that any attempt in the philosophy of right is in vain if right, duty, and practical necessity are nothing but force; power or force do not create law: i.e., if law is nothing but positive (historical or empirical) law resting on social power, there is no non-positive source of right and wrong. Under this condition, the notion of a law of nature or of any other kind of non-positive law becomes empty; philosophy of law and even practical philosophy in general is, indeed, superfluous. The problem, therefore, of how "conformity" of the individual and the general will and even real unity of both can be brought about without recurring to force *has* to be solved if there is to be any *philosophy* of law, right, and the state at all. This is why Hegel *had* to find a new way to solve the problem of free, unforced identification of the individual and the social will as the only possible non-positive source of obligation and right.

69. See *Über Theorie und Praxis*. Einleitung von Dieter Henrich (Frankfurt: Suhrkamp, 1967); compare in particular the arguments exposed by Gentz (110), Rehberg (117f. and 128f.) and Garve (ibid., 157f.) with Hegel GW 4.429, 18–39. It seems obvious to me that Hegel refers—as usual by allusion only—to this debate, to which the last contribution was published just two years before Hegel's essay appeared (sc. Garves "Vermischte Aufsätze" in 1800; see Henrich op. cit. 133). The different points of criticism (e.g., 4.429, 30 "keine Anwendung habe" . . . "und der nothwendigen Praxis widerspreche") reflect the different positions of Garve, Gentz, and Rehberg.

70. See above and GW 4.434, 17–19, 28–30.

71. GW 4.449, 21.

72. Rousseau, *Contrat Social* I 3.

73. GW 4.429, 18–39 and 432, 13–449, 10.

74. GW 4.456, 11–457, 10.

75. Ibid., 457, 11–458, 34.

76. GW 4.425, 30. I take it to be legitimate to connect this feature of the state of nature with Hegel's positive concept of *Sittlichkeit*, for: "Die absolute Idee der Sittlichkeit enthält dagegen den Naturzustand, und die Majestät als schlechthin identisch" (GW 4.427, 15–17).

77. GW 4.453, 27–454, 1–454, 29–31/454, 34–455, 2.

78. Which is reason, subject-object, and spirit.

79. This can already be seen in the *Jenaer Systementwürfe* I–III, GW vols. 6–8.

80. Here I can only point out to the further systematic elaboration Hegel gave to the foundations of practical philosophy, subsumed under the concept of "subjective spirit" and "spirit" in general.

81. This "absolute right of appropriation," as Hegel calls it in § 44 of his *Philosophy of Right*, irresistible by humanity's nonhuman environment which absolutely lacks a self, freedom, and a will (cf. also § 42).

82. See again GW 4.425, 30 and context.

The Contributors

SHARON ANDERSON-GOLD is Associate Professor of Philosophy at Rensselaer Polytechnic Institute in Troy, New York, where she specializes in sociopolitical philosophy and ethics. She has published articles on Kant's ethics, political philosophy, and philosophy of religion and history and is currently working on a book which will integrate these elements of Kant's thinking.

LESLIE A. MULHOLLAND is Visiting Professor of Philosophy at York University in Toronto. He has published *Kant's System of Rights* and articles on Kant's ethics and political philosophy, on Hegel and Marx, and on human rights. His current projects focus on Kant's epistemology and on natural law principles in relation to economic history.

ANTHONY N. PEROVICH, JR., is Associate Professor of Philosophy at Hope College in Holland, Michigan. He has coedited *Human Nature and Natural Knowledge*, and among his articles are several dealing with Kant and with the philosophy of religion. He is currently at work on a study of intellectual intuition in German idealism.

PHILIP J. ROSSI is Associate Professor of Theology at Marquette University. He has published *Together Toward Hope: A Journey to Moral Theology* and articles on Kant's ethics, the role of imagination in philosophical and religious ethics, and human rights. He is currently editing a collection of essays on mass communication, culture, and moral thinking and preparing a monograph on the place of religion and morality within Kant's account of human culture.

JOSEPH RUNZO, Professor of Philosophy and of Religion at Chapman College, and former Visiting Professor at Claremont Graduate School, is the author of *Reason, Relativism and God*, coeditor of *Religious Experience and Religious Belief: Essays in the Epistemology of Religion*, and editor of *Ethics, Religion and the Good Society: New Directions in a Pluralistic World* and *Is God Real?*. His fields are epistemology and philosophy of religion. The recipient of two NEH fellowships, he is the author of numerous articles in the philosophy of religion, the philosophy of perception, and philosophical theology.

DENIS SAVAGE, Associate Professor of Philosophy at Marquette University, is currently working on a book on Kant's theory of empirical knowledge and his theory of morality.

WALTER SPARN is Professor of Theology at Bayreuth University, Faculty of Cultural Sciences, and is chairperson of an interdisciplinary research institute on contemporary religious culture. His main interests focus on modern mentality and on the history of fundamental theology. Among his publications are *Wiederkehr der Metaphysik. Die ontologische Frage um 1600; Leben, Erfahrung und Denken. Materialien zum Theodizeeproblem; Historische Kritik und biblischer Kanon im 18. Jahrhundert;* and *Biographie, Autobiographie, Hagiographie.*

BURKHARD TUSCHLING is Professor of Philosophy at Philipps-Universität. He has published four books: *Metaphysische und transzendentale Dynamik in Kants opus postumum; Rechtsform und Produktionsverhältnisse; Die "offene" und die "abstrakte" Gesellschaft;* and *Kritik des Logischen Empirismus* (with Marie Rischmüller). He has also published a volume entitled *Probleme der Kritik der reinen Vernunft* and several articles on Kant and Hegel. Two volumes on Hegel's philosophy of subjective spirit (one containing Hegel's lectures of 1827–28, the other containing contributions to a conference on the subject) will appear in 1990.

NICHOLAS P. WOLTERSTORFF is Professor of Philosophical Theology in the Divinity School of Yale University and contributing faculty member for the departments of Philosophy and Religious Studies at Yale. He has published a number of articles on philosophy of religion, aesthetics, and metaphysics; he is author of *Reason within the Bounds of Religion, Works and Worlds of Art,* and *On Universals,* along with other books and anthologies. At present, he is finishing a book on the origins of modern ideas of rationality and responsible belief in John Locke.

ALLEN W. WOOD is Professor of Philosophy at Cornell University. His main interests are in the history of German philosophy in the eighteenth and nineteenth centuries. He is co-general editor of the forthcoming Cambridge edition of the works of Immanuel Kant in English translation. As part of this edition, he will serve as coeditor and co-translator of volume 2, *Critique of*

Pure Reason, and volume 6, *Religion and Rational Theology.* He has also edited the anthology *Self and Nature in Kant's Philosophy.* His other previous publications include *Kant's Moral Religion*, *Kant's Rational Theology*, *Karl Marx*, and *Hegel's Ethical Thought.*

Index